Accelerating Health Care Transformation with Lean and Innovation

The Virginia Mason Experience

Endorsements

"This is the 'must read' text for anyone in healthcare who is interested in improvement and innovation. It is easy to read, provides lots of stories and describes how evidence can and has been put into action through real world examples. Many people will recognise that Virginia Mason have been successfully using lean methods, but most will be surprised by their clever use of both innovation and lean methods together, thus creating significantly more value than using either alone and dispelling the myth that lean and innovation methods cannot work in harmony. There is a clear message that patients are the number one priority. We see how they actively seek to deeply understand patients' experiences and how they engage both patients and staff to create innovations that make the biggest difference. To achieve innovation, leaders cannot rely on tools and techniques alone; they have to create the conditions that support staff to excel. Rather than putting this into the 'too difficult' list, we see how Virginia Mason leadership teams have committed to achieving conditions within which innovation can flourish.

As you travel through this book, you will recognise some of the struggles that healthcare teams from around the world face; read on and you will learn valuable lessons about how you too can overcome these to create a thriving organisation that provides an excellent service for patients and an excellent workplace for staff."

Dr. Lynne Maher
Director for Innovation
Ko Awatea
Middlemore Hospital
Auckland, New Zealand

"Few organizations in health and medical care have created a learning system aimed at achieving performance that is better everyday than it was the day before. The system involves every employee, every board member, every patient, and ideas and practices from every industry and geography. Virginia Mason is not a finished product, but if you are interested in learning how to pursue excellence in a non-random way...you should read this book."

Paul O'Neill
Former Chairman and Chief Executive Officer Alcoa
72nd Secretary of the US Treasury

"The practical tools and approaches Plsek offers are helpful for health care providers at all levels. This book demonstrates, through the remarkable journey of Virginia

Mason Medical Center, what can be accomplished when leadership, lean thinking, and creative innovation all align."

Maureen Bisognano
President and CEO
Institute for Healthcare Improvement

"Health care organizations are being asked to do the seemingly impossible: become defect-free by standardizing core processes and reducing waste, while nurturing a culture of innovation. In this superb and highly readable book, management guru Paul Plsek describes how one US medical center—Seattle's Virginia Mason—managed to achieve these twin goals. He argues convincingly that the goals of "lean thinking" and innovation are not in tension; rather, when approached the right way, they are highly synergistic. Plsek writes with insight, experience, and clarity, and the book is chock-full of inspiring examples and practical tools. If I were leading an effort to improve the care delivered by my organization, this would be the first book I would distribute to all of my clinicians, staff, administrators, and board members."

Robert M. Wachter, MD
Associate Chair
Department of Medicine
University of California San Francisco

"Health care is in the midst of massive transformation—a true "100 year storm" that will thin the weak but leave the strong standing even taller. This volume outlines the deep roots, based in Lean quality theory, that can anchor a care delivery group to withstand the blasts and thrive in the gale. It comes from one of the few who truly know—a rare organization that models the principles, and harvests the results, that will form the next generation of health care delivery. Most important, it addresses fundamentals—the core infrastructure from which any world-class organization grows—at a level of sufficient practical detail to actually be useful to others striving for excellence in the field."

Brent C. James, MD, M.Stat
Chief Quality Officer and Executive Director
Institute for Health Care Delivery Research
Intermountain Healthcare

"Lean sounds mean; innovation sounds risky. But both are at the heart of what people do every day at VMMC. With lucid descriptions and riveting examples, Paul Plsek tells us how this top-rated health care organization created the culture and provided the tools so that everyone can innovate and learn. A treasure of insights for all who, like VMMC, strive to provide a 'perfect patient experience'."

Lucian L. Leape, MD
Harvard School of Public Health

Accelerating Health Care Transformation with Lean and Innovation

The Virginia Mason Experience

Paul Plsek

Foreword by Donald M. Berwick, MD, MPP

CRC Press
Taylor & Francis Group
Boca Raton London New York

CRC Press is an imprint of the
Taylor & Francis Group, an **informa** business
A PRODUCTIVITY PRESS BOOK

CRC Press
Taylor & Francis Group
6000 Broken Sound Parkway NW, Suite 300
Boca Raton, FL 33487-2742

© 2014 by Virginia Mason Medical Center
CRC Press is an imprint of Taylor & Francis Group, an Informa business

No claim to original U.S. Government works

Printed on acid-free paper
Version Date: 20130905

International Standard Book Number-13: 978-1-4822-0383-7 (Hardback)

Visit the Taylor & Francis Web site at
http://www.taylorandfrancis.com

and the CRC Press Web site at
http://www.crcpress.com

Just a few requests

Please DO NOT write in the book.

Please DO NOT fold down the pages.

Please DO NOT leave sticky tabs, paperclips or bookmarks in the book.

Please DO NOT leave any personal items such as bank cards or receipts in the book.

Please DO NOT eat, drink or smoke over the book.

**Thank you
for helping us
take good care of our books**

National University Staff - Spectrum Library

Contents

Foreword

Donald M. Berwick, MD
President Emeritus and Senior Fellow
Institute for Healthcare Improvement

In the spirit of innovation, I was tempted to write the shortest Foreword ever. If I had done so, it would be this:

> *If you are in health care and this book doesn't scare you, you are not paying attention.*

But I could not find the courage, so, read on.

Let's start with the overall theme: "Lean Thinking and Innovation." At first impression, that is oxymoronic. Lean thinking invests deeply in standardization; wake up a Virginia Mason Production System expert suddenly at night, and he is likely to mutter something about "standard work." Innovation is the opposite of that, isn't it? What was Picasso's "standard work"?

In this book, the author unmasks "…the myth that creativity and lean form a dichotomy," and blows it up. On the contrary, we learn, it is the very process of removing waste in the pursuit of standardization in the service of excellence that can release the energy of the workforce to think and act anew.

That is just one example of the assumption-busting you, reader, are about to encounter here. As I write this, I am returning from a contentious meeting in which harried nurses and worried patients argued for legislation to fix minimum required nurse-to-patient staffing ratios in the service of patient safety. Well, hold on a moment! What are we to make of a place that can increase the percentage of value-added nursing work time from 35% of the day to 90%? "Too much work… need more nurses" looks like an assumption headed for a hard time.

Try showing up in your clinic or hospital tomorrow and suggest drive-by influenza vaccination through a MacDonald's-like window, and see how far that gets. Or propose to your exhausted colleagues that, in a culture of excellence, "everything matters" or that there is "shame" in having anyone wait. I suspect that the result is less likely to be a change in care than a sudden decrease in your invitations to dinner parties with colleagues.

From the early days of my learning about modern improvement—days enriched immeasurable by my mentoring from and friendship with Paul Plsek—I heard the term, "transformation," and struggled to understand it. On one hand, I have for decades now felt that something was not at all right about the way we have organized health care. I have seen and tried with many colleagues to remedy fragmentation, waste, injuries from care, and indignities, all the time believing in my heart that none of these flaws reflects bad intention on the part of the people who do the work of healing, let alone the people who need the healing. So much improvement had felt like nibbling at the edges of the defects, not going to the heart of the causes. So, indeed, "transformation" sounded promising—more fundamental.

On the other hand, what could that term possibly mean? Transform what? Into what? And, how? Maybe some 16th century shepherd dreamed that people could somehow learn to fly, but he had no image of an airplane. That's me, trying to imagine transformation in health care.

For as long as I have known him, Paul Plsek has been comfortable with contradictions. He revels in connections among concepts that most of us see no connections among at all. He can be in "yes" and "no" at the same time, and keep smiling. And that strength, that synthetic capability, in this book at long last gives me the image of the transformation that health care needs—one that I have been looking for. It is massive; total; scary.

Success comes from the dialectics, the "what-if's," the provocations, and wordplay that Paul has brought into the center of his work to make the world better. "Directed Creativity," he calls it—crafting tools to help us break free of the fetters of assumption.

And the seeds of his mind could not have found more fertile soil than Virginia Mason under Gary Kaplan's leadership. It has taken over a decade, but it seems that constant searching, the discipline of methods learned from Japanese senseis, the investment of the Board, and attention to detail have led to a culture profoundly different from the usual culture of a large and prestigious health care organization. Commitment like that infuses Virginia Mason with a new vocabulary, impressive teamwork, a willingness to take risks, and, I daresay, playfulness. It *transforms* Virginia Mason into something very new. Something highly disruptive. Foreign. Tribal.

Be afraid. Be very afraid. What if that is what it will take to bring health care into a new and far more successful future? What if rescuing health care will require wholly new thought patterns, wholly new interactions, ambition for improvement that says "50% better," "perfect," and "everything matters," and feels just fine about it. What if everyplace needs to be the kind of place where someone says, "Let's set up a window for drive-by flu vaccines," and people (from the Board to the front line) say, "Yeah…Cool…. Let's do it!"

I think this book is a profoundly important contribution to the literature of health care change. It doesn't just push the envelope; it burns the envelope and starts over. And it shows just how much leadership, investment, and hard, hard work change like that takes.

What if that is what it will take in all of our massive health care industry to focus for real—truly—on what patients, families, and communities need from us? What if (a) this is what "transformation" looks like, and (b) it is the only way out?

Which is a long way around to saying: "If you are in health care and this book doesn't scare you, you are not paying attention."

Note about This Book

The work at Virginia Mason Medical Center to integrate lean and innovation in the pursuit of the perfect patient experience is a journey that will never end. This book represents a snapshot describing Virginia Mason's location on its path circa 2013. Applying lean and innovation to healthcare is a difficult task that evolves daily. Processes and workflows described here will undoubtedly change over time. Some improvements and innovation described here may not have spread throughout the organization, others might not have sustained, and still others will be replaced by even better ideas.

Acknowledgments

I always get the shakes when I sit down to write the Acknowledgments section of a book. I just know that I am going to forget someone, and I really do not want to do that. Apologies in advance to anyone I overlook here. I'm just forgetful; please forgive.

First, a general thank-you to my dear friend, Dr. Donald Berwick, who graciously agreed to lend his name to this work by writing the Foreword. Don, and the organization he founded, the Institute for Healthcare Improvement, brought me into healthcare in the late 1980s and I have never looked back. Another general and warm acknowledgment goes to my dear friend, Dr. Lynne Maher, formerly with the United Kingdom's National Health Service's Institute for Innovation and Improvement, and now using her many talents as director of innovation at Ko Awatea in New Zealand. I have learned a lot from Lynne and we had great fun together over many years further developing many of the concepts that you will read about here. A final, general thank-you goes to all my healthcare clients, in the United States and Europe, who have worked with me over the past two decades and helped me learn about creativity and innovation in healthcare.

The work at Virginia Mason Medical Center has been a most wonderful period of my career. There are so many people to thank there and I really tremble now at the fear of forgetting someone. A very warm thank-you goes to chairman and CEO Dr. Gary Kaplan, who has allowed me to serve in this wonderful organization. Lynne Chafetz and Jennifer Phillips have been constant and wonderful companions in this work. None of this would have come to fruition without their efforts. Diane Miller has been a good friend and has guided me through understanding the organization over many years.

I would like to offer special thanks to the Virginia Mason internal review committee comprising Lynne Chafetz, Linda Hebish, Gary Kaplan, Diane Miller, Sarah Patterson, and Jennifer Phillips. This group suffered long through multiple drafts of this manuscript and graciously offered more help than I deserved. In the final draft, Kathleen Paul also offered invaluable comments on a variety of details.

I interviewed over seventy individuals at Virginia Mason as background for this book. Their names are listed in the "Source Notes" section. I want to offer a special thank-you to all of these, not only for the work that you did, but for sharing it so graciously with me and taking the time to review drafts to make sure I had the story straight. In the end, I had enough material for a multivolume set on innovation at Virginia Mason Medical Center. I am only sorry that I could not use all the stories you shared with me, and all the words of wisdom, in this present book. Finally, I'd like to say thank-you to the other several thousand team members at Virginia Mason that I did not have the privilege of interviewing, but whose work is reflected in what I am reporting here. Virginia Mason Medical Center is an outstanding healthcare institution mainly because of the values and character of the men and women who work there. It is an honor to pass you in the halls or see you in the audience on my visits there.

Producing a book like this requires a cast of supporting characters. Jennifer Phillips never seemed to tire of my numerous requests for additional materials, some of which she had already sent me but I was too disorganized to know it. Diana Thordarson provided wonderful project management support. I could not have survived the process without her. Cecelia Carson and her team at WordCrafters NW provided great transcription service, painstakingly converting to text more than sixty hours of interviews. Finally, I wish to thank the editorial and production staff at Taylor Francis for taking all of this and converting it into a published work.

On a personal note, I want to acknowledge my sons, Jonathan and Ryan, and their mother Belinda. The knowledge represented in this book was accumulated over time through travels to many places, with many nights away from family. Thanks for allowing me that life. I would also like to thank my dear friend Jan who put up with my work schedule and occasional rants during writer's block over several months as the book took form. A week before the final manuscript was due to the publisher, my condo was flooded and I was forced to vacate. Luckily, I got my computer and files out. Jan gave me a comfortable place to work, a glass of wine in the evening, and much-needed support. Her dog, Bubba, slept under the table where I worked, providing a wonderful sense of peace in an otherwise stressful situation.

Paul Plsek
Roswell, Georgia
July 1, 2013

About the Author

Paul Plsek (plea'-sick) is an internationally recognized consultant on improvement, innovation, and large-scale change in complex organizations and systems. Before starting his own firm, he led engineering teams at Bell Laboratories and was director of corporate quality planning at AT&T. The developer of the concepts of DirectedCreativity™ and PatternMapping™, his work with leaders can be described as *helping organizations think better.* He has an extensive list of healthcare clients in the United States, United Kingdom, Norway, Sweden, and Canada. Paul is the author or coauthor of dozens of journal articles and seven books, and was an advisor on complex systems design to the US Institute of Medicine's Committee on the Design of the 21st Century Healthcare System that authored the *Crossing the Quality Chasm* report. He is also currently the Mark Hutcheson Chair of Innovation at the Virginia Mason Medical Center in Seattle; a member of the editorial board for the AHRQ Innovations Exchange; and an Innovator-in-Residence at the MedStar Institute for Innovation. He can be reached at PaulPlsek@DirectedCreativity.com.

Chapter 1

Virginia Mason, Lean, and Innovation

We want to make sure we are in existence 100 years from now, and you can only do that if you are innovative. You cannot just tread water and not embrace change because you will die. So, you've got to always be figuring out some way to grow, and that requires being willing to look at things differently.

—Mark Hutcheson
Past Virginia Mason Medical Center Board Chair

Janice (not her real name) is a 63-year-old woman who is a patient of Virginia Mason provider Dr. Keith Dipboye. When she arrived for a routine primary care visit in May 2007, she was unaware that what happens routinely behind the scenes at Virginia Mason Medical Center would save her life.

When Dr. Dipboye started practice in 1999, determining a patient's preventive care needs, such as when a person was due for colon cancer screening, involved flipping through a paper chart searching for the most recent tests performed. Most doctors did not have time to do this, so unless a patient came in for a longer annual physical, cancer screening was generally not addressed.

But Dr. Dipboye participated in an effort that changed all that in early 2007. A Virginia Mason team developed an innovative combination of computer tools that can display in seconds all of the tests a patient needs on one screen in the electronic medical record. As we will explain in this book, the culture and systems at Virginia Mason actively support such innovations in the daily delivery of care.

But innovative computer tools for prevention and health maintenance are of little value if they are not used for each and every patient. Fortunately, the culture and systems at Virginia Mason also support the concept of standard work, which defines how common tasks should be done each and every time. It is a part of what is called *lean thinking*. In primary care at Virginia Mason, checking the health maintenance module screen during every patient visit is standard work.

Dr. Dipboye's flow manager, Misty Benham, was following the standard work as she set up the health maintenance module screen in the exam room. Dr. Dipboye noted that Janice was due for a colonoscopy and he scheduled the test.

On July 20, 2007, Janice sent a handwritten note reading, "Dear Dr. Dipboye: I wanted to write and thank you for scheduling a routine colonoscopy for me this June. A cancerous tumor was discovered and I had surgery on July 9 removing the mass before it had the opportunity to spread. Without the screening, I would not have known about this tumor as I had no symptoms."

At Virginia Mason Medical Center, the culture and systems support both the development of innovation and the discipline of lean thinking in an overall effort to transform care. Janice is just one of many beneficiaries.

═══════════════════════════════════════

Innovation is in the genes of Virginia Mason Medical Center. In 1920, eight physicians from the Mayo Clinic and University of Virginia came to Seattle to found a healthcare organization based on the innovative ideas of working together across disciplines to create *team medicine*, and providing *one-stop shopping* for virtually any medical problem. That was just the beginning of a rich pattern of innovations and firsts at Virginia Mason in its over ninety-three year history (see box).

Virginia Mason was established as a 21-physician group practice, with 6 clinics and an 80-bed hospital. Since then it has grown to include a 336-bed acute-care and teaching hospital, a primary and specialty care group practice of more than 450 employed physicians in over 45 fields, and a network of clinic locations throughout the Puget Sound area. A nonprofit regional healthcare system employing nearly 5,000 people and generating almost $1 billion in revenue annually, Virginia

A PARTIAL HISTORY OF INNOVATION AT
VIRGINIA MASON MEDICAL CENTER

1920	Virginia Mason multispecialty group practice, clinics, and hospital established.
1923	First use of insulin to treat diabetes west of the Mississippi.
1925	First in the region to form a school for patients with diabetes on insulin.
1937	First deep therapy X-ray.
1940s	Virginia Mason becomes one of the first hospitals in the nation to allow fathers in the delivery room.
1956	Research center opens. This would later become the Benaroya Research Institute at Virginia Mason, internationally recognized for its breakthrough discoveries on autoimmune diseases, such as Type 1 diabetes, multiple sclerosis, Crohn's disease, and rheumatoid arthritis.
1957	First cobalt cancer therapy.
1974	First use of electromagnetic imaging.
1985	The region's first lithotripter is installed for treating kidney stones without surgery.
1992	Bailey-Boushay House established; the first facility in the United States designed and built specifically to meet the needs of people living with HIV/AIDS.
1996	First in the region to use the Mammotome® Biopsy System for early detection and treatment of breast cancer.
2001	First bilateral cochlear implant surgery in the Pacific Northwest.
2002	First health system to declare the principles of the Toyota Production System as its management system, with a goal to eliminate waste, and improve quality and safety.
2005	First medical center in the Pacific Northwest to offer a drive-through influenza immunization clinic and the first nonprofit hospital to implement a 100% staff influenza immunization goal and a fitness-for-duty requirement as an important patient safety effort.

Mason serves thousands of patients and families across the Pacific Northwest. The system also includes an innovative HIV/AIDs care facility, an internationally recognized research institute, a fundraising arm, and a nonprofit educational institute that reaches out to help other healthcare organizations replicate Virginia Mason's success.

This chapter introduces Virginia Mason Medical Center, along with the basic concepts of lean thinking, creativity, and innovation as essential background for the story of how Virginia Mason has integrated innovation and lean in its pursuit of the perfect patient experience.

A Leader in Lean Thinking in Healthcare

While Virginia Mason's innovations have had major positive benefits for the patients, families, and team members involved in each instance, the innovation with the most pervasive impact on the entire medical center has been the adoption of the Toyota Production System principles (also known as *lean manufacturing*, or simply, *lean*). This story is told in Charles Kenney's book, *Transforming Health Care: Virginia Mason Medical Center's Pursuit of the Perfect Patient Experience*. Its effect can be measured across all the dimensions of the balanced scorecard by which organizational success is traditionally measured: clinical outcomes, safety, patient satisfaction, process indicators, staff engagement, and economics.

In terms of clinical service delivery, Virginia Mason achieves top performance on several of the Medicare Fee-For-Service Quality Report indicators of preventative care, including mammograms within 24 months, colorectal cancer screening, influenza immunization, and pneumococcal vaccine. Hospital-acquired pressure ulcer prevalence dropped from 5.0% to 1.7% during the period 2007 through 2012. Monthly indicators of medication reconciliation rates on admission and discharge routinely hit 100%. Over the period from 2009 through 2012, a series of lean improvement projects dropped average length of stay for orthopedic patients by half a day (from 3.7 to 3.2 days), with good clinical outcomes and return to functioning for patients.

Utilizing a rapid medical examination concept created by Virginia Mason team members in a lean thinking workshop, the emergency department (ED) reduced the time for patients discharged to home by 43%. Flow improvement work in the ED also dropped the average time from the arrival of a suspected heart attack victim to cath lab intervention (commonly referred to as *door-to-balloon time*) to 42 minutes, besting by half the goal of 90 minutes or less recommended by the American College of Cardiology and the American Heart Association. Other work, focused on a potentially deadly medical condition called *sepsis*, decreased the time from patient arrival to the start of antibiotics from 160 to 25 minutes.

Virginia Mason also scores high on a variety of recognized indicators of clinical excellence where the only ethical goal is 100% compliance, or zero defects. For example, in 2011:

■ 100% of surgical patients had venous thromboembolism (VTE) prophylaxis ordered, compared to the national average of 98%.
■ 100% of heart attack patients were given aspirin on arrival, evaluated for left ventricular systolic function (LVF), discharged on one of the several medications appropriate to their condition, and provided with discharge instructions, compared to the national average range across these indicators of 92% to 99%.

One indicator of the overall success of Virginia Mason's efforts directed at creating a climate of clinical excellence, safety, and the perfect patient experience is the fact that the medical center's professional liability insurance premiums have dropped by 60% since 2004, and this in a state without tort reform. Insurance carriers are asking Virginia Mason to teach others its approach to risk mitigation.

A series of efforts has made it easier for patients to get a clinic appointment when they want one. Phone service levels, as measured by the percentage of calls answered in twenty seconds or less—approximately three rings—improved by more than 21% in 2012. This work, coupled with better internal handling of telephone requests, also resulted in decreasing the number of calls coming into one 10-physician group by 1,100 per week, because patients were getting what they called for the first time they called. "I love how your system is set up," wrote one patient on a satisfaction survey, "That is why I continue to call Virginia Mason when I need a doctor."

Over the past seven years, patient satisfaction has steadily improved across the domains of the standardized survey used to judge US hospitals (see Figure 1.1). Virginia Mason now ranks in the top 15% nationally in overall satisfaction. Staff also benefit directly from all the improvement work. For example, as a result of efforts to reduce motion and waste in nursing work, nurses at Virginia Mason now walk an average of 0.6 miles per day, instead of the 5 miles measured at baseline. These and other improvements make it possible for nurses to spend almost 90% of their time on direct patient care, up from less than 40% just a few years ago. In primary care clinics, providers now see more patients, in shorter workdays, with better quality care. Primary care doctors, who previously stayed until 8:00 p.m. or 9:00 p.m. doing paperwork, now routinely leave by 6:00 p.m. because everything throughout the day flows so well.

Team members at Virginia Mason know that the organization listens to them. This is demonstrated in measures of staff engagement. For example, in 2012, more than 90% of staff voluntarily participated in the annual Culture of Safety survey that the Agency for Healthcare Research and Quality uses for national benchmarking, compared to the national average participation rate of 51%.

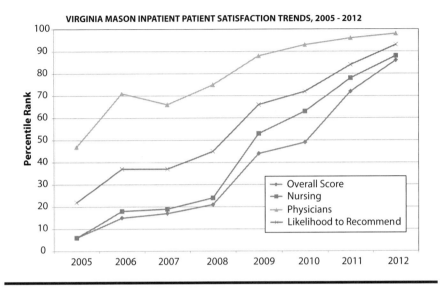

Figure 1.1 Virginia Mason inpatient patient satisfaction trends, 2005–2012.

Toyota Production System methods are also applied to corporate and support functions. Lean project work to continually root out waste in 2012 reduced inventory of supplies on hospital floors by over $40,000, without compromising quality, safety, or staff productivity. Systematic waste reduction efforts in the surgery supply chain, involving 404 procedure types and 93 surgeons, resulted in a reduction of over 37,000 individual supplies, decreasing the weight of pans carried to and from the operating room by over 83 tons annually. Overall, supply chain cost reductions such as these have netted $2 million in savings in the year they were implemented, yielding an ongoing stream of cost avoidance in future years.

These and other results have been externally evaluated and widely recognized. The Virginia Mason Medical Center story has been the subject of reports in the *New York Times, Wall Street Journal, AARP Magazine, CBS Evening News,* and *PBS News Hour.* Virginia Mason received the 2013 Distinguished Hospital Award for Clinical Excellence™ for the third year in a row from Healthgrades, placing it among the top 5% of hospitals nationwide. For the seventh consecutive year, Virginia Mason was also named a Top Hospital by the Leapfrog Group. It is one of only two hospitals in the country to receive Top Hospital distinction every year since the recognition program's inception in 2006, earning both organizations the honor of being named Top Hospitals of the Decade.

All this quality does not cost more; quite the contrary. After two years of operating losses in 1998 and 1999, Virginia Mason Medical Center has steadily made margin over the years, in a healthcare financing and reimbursement climate that has others struggling. In 2012, it had a margin of $30 million on total revenues of $934 million. Leaders uniformly attribute this success to the 2002 innovation of the adoption of Toyota Production System principles.

Lean Thinking Basics

Lean thinking is based on an approach to managing high-quality production pioneered by Taiichi Ohno at Toyota in Japan. The Toyota Production System (TPS) grew out of principles of quality control that Japanese manufacturing leaders learned from American experts such as Joseph Juran and W. Edwards Deming as part of the effort to rebuild that country after World War II. The term *lean thinking* was first given to the approach by John Krafcik in a 1988 article, and was later popularized in the 1996 book by the same name by James Womack and Daniel Jones.

TPS grew pragmatically from the 1940s onward as Ohno and his followers sought to reduce three categories of waste: *muda* (non-value-added work), *muri* (overburden), and *mura* (unevenness).

- *Muda* is anything that does not add value for the customer. Non-value-added waste can occur in processing, motion, transportation, defects, inventory, overproduction, and time.
- *Muri* occurs when one asks an individual, a piece of equipment, or a system to do that which it is not capable of doing. TPS includes an emphasis on the design of work, tools and training, and the development of people, in order to eliminate muri.
- *Mura* focuses attention on creating smooth and harmonious flow, a central concept in lean thinking. Author John Black, who introduced Virginia Mason to TPS, cataloged seven flows that must be coordinated and made smooth in manufacturing. Virginia Mason adapted these to healthcare to create the seven flows of medicine: patients, providers, medications, supplies, information, equipment, and process engineering (for example, instrument, tools, and instructions that guide the work). They later added an eighth—the flow of families.

In the 1990s, various authors attempted to codify the evolved TPS approach into a set of principles to aid teaching the methods to others. Over time, these have coalesced into five generally agreed upon themes.

- *Define value from the customer's perspective.* The most important perspective on any product, service, or process is that of the customer. It is essential to know this perspective in detail. Anything in the process that the customer would be unwilling to pay for is waste.

■ *Identify the value stream and remove waste.* The value stream is the sequence of events in the production of a product or service. It comprises the eight flows described above, although not all value streams will have all eight. Waste can be muda, muri, and mura.

■ *Make value flow without interruption.* A continuous flow of activity toward the goal of providing value to customers, and doing only what provides value, is the desired state in lean thinking. Anything that impedes flow, or the coordination of flow among various processes, is to be eliminated.

■ *Help customers pull value.* Because excessive inventory and overproduction are muda, production at any step of a process should be initiated only when the next step in the process requests, or *pulls* it. This thinking goes all the way down the value stream to include the ultimate customer—the patient in the case of healthcare. The concept of just-in-time production follows directly from this principle.

■ *Pursue perfection.* After implementing the four principles above, continue refining the understanding of the customer, eliminating waste, and creating continuous flow and pull systems until perfection is reached—perfect value with zero waste.

Lean practitioners use a range of approaches, methods, and tools to implement these concepts. For example, mistake-proofing, what the Japanese call *poka-yoke,* is a set of generic approaches to preventing, correcting, or drawing attention to human errors as they occur in order to reduce muda. The computer cable connector that will only engage one way is an example of mistake-proofing.

A critically important principle in lean thinking is *standard work.* Standard work captures the current best-known way to do something. Typically, this has been carefully worked out based on evidence and testing, and takes into account the coordination of flow with others in the value stream. Variation from standard work simply based on the personal preferences of the one doing the work is considered waste.

Another important aspect of lean thinking, and most other approaches to improvement, is the concept of learning from small tests of change. In the 1920s, statistician Walter Shewhart developed a simple four-step cycle for testing ideas for change. He suggested that one must first plan the change and then actually do it. This was to be followed by reflection in a third step that he originally called *check*, but others have since called *study.* The final step was to act on what was learned in the test by continuing to test, modifying the idea, or abandoning the idea. W. Edwards Deming popularized Shewhart's plan, do, study, act (PDSA) cycle, and this simple change model has been the foundation of nearly all approaches to improvement since the 1930s.

Practically speaking, most people learn the concepts and tools of lean thinking initially in the context of structured projects, often called *workshops* or *events.* A workshop is typically formed around an improvement goal associated with a product, service, process, or topic of interest. It comprises a team of frontline staff and managers whose work is directly associated with the topic of interest, and may also include customers, individuals not normally associated with the topic who bring fresh points of view, and highly skilled lean practitioners who facilitate the work. These events can range from a few hours to a few days and typically involve understanding the current state, envisioning better ways, prototyping and testing ideas (often in the actual work setting itself), and creating tools and other items to support sustainable implementation of the best ideas.

After engaging with lean thinking in this structured context, most individuals begin to see applications of the concepts all around them in their daily work. In essence, an organization can develop a pervasive culture of lean thinking such that these concepts become the way everyone thinks about what they do. As described in Kenney's *Transforming Health Care,* this is precisely what has evolved through disciplined effort and leadership at the Virginia Mason Medical Center.

Creativity and Innovation Basics

As if maintaining the discipline of lean thinking was not enough, Virginia Mason has also succeeded at integrating additional creativity and innovation methods into its application.

The literature on organizational innovation and the stimulation of creative thought goes back to the 1930s. While the classic literature describes methods derived pragmatically over time, more recent research from the fields of psychology and cognitive science has provided underlying principles that give rise to general classes of methods.

Natural thinking as mental valleys. To understand creative thought, it is important to understand first how thought proceeds normally. The mind processes language by activating patterns of neurons that unfold a word into a rich set of images and concepts, based on past learning. This is illustrated by Edward de Bono's mental valleys model of the mind (see Figure 1.2). Just as randomly falling rainwater gets organized into streams at the bottom of valleys through years of erosion, so the mind learns to organize the otherwise random sounds of a spoken word into an associated stream of thought.

Thus, when one thinks of a clinic, he or she immediately thinks of a physical location, with a receptionist and waiting area, where the nurse calls you back into an exam room before you see the doctor, and so on. This thinking process occurs with minimal conscious effort and gives rise to the fact that most clinics, and their processes, are quite similar.

Creativity occurs when we rise out of the usual mental valley to explore other possibilities. A video consultation with a healthcare provider over the Internet is a creative idea because it lies outside the current mental valley of *the clinic*. However, it is not completely unheard of; the mental valley of the Internet includes the concept

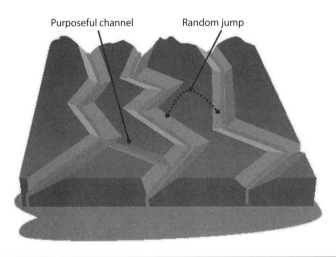

Purposeful channel   Random jump

Figure 1.2 Natural thinking as mental valleys (© 1999 Paul E. Plsek).

of distant video connections. Creative thinking almost always involves connecting and rearranging information in our mental valleys. The connection can be made either purposefully or randomly. The terms *mental model, assumption, paradigm, rule, the way we do things, mental box,* and similar are roughly equivalent to what de Bono calls a mental valley. The point is to rise out of a valley and explore other possibilities (see Figure 1.2).

Definition of creativity. Creativity is the connecting and rearranging of knowledge—in the minds of individuals who allow themselves to think flexibly— to generate new, often surprising ideas that others judge to be useful. This definition summarizes the five themes most often found in the creativity literature. First, as we have seen previously, creative thinking occurs when one rises out of current mental valleys and connects with concepts in other valleys. Second, self-censorship kills creativity, while flexible, freewheeling thinking feeds it. Third, creative ideas must represent something that is new in some way. This can range from something that no one has ever thought of in the history of the world, to an idea that is quite normal in one context, but quite novel when applied in another. Fourth, creative ideas are often greeted with surprise; both laughter and initial rejection are natural reactions and should not deter us. Finally, creativity is socially constructed; a marketplace is always the ultimate judge of an idea.

Creative thinking requires attention, escape, and movement. The process of rising out of and exploring mental valleys in order to come up with new and useful ideas relies on three deliberate mental activities—attention, escape, and movement. We must pay attention to our mental valleys, assumptions, and traditions, and not allow thought to simply rush forward in the usual way. We must be willing to challenge these and escape, even if only for a few moments in our mind, in order to wonder "what if…?" We must also overcome the self-censoring that would draw us back into comfortable patterns of thought, and instead move on to create a brainstormed list of ideas and possibilities that arise out of the attention and escape. These three principles, in some sequence and relative emphasis, lie behind all methods for creative thinking.

Seven levels of change. The range of what might constitute a new and useful idea, coupled with the endless possibilities that arise out of attention, escape, and movement, leads to the observation that the degree of creativity of a given idea lies along a gradient. Author Rolf Smith describes this gradient in his seven levels of change (see box). The seven levels can be used to reflect on the output from idea generation, or to deliberately focus an idea generation session to stimulate certain classes of ideas.

SEVEN LEVELS OF CHANGE*

Level 1: Doing the right things
Effectiveness, focus, and working to priorities

Level 2: Doing things right
Efficiency, standards, and variation reduction

Level 3: Doing things better
Improving, thinking logically about what we are doing, and listening to suggestions

Level 4: Doing away with things
Cutting; asking "Why do we do this?"; simplifying and stopping what really doesn't matter

Level 5: Doing things that other people are doing
Observing, copying, and seeking out best practices

Level 6: Doing things no one else is doing
Being really different, combining existing concepts and asking "Why not?"

Level 7: Doing things that cannot be done
Doing what is commonly thought to be impossible, questioning basic assumptions, breaking the rules, and being a bit crazy

* Adapted from R. Smith, *The Seven Levels of Change: Different Thinking for Different Results, 3rd ed.*

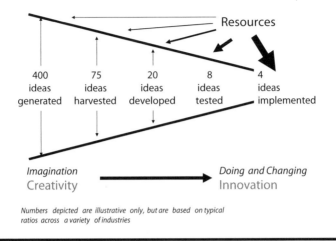

Figure 1.3 Innovation funnel (© 1999 Paul E. Plsek).

Innovation funnel. Research on innovation processes in organizations reveals that it is not a linear, deterministic process. That is, it almost never happens that a team comes up with a single idea, their first prototype is perfect, and they seamlessly transition to successful full-scale implementation. Trying many new things, and failing on most but learning and adapting as you go along, is an essential part of the process.

This observation is summarized in what the innovation literature refers to as the *innovation funnel* (see Figure 1.3). The 100:1 ratio of ideas initially generated in freewheeling brainstorming to successful new products and services highlights the importance of not restricting idea generation, while the narrowing of the funnel calls attention to the need for progressively applying judgment regarding investment of resources as the process moves along over time.

Directed creativity and innovation. While it certainly can happen that a creative thought might occur to anyone at any time by chance, the concepts discussed previously support the proposition that creative thinking can also be a deliberate process, directed to specific ends. We can facilitate attention, escape, and movement out of our existing mental valleys aimed at producing ideas for change at one or more of the seven levels. We can also systematically harvest and develop ideas along the pipeline illustrated by the innovation funnel. Directed creativity is a real possibility. Organizational innovation can therefore be defined as *directed creativity implemented.*

These basic concepts give rise to methods, tools, and processes to facilitate creativity and innovation in an organization. An organization that encourages those within it to challenge traditions and assumptions, freewheel in thinking from time to time, manage the risks inherent in trying out new things, learn from failure, and develop ideas into practical realities can be said to have a culture that supports innovation. Virginia Mason Medical Center has aligned these concepts, methods, and elements of culture with their counterparts from lean thinking to create a powerful engine for transformation.

Virginia Mason's Chair of Innovation

I play a supporting role in the story of Virginia Mason's integration of innovation and lean, so it seems appropriate that I should also introduce myself. I serve the organization as the Mark Hutcheson Chair of Innovation. This role was established in a May 1, 2003 Virginia Mason internal announcement about the new position to "(a) assist Virginia Mason in developing and enhancing expertise and methodology for generating and implementing innovations; (b) assess and identify tactics to enhance the culture of innovation; and (c) provide training and education in innovation techniques." I am external to the organization, visiting several times a year for a few days at a time and providing consultation as needed via email and telephone.

An engineer by background, I started my career at AT&T Bell Laboratories, which during the 1970s and 1980s was among the premier research and development organizations in the world. Innovation was what we did. I held various positions overseeing quality planning, control and improvement efforts in product design and manufacturing, and was AT&T's Corporate Quality Planning Manager in the mid-1980s. I left AT&T and started a consulting practice in 1985.

In 1987, I met individuals who would later establish the Institute for Healthcare Improvement (IHI), a nonprofit organization based in Boston that led the adaptation of continuous quality improvement methods from industry into healthcare. The institute's founder, Dr. Donald Berwick, a team of several others, and I created some of the first courses on industrial quality improvement ever offered in healthcare. I met Virginia Mason leaders in 1989 when they engaged Berwick and me to teach them these improvement methods, which at the time were novel in healthcare.

In the mid-1990s, I studied the creativity literature and subsequently helped healthcare clients in the United States and the United Kingdom adapt a variety of tools and methods for use in improvement and innovation. I wrote *Creativity, Innovation and Quality* in 1997, the first book to bring creative thinking techniques into the field of quality improvement, and in 1999 published the first article ever to appear in a major healthcare journal, the *Annals of Internal Medicine*, on the application of directed creativity methods to healthcare.

In February 2003, I was invited back to Virginia Mason to conduct an all-day learning event, help develop common understanding about the application of innovation methods in healthcare, and assist the organization in its strategic goal to promote a culture of innovation. Executive vice-president, chief information officer, and chief financial officer Sue Anderson recalls, "I think that was the first time, at least for me, that I understood how innovation can actually have legs in terms of what we would do." Following that visit, I was asked to serve as the chair of innovation, a role I am privileged to fill.

The Marriage of Lean and Innovation at Virginia Mason Medical Center

The lean thinking concept of standard work is a particularly troublesome one to many healthcare professionals. This has led many in healthcare to believe that lean thinking is anti-innovation. Standard work, they say, stifles creativity and the foundational freedom to think and do differently, which is at the heart of innovation. So, to many in healthcare, it is remarkable to learn that the Virginia Mason Medical Center has *integrated* innovation and lean at both the strategic and operational levels. However, it turns out that creative thinking goes hand in hand with lean thinking. That remarkable concept—how it evolved and how it has contributed to the organization's success story—is the subject of this book.

Chapter 2 describes Virginia Mason's strategic approach to innovation. You will see that innovation is addressed systematically and deliberately, with involvement of the whole organization from the board of directors to the front line. Innovation in healthcare needs to be more than simply a word in a vision statement, or a wishful exhortation.

Chapter 3 goes to the heart of the matter in providing examples of the integration of creativity and innovation methods into lean. You will learn that the concepts and methods from the literature on creativity and innovation fit nicely with lean methodology and help to stretch thinking beyond incremental improvement and across all seven levels of change. Lean is not anti-innovation after all.

Chapter 4 focuses on how Virginia Mason builds leadership knowledge and capabilities with regard to innovation. When leaders *know* better, via systematic learning and unlearning, they can *do* better to catalyze and support innovation. Anyone can learn to be more creative and innovative.

Chapter 5 describes how the organization measures and improves those elements of its culture that are known to support innovation. Organizational culture is key to success in both lean and innovation, and it can be created through deliberate and systematic effort.

Chapter 6 covers Virginia Mason's infrastructure for innovation. In contrast to many other healthcare organizations that are focusing on innovation, Virginia Mason maintains a minimal infrastructure that supports, facilitates, and teaches others, rather than creating a separate, centralized structure where innovative thinking occurs mainly outside the daily work of healthcare service delivery. Virginia Mason Medical Center believes that freedom to innovate is everyone's privilege, not just that of a separate workgroup.

Chapter 7 follows on naturally from the discussion about culture and minimal centralized infrastructure to highlight examples of creativity and innovation in the daily work of frontline team members. At Virginia Mason, frontline staff regularly take advantage of the opportunity to be innovative.

Chapter 8 focuses specifically on how the voice of patients and families inspires innovation. Innovation is often triggered when we deeply understand the experience of patients and families, but it requires that we observe and listen well, and to the right things. Bringing into its lean efforts an innovative approach called *experience-based design*, Virginia Mason is showing that the patient and family experience can be measured and improved upon in ways that patients and families truly appreciate.

Chapter 9 concludes by looking ahead strategically. While stories of success are already evident, the journey of the integration of lean and innovation has only just begun at Virginia Mason, and within American healthcare in general. Virginia Mason Medical Center has come a long way, but knows that it still has a long way to go.

To make concrete an invitation to travel with Virginia Mason on its mission to transform healthcare, each chapter ends with a section that summarizes key points and raises challenging questions for reflection. This section is ideal for creating dialogue among leadership teams that are contemplating adding a deliberate effort on innovation to their healthcare organization's strategy.

Chapter 2

Strategy as Innovation, Strategy for Innovation

Innovation is always a surprise. By definition, it is something no one has thought of before. Its very existence shows that reality is not fixed in predictable patterns. Instead, creative new possibilities can emerge in any field, in any industry. To succeed, we must imagine possibilities outside of conventional categories, envision actions that cross traditional boundaries, anticipate repercussions, take advantage of interdependencies, make new connections, or invent new combinations.

—**Dr. Gary Kaplan**
Chairman and CEO, Virginia Mason Medical Center

Nearly every presentation in Virginia Mason Medical Center begins with the same slide—the organization's strategic plan pyramid (Figure 2.1). "I've never seen anything like it," says board member Bob Lemon, who has worked with many organizations over three decades as a partner at consulting giant Accenture. "That's the ritual. It is just part of the culture, and everyone gets it." Executive vice president and chief operating officer Sarah Patterson adds, "We don't just put it up and go through a rote process of going 'Here's the plan.' Actually, the conversation is often very, very rich."

While nearly every healthcare organization has a strategic plan, few make it as visible and meaningful on a daily basis as Virginia Mason. As one strolls through the corridors, in both administrative and patient care areas, the pyramid is everywhere—as workstation wallpaper, bulletin board poster, or laminated desk mat.

Figure 2.1   Virginia Mason Medical Center Strategic Plan.

You cannot miss it. Importantly, the constant communication appears to work. Partnership survey scores indicate that over 92% of staff members say they know what the organization is trying to accomplish and how their workgroup contributes.

Virginia Mason Medical Center's strategic plan has several features that were driven by innovative thinking, and that now, in turn, drive the approach to innovation across the organization. In this chapter, we will explore the plan, describe its origins and evolution, and see how its elements work together to create a sustainable culture for innovation.

The Challenge of Innovation in Healthcare

Innovation, transformation, and *radical change* have become oft-used words in healthcare over the past decade. The 2001 landmark publication by the Institute of Medicine (IOM), *Crossing the Quality Chasm: A New Health System for the 21st Century,* laid out six aims for the twenty-first-century healthcare system—effectiveness, safety, efficiency, timeliness, equity, and patient-centeredness. Critically, the report gave evidence that American healthcare was suffering a huge performance gap in each of these dimensions. The IOM expert committee concluded, "This challenge demands a readiness to *think in radically new ways* about how to deliver healthcare services" (italics added for emphasis). Reviewing health policy documents from several countries, British researchers writing in 2004 in the journal *Quality and Safety in Health Care* similarly concluded, "Healthcare systems around the world are engaged in striving to make *radical and sustainable changes.* ... The words leave no doubt that what is being envisaged is *big, bold, transformational change.* ... Internationally, there is a parallel realization and understanding that the design of the existing healthcare system will not deliver what is required for the future" (italics added). Most recently in the United States, the Patient Protection and Affordable Care Act promised to "accomplish a *fundamental transformation...*" (italics added).

The drivers behind these calls for innovation are many. In the United States, per capita annual healthcare spending is over $8000, two-and-a-half times more than most developed nations in the world. Yet the increase in life expectancy at birth in the United States between 1960 and 2010 was less than the average increase in the 34 nations in the Organisation for Economic Co-operation and Development (OECD). Research conducted by the Dartmouth Institute has documented large variations in medical practice across different regions in the United States that cannot be explained by differences in population structure or illness. For example, they found that the rate of coronary bypass was 5 times greater in certain hospital referral regions compared to others. While high-end specialty care in the United States is quite good—2012 data shows that breast cancer survival rates in the United States are the best among OECD nations—other aspects of care are not doing so well. For instance, while asthma and chronic obstructive pulmonary disease (COPD) should be largely managed in primary care, US hospital admission rates for these two conditions were the highest among the OECD nations. These statistics are just a quick sample from among the lengthy list of performance challenges facing the US healthcare system. While other countries surpass the United States on some indicators, they lag in other areas, making the call for innovation a universal phenomenon, even if for different reasons.

Unfortunately, innovation often faces both mental and structural barriers in healthcare. It requires the insight and courage to challenge the mental valleys of traditions, assumptions, roles, and "we've always done it this way" thinking. This is what the IOM report seems to be highlighting in calling for the "*readiness to think in radically new ways...*" (italics added). Healthcare professionals and the organizations they work in have a long history steeped in tradition and are notoriously change averse (see box).

While this cautiousness is often appropriate, it can be overplayed, and in some cases, have a self-serving motive to preserve the status quo with regards to power, status, autonomy, or preference. Disruptive innovation guru and Harvard professor Clayton Christensen, along with physician colleagues Richard Bohmer and John Kenagy, studied several modern healthcare innovations that failed to get backers

A LONG TRADITION OF CAUTION REGARDING INNOVATION

A letter to the editor of the *Times* of London, written in 1834 by a physician concerned about the introduction of the then-innovative stethoscope, describes a conservativeness that often still pervades healthcare thinking. He wrote, "That it will ever come into general use, not withstanding its value, is extremely doubtful because its beneficial application requires much time and gives a good bit of trouble; both to the patient and practitioner. Its hue and character are foreign and opposed to all our habits and associations."

and concluded, "Health care may be the most entrenched, change-averse industry in the United States." They noted that the mental barriers to innovation are reinforced structurally in the healthcare marketplace by such things as payment systems, professional standards on scope of practice, and regulatory policy.

Complicating the matter further is the multifaceted nature of the focus that innovation can take in any industry. A healthcare organization can choose to innovate in the areas of basic research, treatment protocols, surgical procedures, new models of care delivery, more patient-centered delivery of existing services, new lines of business, novel revenue sources, partnership arrangements, organizational development, or internal processes. Consequently, an organization might develop a stellar reputation for innovation in one or more of these areas, while being quite average, or worse, in others.

Addressing all these challenges and meeting the need for innovation requires that an organization have a deliberate approach—a strategy that channels the organization's attention and effort. In which aspects of healthcare do we wish to innovate? What goals are we trying to achieve? How will we create and sustain the underlying capacity and capability to be innovative? These and other questions must be debated thoughtfully, with answers translated into plans, actions, and communications that align the organization's efforts from top to bottom in the pursuit of its goals.

Seat-of-the-Pants versus Deliberately Planned Innovation

These challenges and needs came into sharp focus for Virginia Mason Medical Center as it entered the new century. The organization was in trouble. In 1998 and 1999, the system lost money for the first time in its history. Competition in the Seattle marketplace was sharp and there were two other larger players in town. In the wake of the 1999 IOM report, *To Err Is Human: Building a Safer Health System,* which estimated upward of 96,000 preventable deaths annually in American hospitals, key clinical leaders at Virginia Mason were soul-searching. They wondered if what the IOM said was routinely happening across American healthcare wasn't also true at Virginia Mason. They could certainly find no proof to the contrary.

At an October 2000 professional staff meeting, chairman and CEO Dr. Gary Kaplan declared, "We change or we die." This realization led them to the drafting of a new *compact* defining a fundamentally new arrangement between the medical center and the physicians. It was emotionally challenging work, with many feeling a sense of loss for the past. (A fuller accounting of these events, and several others throughout this book, is provided in Charles Kenney's, *Transforming Health Care: Virginia Mason Medical Center's Pursuit of the Perfect Patient Experience*.)

Refusing to be discouraged, Virginia Mason Medical Center also brought to these challenges both its long history of innovation and a willingness to be more strategically deliberate. With its litany of firsts, Virginia Mason had always attracted people who wanted to be involved in innovation. "But," CEO Kaplan explains, "it just sort of happened and was not planned. We have now come to be much more thoughtful and deliberate about building a culture of innovation. What happened before maybe was innovation by the seat of our pants, as opposed to more of a deliberate creation of a culture where people are encouraged, stimulated, and incentivized to innovate." Over the ten-year span from 2002 to 2012, Virginia Mason Medical Center has continuously evolved a deliberate, strategic approach to innovation that contributes to its being named by the Leapfrog Group as one of only two "hospitals of the decade."

Are You Guys Kidding Me? The Patient at the Top of a Pyramid!

Medical center executives and the board decided that Virginia Mason needed a new strategic plan to address its challenging situation, and so created a committee comprising board members, physicians, executives, and key staff people. The strategic planning committee completed its work through a series of retreats and regular board meetings throughout 2001.

One of the goals that emerged from discussions at the board meetings was to avoid simply creating a binder full of materials that people put on a shelf to gather dust. Sadly, this is often the case with many healthcare organizations' strategic plans. As they reviewed prior plans, committee and board members concluded that they were all too long, too complicated, with far too many goals. Then board chair Mark Hutcheson recalls, "We said we wanted to have something short, sweet, and to the point. If we could end up with some way to get it all on one page that would be even better."

After the committee and board had completed its work to identify all the elements necessary to form the strategy, a staff working group structured the plan graphically in a pyramid. The appeal of a pyramid framework is that it clearly shows the pinnacle, the highest goal, and what elements can be supportive if focused on building toward that goal. The vision was to make the new strategic plan something that would facilitate organizational alignment of effort and that individuals throughout the organization recognized, resonated with, and talked about more broadly.

Creativity often arises from a challenge to, or dramatic reversal of, a tradition or trend. For example, the automobile glass repair service that comes to replace your windshield in your driveway, instead of you having to go to their repair shop, is a creative and attractive reversal of thinking. Likewise, it was innovative for Virginia Mason to break with tradition and challenge the assumption that a strategic plan for an organization in a complex situation needed to be equally complex. Instead, they opted to communicate their strategic plan on a single page, in a graphic, in order to spawn organizational dialogue that deepened understanding and consensus.

An even more deeply held assumption was challenged as the discussion turned to what should go at the pinnacle of the pyramid. For years, physician recruiters, including CEO Kaplan, promoted Virginia Mason to other doctors as a physician-driven, physician-led place. Virginia Mason was not unique in this practice. "Everything was designed around us,'" Kaplan says. "Most in healthcare won't admit it, but patient-centeredness is a huge cultural change. It is one of the IOM six aims, and everybody says they embrace it, but they don't know what it means."

So, it was not surprising that the discussion regarding what to cite as the goal at the top of the pyramid might touch a nerve. However, the "change or die" message and new compact discussion from the October 2000 professional staff meeting, along with soul-searching regarding patient-centeredness, led to a deep dialogue at board meetings that resulted in the patient being placed at the pinnacle of the pyramid.

Twelve years on, no one I interviewed at Virginia Mason Medical Center disagrees today about the patient at the top. Indeed, today, many healthcare organizations display planning diagrams that show the patient at the top of a hierarchy, or center of attention. But this was not this case in 2001. Having challenged the assumptions and worked constructively through the controversy regarding what it would truly mean to achieve what, at the time, was an innovative strategic decision; Virginia Mason has gone on to a multiyear head start over most others in operationalizing patient-centeredness.

This initial example of a principle underlying innovative thinking—that it challenges traditions and contradicts assumptions in ways that are often greeted initially with some degree of controversy—also hints at another important point about innovation. An innovative idea is context dependent. That is, an idea or practice that might be common in one industry can be seen initially as controversial, but then as highly innovative, if adapted to another. Immediate past board chair

Carolyn Corvi, a former Boeing executive, recalls her reaction when she first joined the board shortly after the creation of the strategic plan pyramid. "They put up the pyramid and were really feeling great about the fact that they had put the patient at the top. Of course," she went on with a laugh, "if you join the board, coming from a private sector company like Boeing, you're a bit shocked to think that it wasn't like that before. I was coming from the other direction and thinking, 'Are you guys kidding me?' But it was good; a very pleasant conversation to have." Exploring mental valleys outside one's own realm, and actively seeking to adapt what you find others doing, even if they and their situation seems quite different from your own, is one of the many deliberate approaches to stimulating innovation. It is an approach that underlies much of the Virginia Mason story of innovation.

Four Strategic Pillars Support Pursuit of the Perfect Patient Experience

Over the series of meetings in 2001, the strategic planning committee identified the necessary elements of the strategy and eventually arranged them to comprise the complete strategic pyramid. Vision, mission, and values—common elements in any strategic plan—were placed at the top belowthe patient. These were not controversial and were consistent with the history of the organization. Fundamental elements critical to success—strong economics, responsible governance, integrated information systems, education, research, and the Virginia Mason Foundation (fundraising efforts)—were arranged as a foundation. The very base of the pyramid, the Virginia Mason Production System, did not yet exist and was added later.

The keys to the achievement of the perfect patient experience are the four strategic pillars in the middle of the pyramid. These emerged as clear themes from discussion about what it would take to truly *put the patient at the top* and achieve the vision and mission. These key strategies (pillars) are:

People: We attract and develop the best team.
Quality: We relentlessly pursue the highest quality outcomes of care.
Service: We create an extraordinary patient experience.
Innovation: We foster a culture of learning and innovation.

The people pillar emerged easily with almost no debate. On the other hand, the service and quality pillars required some dialogue. Physicians naturally wanted to focus on quality of care as meeting the central need of patients, but others pointed out that when patients interact with any healthcare institution, they expect high-quality care. This is a *minimum* expectation, not a differentiator. To distinguish itself in the marketplace, a healthcare provider must recognize the service element that is often missing. Therein lies the strategic opportunity. In the end, both service and quality were created as equal pillars.

The emergence of the innovation pillar was interesting. Executive vice-president Sue Anderson, the organization's chief financial and information officer, says, "When we developed the strategic plan in 2001, we knew that innovation was really important and we wanted it, but we weren't really sure what form that strategy would take over time." Lynne Chafetz, senior vice president and general counsel, and also the executive sponsor of the innovation pillar, puts it more bluntly, "I think most organizations say that they want to be innovative but they don't really know what they mean when they say it." On the other hand, board members like Hutcheson, Corvi, and Lemon describe the innovation pillar as simply a natural trait of the organization, citing the historical list of firsts as evidence.

Perhaps these differing points of view are best reconciled via CEO Kaplan's insight that there are two paths to the result of innovation; "innovation by the seat of our pants ... as opposed to more of a deliberate creation of a culture." Board members, who are naturally somewhat detached from internal operations, only witnessed the historical results of innovation by the seat of our pants, but executives knew that the organization needed more deliberate creation of a culture. Looking back, Chafetz reflects, "It's been really rewarding to watch the evolution of the organization's understanding of what we mean by innovation, how we embed it into our processes, and how we build it as a culture."

Virginia Mason Medical Center's strategic plan pyramid says so much on one page. The organization's strategy is to maintain a solid foundation, attract the very best people, and put them in a culture that encourages innovation, in order to focus on delivering outstanding quality and service, while exemplifying a core set of values. All of this is constantly aimed at the implicit question at the pinnacle of the pyramid: What is best for the patient? *How will we do all that?* is a question that is asked periodically of a cadre of leaders who sponsor, lead, and staff the various committees set up to plan annually and review regularly each of the elements of the pyramid. *Are we doing that today?* is a question that is implicitly asked in every corner of the medical center, every day.

Looking Outside for Insight: The Birth of the Virginia Mason Production System

Around the same time that Virginia Mason Medical Center was developing its innovative strategic plan, the organization was also embarking on a journey that would eventually produce what many leaders and staff now cite as perhaps its biggest innovation.

Sizing up the growing crisis as it entered the new century, Virginia Mason's leadership team knew that piecemeal approaches would not work; they had tried quite a few in the past. Like many healthcare organizations, they could produce a successful pilot project or do something highly effective in one area, but were never seemingly able to spread the success and embed it across the entire organization in a way that would stick. What the organization lacked was a tangible method for achieving goals systematically and sustainably across the entire organization.

The leadership team embarked on a search to find a healthcare organization that had figured out how to transform itself into one capable of providing the best possible patient-centered care. In an industry with millions of the finest minds, someone should surely have figured it out. Tapping a wide network of contacts, Virginia Mason leaders visited many of the best healthcare organizations in America. While these organizations were doing great work in particular areas, none had transformed into the kind of patient-centered entity Virginia Mason aspired to be. Virginia Mason leaders gained many insights regarding the quality, cost, and safety challenges the organization was facing, but they did not hear a *systematic management* method.

CEO Kaplan posited in hindsight that this might have been due to several factors, an important one of which was the somewhat insular nature of healthcare. "The natural trajectory of the profession and the industry was not to look outside of itself. Healthcare professionals have always felt that we had a noble calling, that we were serving our communities and our patients, and with that sometimes comes, I think, a certain amount of elitism—some might call it arrogance—and an unwillingness to look outside. So one construct is that all we really had was ourselves to benchmark against. When you don't look outside, you don't necessarily see what's possible."

What would turn out to be a breakthrough in the search happened quite by chance in November 2000. Former Virginia Mason president Mike Rona found himself seated on a long flight next to John Black, a former leader at Boeing, who had gone on to set up his own consulting practice. Black introduced Rona to the Toyota Production System and lean thinking. Rona was fascinated. Perhaps other industries operating in competitive global marketplaces might have lessons to benefit healthcare?

The central premise in Black's book, *A World Class Production System*, is that most organizations can do twice what they are doing today with the same resources, while creating a higher-quality, defect-free product. A compelling premise indeed for an organization with the challenges facing Virginia Mason in late 2000. In discussions over the next several months, both the executive leadership team and the board became convinced that further exploration of the Toyota Production System and Black's ideas was warranted.

The story of Virginia Mason's willingness to learn about the lean management system from others *outside* healthcare—Toyota (automobiles), Boeing (aerospace), Genie (industrial equipment), Wiremold (electrical systems), and others—is fully documented in *Transforming Health Care*. Virginia Mason was among the very first health systems to adopt lean methods. Chihiro Nakao (one of only two living *senseis* to study directly with Toyota Production System founder Taiichi Ohno) states emphatically that Virginia Mason leads the world in applying these methods to healthcare. Further, many of the medical center's most famed innovations resulted from adaptation of practices that Virginia Mason team members witnessed on visits to Toyota. A prime example is the Patient Safety Alert (PSA) system, in which all members of staff are expected to *stop the line* by raising an alert if they encounter a situation likely to harm a patient. The alert creates immediate attention, slows or stops an unfolding process that might be error-prone, and results in the convening of senior clinical and administrative leaders to fix the system. This mimics what happens on automobile assembly lines in Japan when a worker spots a potential problem.

In subsequent chapters we will explore how Virginia Mason has further evolved its version of lean methodology, the Virginia Mason Production System (VMPS), by integrating concepts and methods from the creativity and innovation literature. Suffice it to say for the moment that the linkage between lean and innovation occurs in at least four ways. First, adapting lean methodology to healthcare was a highly innovative act in itself. Second, the lean management approach provides a systematic methodology for executing innovative ideas once they arise within the organization. Third, classic lean methods alone often stimulate innovative thinking because they create attention, escape, and movement. They often require managers and staff to view work through a new lens that sees bottlenecks, waste, and activity of low value to the patient or other customer. Fourth, the addition of more tools from the creativity and innovation literature sparks even more innovative thinking. The Virginia Mason Production System, based on the Toyota Production System, was adopted as the organization's management system in 2002, and subsequently added as the foundation of the strategic pyramid.

Gaining Outside Insight on Innovation

The realization that no one was quite sure how to translate the innovation pillar's goal to "foster a culture of learning and innovation" into tangible actions led to further search outside the walls of the institution. In 2002, Virginia Mason commissioned a team from the University of Washington's Masters of Health Administration program to research the academic innovation literature for definitions, organizational characteristics, and specific tactics and methods. The report brought some clarity around basic concepts, helped ensure that leaders had some foundational knowledge about innovation, and gave insight into how they might think about acting to realize it. However, as leaders thought about making innovation a tangible organizational capability, they saw they needed specific expertise in the how-to of innovation. They decided it would be useful to have an outside challenger with an unencumbered perspective to advise them, an *innovation sensei* like the ones they had to stimulate progress in the lean thinking effort that was going on in parallel.

Chafetz recalls the somewhat delicate context in those early days. "We were trying to bring innovation from a somewhat amorphous concept to something more tangible and directed. At the same time, we came to recognize the need for the priority focus to be on the cultural transformation associated with adopting VMPS as our management method. We knew that there was only so much change in culture, language, and process improvement that the organization could effectively absorb." It was important, therefore, to adapt a supportive *integration* of lean and innovation, rather than having the two initiatives appear as competing concepts. Leaders of the innovation strategic planning effort, therefore, wanted someone who could help define innovation *for Virginia Mason,* and help think through how to connect seamlessly with the nascent Virginia Mason Production System.

I was asked in June 2003 to establish an ongoing relationship with the organization as its external chair of innovation to provide these "challenging outside eyes." This is the innovation process role that Harvard professor Michael Tushman calls a "boundary spanner." Tushman's study of large research and development laboratories highlighted the boundary spanner's contribution as the one who linked an organization's internal networks with external sources of information, bringing new ideas into the organization. As the executive sponsor of the innovation pillar in the strategic plan, Chafetz noted the establishment of the chair as an important milestone in the organization's journey. "Early on, bringing in outside eyes with expertise who could challenge our thinking was just like bringing Toyota in from the outside. It helped us move."

Learning from a variety of other industries, as well as purposely inviting in outside eyes to challenge thinking, illustrates another key concept. Exploring outside one's existing mental valleys, boundaries, and comfort zone is a powerful method for stimulating innovation. It is what Virginia Mason Medical Center does now by strategic intent.

Evolution of the Strategic Innovation Plan

Teams were formed shortly after the development of the pyramid to further define the four strategy pillars of people, quality, service, and innovation. A senior executive sponsors each team. The teams are chartered to create, monitor, integrate, and periodically refresh strategic plans in each of the four areas. Multiyear plans provide overall goals and direction, while annual plans focus on specific strategies and projects. The pillar planning cycle stimulates external searches for best practices and new ideas, while the resulting action plans and accountability structures assure continuous development of capabilities, infrastructure, and organizational culture.

The evolution of the innovation strategy is summarized in Table 2.1. Three important strands have played out over time: (a) increasing clarity about definitions and mission, (b) paying attention to the creation of capability and sustaining structures, and (c) directing focus to the highest-impact issues in the marketplace or environment.

Table 2.1   Virginia Mason Medical Center Strategic Innovation Plan

Strands of evolution:

a. Increasing clarity about definitions and mission

b. Paying attention to the creation of capability and sustaining structures

c. Directing focus to the highest impact issues in the marketplace or environment

Timeframe	Key Innovation Goals
2002	• Rapidly adopt proven innovations and Virginia Mason accepted standards of care. • Increase bench-to-bedside research. • Implement Rapid Process Improvement methods across the entire system.
2003–2006	• Create a strong structure and environment for innovation. • Link innovation to the strategic quality plan. • Link innovation to the strategic plan for people. • Link innovation to exceptional patient service. • Grow bench-to-bedside research.
2006–2009	• Continue to develop the culture for innovation. • Direct innovation efforts to implementation of organizational and divisional goals. • Promote spread and implementation of ideas and standards.
2009–2012	• Achieve 100% staff satisfaction on key indicators of an innovative workplace. • Develop a waste-free pipeline that supports the flow of ideas from generation to implementation. • Create systems and supports to enable staff and patients to generate 100,000 ideas per year, with 90% adopted or abandoned/closed based on evaluation and testing. • Differentiate Virginia Mason as a breakthrough innovator.
2013–2017	• Sustain and nourish an innovative workplace. • Develop a high-volume, waste-free pipeline that supports the flow of ideas from generation to implementation. • Differentiate Virginia Mason as a breakthrough innovator. • Share our knowledge to transform healthcare.

Increasing clarity about definitions and mission. The initial, 2002 strategic innovation plan, written before substantial input from outsiders, focused on Virginia Mason's traditional history of clinical innovation, and on connecting innovation to general change methodology and the adoption of "proven innovations" and "accepted standards of care."

Implicit in these goals was a definition of innovation that is widely used in healthcare but is somewhat problematic. In his research on the spread of ideas in social systems, documented in the 1962 text, *The Diffusion of Innovation,* Everett Rogers defined *innovation* as "an idea, practice, or object that is perceived as new by an individual or other unit of adoption … if an idea seems new to the individual, it is an innovation." This broad definition includes any sort of change, at any of the seven levels of change, not necessarily the radical, transformative type called for by healthcare policy makers around the world. To be fair, Rogers' interest was on the spread of ideas, not the innovation process per se. Unfortunately, this definition of innovation is widely quoted in healthcare today, creating confusion between the terms *improvement* and *innovation.*

When an organization defines innovation this way, it often implicitly adopts a *follower strategy.* In essence, it hopes that others will have innovative, breakthrough ideas, which it can then replicate. There is nothing wrong with this; it is a valid strategic choice. While it does little for an organization's reputation as an innovator, it has the advantage of being low risk. Of course, if everyone in an industry adopts a follower strategy, the industry evolves slowly and incrementally, not radically and quickly, as is the need in healthcare today.

By 2003, learning from outside experts, Virginia Mason leaders moved toward the more transformative definition of innovation as *directed creativity implemented.* At Virginia Mason, each of these three simple words is filled with meaning. *Directed* means that it is strategic and focused on organizational goals and aims where, according to the pyramid, the patient is of first importance. *Creativity* suggests thinking outside the box, escaping mental valleys, and challenging traditions, norms, and assumptions. It is about doing things that no one else in healthcare is doing, and therefore demands thought leadership that goes beyond a simple follower strategy. The final word, *implemented,* stresses that ideas, by themselves, are of little value. What matters is what one does with an idea, and whether it makes an impact on health or the marketplace.

The Rogerian definition of innovation focuses on implementation alone, but implementation of current best practices is not sufficient if the ultimate aim is radical transformation of the healthcare system. A full innovation definition must involve both sides of the coin—creative idea generation *and* determined development and implementation. Both CEO Kaplan and innovation pillar executive sponsor Chafetz cite establishment of Virginia Mason's definition of innovation as a major milestone. It transformed the thinking behind later iterations of the innovation plan, and focused the mission on generating new ideas for achieving organizational goals.

Paying attention to the creation of capability and sustaining structures.
Early on, Virginia Mason leaders made an important strategic decision—another
one that they cite as a major milestone—by establishing a deliberately *small*, centralized resource to support the innovation effort. Since its inception in 2003, the
Center for Innovation has never been more than two full-time equivalent positions,
and at times has been only its director, Jennifer Phillips. However, Phillips and
executive sponsor Chafetz have been involved, often behind the scenes or through
developing skills in others, in nearly all of the work described in this book. The
small size makes it clear that the Center for Innovation is a facilitative structure,
one whose aim is to challenge thinking and accelerate progress, rather than to be
the innovator itself. At Virginia Mason, innovation only happens when operational
leaders and frontline staff get involved.

This strategic choice is in contrast to the path taken by other healthcare organizations. For example, the Mayo Clinic's Center for Innovation has more than fifty
full-time staff including service designers, project managers, and others working to
develop healthcare delivery solutions, which must then be transferred to operations.
Only time will tell which structural option provides the quickest and most sustainable path to healthcare transformation. I will return to this topic in Chapter 6 on
infrastructure for innovation.

The small size of the Center for Innovation is reflected in the innovation strategic plan by a focus on goals that explicitly link with other efforts to create capability
and a culture for innovation. Over the years, the Center for Innovation has helped
develop a set of core competencies and a training curriculum on creativity and innovation, as well as indicators and management aids to improve the overall culture for
innovation. A growing number of leaders have developed skills in these areas and
are embedding them into lean workshops and daily management practices.

An additional internal strategy, first explicitly introduced in the 2009 innovation pillar strategic plan, has been to build and support a sustainable, free-flowing
pipeline that can spread ideas throughout the organization. This is related to the
concept of the innovation funnel in Figure 1.3. Conceptually, an organization
ought to be able to trace, and therefore manage, a constant flow of ideas from initial
generation, through testing and refinement, and on to widespread implementation.
Unfortunately, in many healthcare organizations, hundreds or even thousands of
ideas from staff, patients, and families go nowhere. Virginia Mason aims to prevent
this waste.

***Directing focus to the highest impact issues in the marketplace or environ-
ment.*** The evolving culture, capacity, and capability for creativity at Virginia
Mason has been strategically directed over the years to support high-impact goals,
in both clinics and hospital, in the areas of service, access, safety, and flow. In the
2009 innovation plan, the organization also began to explore what it might mean
to pursue truly transformative, breakthrough innovation on a few high-impact
issues directly connected to the strategic pyramid vision to transform healthcare.

Over 60 years ago, in his teaching to Japanese leaders, Dr. W. Edwards Deming famously cited fourteen principles for excellence. The first of those principles was "establish constancy of purpose." Virginia Mason Medical Center's decade-plus attention to its clear, simple, yet powerful, strategic pyramid with the patient at the top, and its persistent development of the three strands of evolution in its innovation strategy, are great examples of the constancy that Dr. Deming was talking about.

Listening to the Voice of the Future

In addition to overseeing the innovation strategy and working to create constructive synergy with other pillar plans, the Center for Innovation team has also brought specific innovation concepts to service-line strategic and tactical planning efforts. In 2003, a paper for the Virginia Mason board introduced the concept of the *voice of the future*, which has now been incorporated into the organization's environmental scanning process that precedes strategic planning and annual goal setting.

Lean, and improvement thinking in general, emphasizes listening to the voice of the customer (regarding needs and experience) and the voice of the process (regarding unnecessary complexity and variation in performance). These voices are typically used as inputs to strategic planning tools such as the strengths, weaknesses, opportunities, and threats (SWOT) analysis method. Innovation can be stimulated by adding the voice of the future to SWOT analysis in terms of trends in medical, surgical, and pharmaceutical research; general technology; lifestyles and demographics; public policy; financing; the environment; workforce and education; and so on. One need only look at the fate of banks that continued to invest capital in traditional bank buildings at the advent of the age of the ATM and Internet banking to see how disastrous it can be to fail to hear the voice of the future.

For a healthcare organization, the voice of the future raises many strategic questions. For example: What are the implications for construction of new facilities if illnesses that are currently handled by surgery will tomorrow be treated by drugs, diagnosed by genetic markers years before the appearance of symptoms, or handled by the injection of nanotechnology robots who perform the repairs from inside the patient's body while the patient sits in an easy chair?

The Center for Innovation recommended to the board in 2003 that Virginia Mason ensure that the voice of the future is heard widely throughout the organization. This led to a series of facilitated sessions, spanning several years, with individuals responsible for the strategic planning associated with the quality, service, people, and VMPS elements of the pyramid, as well as those involved in annual goal planning for the organization's various lines of service. Dialogue initiated in these events has led to an ever-increasing level of sophistication in the environmental scanning that Virginia Mason uses in conjunction with its annual planning. While those responsible for environmental scanning continually see room for improvement in the process, the widespread involvement and substantial progress to date has heightened awareness of its importance.

Stimulating Breakthrough Innovation

Another area of influence on the organization's overall strategy and tactics is around the concept of breakthrough innovation, or what Harvard professor Clayton Christensen calls *disruptive innovation.* He defines it in healthcare as "cheaper, simpler, more convenient technologies, products or services that ultimately let less expensive professionals provide sophisticated services in affordable settings, or enables patients to service themselves." Examples of disruptive innovations in other industries include personal computers replacing mainframe computers, or ATMs and Internet banking replacing large buildings and tellers.

In healthcare, retail primary care clinics staffed by nurses and nurse practitioners, angioplasty as an alternative to thoracic surgery, and home blood glucose monitors are examples of disruptive innovations. Ideas that effectively move the site of care to those of decreased intensity (from the hospital to a clinic or home) and delivery of care toward decreased expertise (from specialists to nurse practitioners or patient self-service) typically result in cheaper, simpler, more convenient care. This is often enabled by the evolving science that shifts the method used to diagnose and treat disorders from an unstructured problem-solving process, demanding high levels of professional expertise, toward a simple protocol-based regime.

Virginia Mason Medical Center, like most forward-thinking healthcare organizations, naturally embraces many disruptive innovations in an *early follower strategy.* The adoption of shared medical appointments where a group of patients meet with a multidisciplinary team instead of relying on one-at-a-time consults with a physician, or the use of chemotherapy in pill form that a patient can take at home, are examples of this.

In addition, as illustrated by the Spine Clinic case study in the box, Virginia Mason has also taken the opportunity to set up structures and processes to become a creator of disruptive innovation. The Spine Clinic breakthrough innovation work is not an isolated case. Similar marketplace collaboratives have been formed around other conditions (for example, the treatment of migraine headaches). These are supported by a small team at the Center for Health Care Solutions at Virginia Mason which, like the Center for Innovation, facilitate work in partnership with frontline clinical leaders and staff relevant to the topic of interest.

In 2009, "differentiate Virginia Mason as a breakthrough innovator" was added to the strategic innovation plan. The innovation team preferred the term *breakthrough* over Christensen's term *disruptive* because the former was more in line with what would likely resonate best with patients. Patients could not be faulted for feeling perhaps that modern healthcare is already disruptive enough to their lives. The hope of a breakthrough to something much better is a more attractive proposition.

WHY DON'T YOU START WITH THAT?
THE SPINE CLINIC CASE STUDY*

Background: In 2004, several large, Seattle-based, self-funded employers and their health plans challenged leaders about the amount they and their employees paid for healthcare at Virginia Mason. Rather than reacting defensively, Virginia Mason created the first "marketplace collaborative" in which all parties meet in an environment of uncommon transparency and open communication to address issues. Access, quality, rapid return to functioning, and costs associated with the treatment of back pain was a problem of particular concern to the employers.

 Analysis: A team of clinicians and managers used lean methodology and evidence-based practice tools to study the current value stream. They found a huge amount of variation and the use of expensive diagnostic resources of questionable value on 80% of patients who had uncomplicated back pain. The only thing that the evidence showed consistently had value was physical therapy, and that was the last thing most patients received! Upon hearing this at a marketplace collaborative meeting, an employer's benefits manager asked the provocative question: "If the only thing giving value is physical therapy, then why don't you start with that?"

 Actions taken: Virginia Mason took this provocation to heart and completely rethought the process of care for back pain. Today, the Virginia Mason Spine Clinic features same-day access to physical therapy appointments and an initial-assessment process that is based on rigorous evidence appraisal.

 Results achieved: The defect of diagnostic scans of questionable value for patients with uncomplicated back pain has been reduced to nearly zero. In 2007, Virginia Mason patients had a greater reduction in pain, greater improvement in function, greater perceived improvement, and much less lost work time than those treated at other facilities in the Seattle marketplace. Compared to marketplace peers, Virginia Mason created these outcomes in one-third of the total elapsed time from initial complaint to resolution, with 23% fewer MRIs, 40% fewer physical therapy visits per patient, and at a total estimated annual savings of $1.7 million for the employers. Starbucks and its health plan renegotiated its rates for physical therapy to align more with its value, in part enabling Virginia Mason's physical medicine and rehabilitation service to go from a negative contribution margin to a slightly positive one.

 Discussion: The traditional mental valley was that it is important first to completely rule out complicated back pain via visits to medical specialists and extensive tests before recommending simple physical therapy. This was supported by the payment system. The Virginia Mason Spine Clinic model creatively turns that assumption on its head and is, therefore, an innovation. It also clearly meets Christensen's definition of disruptive innovation. This work has been widely praised as highly innovative, and nationally recognized by published papers and an article in the *Wall Street Journal*.

* Adapted from Charles Kenney, *Transforming Health Care: Virginia Mason Medical Center's Pursuit of the Perfect Patient Experience*, 129–148.

> ## VIRGINIA MASON'S DEFINITION AND FOCUS OF BREAKTHROUGH INNOVATION
>
> An idea or unique adaptation in healthcare, that Virginia Mason led, that:
>
> a. breaks mental models (achieving level 5, if adapted from outside healthcare, 6, or 7 of the Seven Levels of Change), **and**
> b. has the potential to make a significant jump in an important metric in an urgent timeframe (with *significant* and *urgent* to be defined on a situational basis).
>
> We seek to stimulate and fund development, adoption, and diffusion of breakthrough innovations in four domains: (1) service, (2) internal process, (3) clinical, and (4) business models/marketplace.

In line with the first of the three strands of evolution in the overall strategic innovation plan, considerable time was given to clarifying the definition, and identifying the potential domains, of breakthrough innovation (see box).

Creation of capability, the next stage of evolution, was accomplished through a variety of efforts, including presentations on the topic at board retreats and various executive and managerial group meetings.

The third strand, directed focus to the highest-impact issues, has evolved from awareness raising and informal discussions with those accountable for strategic and operational goals, to a more deliberate, leadership-driven process linked directly to the organization's structures for operational planning.

Virginia Mason Medical Center translates its highest-level strategic intentions into annual operating goals and plans using the *A3 tool*. This is a method associated with *hoshin kanri,* an approach to planning widely used in companies using lean thinking methods. "The idea," says chief operating officer Sarah Patterson, "is that you should be able to describe succinctly and clearly on one A3-sized piece of paper: What is the problem? Why does it require organizational resources? and What are the metrics that you can use to measure success?"

Consistent with the principles of hoshin kanri, the central value in the A3 process lies in the discipline of getting all leaders to participate in a dialogue that gets the list of organizational goals down to a relatively small number that are large in scope and recognized as high impact and urgent by nearly everyone. This is in contrast to the long lists of goals in most healthcare organizations, a statement that was also true of Virginia Mason at times in the past. Accepted A3s get monetary and knowledge resources assigned to them, along with high expectations regarding delivery. Therefore, they are natural candidates for dialogue about the potential for challenging existing mental models and going for breakthrough innovation.

Coincident with adding the item on breakthrough innovation to the 2009 strategic plan, the Center for Innovation began working with leaders of A3s looking for opportunities to challenge assumptions. In 2012, each was interviewed early in the planning process, specifically to identify candidates for breakthrough innovation. This has resulted in work that is just getting underway in 2013 to actively stimulate breakthrough innovation on two important organizational goals: transition out of the hospital for complex patients and reduction of hospital-induced delirium. Both of these are important issues involving patient experience, quality of care, and cost in health systems across the United States and internationally, and both have been the subject of painfully slow progress over the years. Breakthrough ideas—doing what no one else in healthcare is doing (level 6 change)—would be a huge step toward Virginia Mason's mission to transform healthcare.

The Board's Role in Strategy and Innovation: You Have to Be on the Team

Any discussion of organizational strategy naturally begs questions about the role of the board of directors. Strategic decisions are the most important that any organization makes. Consultation with the board, and its ongoing approval and support, is critical.

Virginia Mason board members tend to be passionately involved with the organization. Board members played an active role in the development of the strategic pyramid plan, and two board members sit on the Innovation Leadership Team that gives ongoing advice quarterly to the effort. During their first three-year term, board members journey with Virginia Mason leaders on a two-week trip to Japan to learn firsthand about lean methodology. Board members and executives support one another in putting the patient first and maintaining the leadership courage and constancy of purpose required to bring about the long-term shifts in deeply held mental models that innovation demands.

When asked what advice she might give to a board chair of another health system that wished to follow Virginia Mason's path regarding lean and innovation, past board chair Carolyn Corvi was emphatic about the need for this level of board commitment and involvement. "The first thing board members have to do is learn. It's not enough to say to the leadership, 'Well, the board supports you, go off and do that.' You have to get your hands dirty and learn how to do it; you're going to have to invest time in this yourself. This isn't about just going to the board meeting and you can't just read a book about it. You have to be on the team."

Transforming Healthcare: What Others Can Learn from Virginia Mason's Innovation Strategy

The Virginia Mason Medical Center experience clearly suggests that innovation in healthcare should be approached systematically and deliberately, with involvement of the whole organization, from the board to the front line. Strategy must be clearly articulated and persistently communicated in both the words and actions of senior leaders in every decision. While high-level goals and strategy require what Deming called constancy of purpose, action plans can evolve and progress over time. As the Virginia Mason experience indicates, the more explicit an organization is about its plans and evolutionary principles, the more successful it can be. Innovation needs to be more than lip service and wishful thinking; more than what CEO Kaplan called "innovation by the seat of our pants."

Leaders in Other Healthcare Organizations Should ...

Reflect on the constancy, complexity, clarity, and communication of their organization's strategic plans. The Virginia Mason story demonstrates the critical role of these four C's.

- As board- and executive-level leaders, are we able to hold a strategic intention and direction over time?
- Is our strategy concise and plain enough to be understood by over 90% of our staff?
- Is our main goal clear in establishing priorities for decision making?
- How many strategic and operational goals do we have?
- How visible is our plan?
- How do we see innovation supporting the larger goals of our organization?

Seek to understand what innovation means and what it requires. Virginia Mason's simple definition—directed creativity implemented—sums it up nicely. They understand the need to challenge traditions, assumptions, and mental models, and to accept such challenges from others as invitations to innovation rather than invitations to explain why the status quo must be maintained.

- How do we define innovation?
- In what aspects of healthcare do we wish to innovative?
- Do we really have what the IOM report called a "readiness to think in radically new ways"?
- Can we already identify some traditions and assumptions that we would like to target for challenging attention, escape, and movement, and can we imagine how that might unfold?
- How will we begin to bring the voice of the future into our organization?

Be willing to actively look outside the healthcare industry for concepts, technologies, and practices that might be imported into healthcare, and to approach these with genuine curiosity and the humility of a learner. In 2002, the initial group of Virginia Mason clinical and executive leaders felt like fish out of water as they traveled to Japan and sat in manufacturing facilities to learn about lean. While some leaders who were invited initially felt somewhat insulted by the suggestion, nearly all who went returned enriched by the experience. Back home, they engaged in dialogue with board members, patients, and other team members who had vastly different points of view and experiences from themselves, but they listened and learned. These learning journeys continue with new groups annually.

- How do we generally react to those from outside of healthcare who say that they have ideas to make healthcare better?
- How patient and open would we feel sitting in a manufacturing factory or other foreign environment in order to learn something new that might apply to healthcare?
- Who plays the role of *boundary spanners* for our organization, bringing in challenging new ideas in from the outside, and how do we support those individuals?

Plan to create a culture that supports innovation, via careful evolution over time. The three strands of evolution that have played out in Virginia Mason over a ten-year period are often seen in the development of a successful, long-term organizational strategy on any topic.

- How will we patiently increase clarity about what innovation means in our organization?
- How will we build organizational capability for innovation, and support and sustain that over time?
- What high-impact issues are our best opportunities for innovation?
- How will we engage the stakeholders on those issues to see the need for the radical rethinking?
- Do we want to be a *follower*, focused mainly on implementing innovations developed by others, or do we wish to be a thought leader capable of creating breakthrough innovations of our own (or maybe some mix of both)?

Chapter 3

Integrating Innovation and Lean in Practice

> By virtue of the Virginia Mason Production System being our management method, we are taking innovation to the next level. Lean encourages you to constantly think in innovative ways because you are constantly trying to improve things. It also gives you a culture, a discipline, and an infrastructure dedicated to bringing about change.
>
> **—Bob Lemon**
> *Board Member, Virginia Mason Medical Center*

The belief that lean thinking and innovation do not mix well is based on a superficial understanding of both. Yet, it is common. "When we first raised the notion of standard work, our doctors were aghast," recalls CEO Dr. Gary Kaplan. "You heard, 'This is cookbook medicine, standardized mediocrity,' and so on." Similarly, Hospital Quality and Safety administrative director Joanie Ching, RN, recalls that when she was considering taking a job at Virginia Mason several years ago, friends counseled her to reconsider, saying that with its emphasis on lean she would not be allowed to be as creative as they knew she liked to be.

Ching found the opposite to be true. Over a decade of experience at Virginia Mason Medical Center further suggests that lean and innovation can be mutually supportive partners in the transformation of healthcare. In fact, Kaplan now calls standard work "the foundation for innovation." Practicing primary care physician and director of Primary Care Quality and Innovation, Dr. Kim Pittenger, goes so far as to say, "I think that the most groundbreaking innovation we have to offer the majority of American medical practices is standardization."

In this chapter, I will dispel the misinformed notion that lean and innovation are antithetical. Rather, I will show how they are conceptually and practically synergistic. When applied in the right cultural context, lean thinking both enables innovation, and helps spread and sustain it. We will look at some specific concepts and tools that support this synergy, and explore examples of how these are used within the Virginia Mason Production System (VMPS).

Debunking the Myth

Most myths are based in a semblance of logic, or they would not endure. It is indeed true that lean emphasizes standardization and elimination of unnecessary variation, while creativity and innovation is all about purposefully violating the current standard and temporarily creating variation for the purpose of testing. However, rather than being polar opposites that can never meet, it is more correct to see these as complementary points in a upward spiral of improvement (see Figure 3.1). In the presence of a supportive organizational culture—which, as you see in the remainder of this book is no trivial task—standard work and innovation go hand in hand.

First, it is important to note that there is mounting evidence that standardization in some aspects of medicine is good. Reviewing healthcare safety and quality practices in the *New Yorker,* surgeon and author Dr. Atul Gawande concluded that "standardization has led to vastly better outcomes." Supporting Pittenger's point, standardization can be an innovation in and of itself.

Going beyond this direct benefit and supporting Kaplan's point, standardization and elimination of variation further provides a stable substrate on which to generate and experiment with innovative ideas for transformation. Standardization of the current way of doing things at least makes it clear what the current mental valleys are, so that one can practice the creative actions of attention, escape, and movement. Further, without standardization, baseline measurement of performance has so much variation that it is difficult to determine if a new way is better. Finally, as internal medicine physician Dr. Dennis Rochier observes, "once you

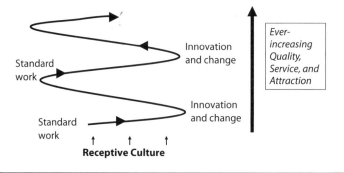

Figure 3.1   Lean and innovation are mutually supportive (© 2004 Paul E. Plsek).

start standardizing the day-to-day work, it really frees up your ability to innovate elsewhere. You don't have to think about those things anymore. Those are sort of automatic and it gives you the benefit of time and energy that you can invest in new ideas."

When the performance of the current way of doing things is no longer meeting needs, it is time for a change. The seven levels of change framework guides a spectrum of thinking from the logical and linear, to the creative and lateral. Generally speaking, change at the initial several levels is called *improvement,* while change that ventures into the latter levels is called *innovation,* but there is not a sharp demarcation.

Lean provides several provocations to think differently in search of useful change. For example, the lean concept of continuous flow encourages one to see waiting states as wasteful and unnecessary, and therefore candidates for new thinking. This is a manifestation of the process of attention, escape, and movement that we find in the innovation and creative thinking literature. The methods of directed creativity add even more approaches for stimulating this process in the search for better ways to do things. Creative thinking techniques are not antithetical to lean, they are a complement to it. In addition, the methods for small-scale tests of change that we find in lean thinking and traditional quality improvement—for example, the Shewhart-Deming cycle of plan, do, study, act—provide structured ways to further develop and test new ideas against the performance of the current standard work.

In a sophisticated organizational culture, like that at Virginia Mason, leaders and staff have no difficulty understanding that they are sometimes in the zone of standardization in the spiral in Figure 3.1, and sometimes in the zone of challenging the current standard and testing innovative new ideas. There is complexity, but no dichotomy. One follows the other naturally.

When an innovation has proven its value in achieving a new level of performance, it then makes perfect sense to standardize the practice and spread it widely, the hallmark of lean thinking. This completes a loop around the spiral. However, the culture of lean and innovation does not allow a standard to become the proverbial *we have always done it this way* that blocks subsequent innovation and change. Rather, the new standard practice is seen as just another temporary phase on the upward journey to better and better performance. In a supportive culture, nothing ever becomes the way we have always done it. Instead, everything is simply the way we are *currently* doing it across the organization. Standard work is meant to be improved and innovated upon. This is the essence of the concept of continuous improvement, *kaizen.*

Consistent with the lean principle of pursuing perfection, the upward spiral of standardization and innovation never ends. Transformation emerges over the various cycles of this spiral across a value stream.

The complementary nature of lean and innovation is not a new idea. It has been embedded in the Japanese tradition of lean since the 1950s. Japanese improvement guru Shigeo Shingo authored *Kaizen and the Art of Creative Thinking* in 1959 in

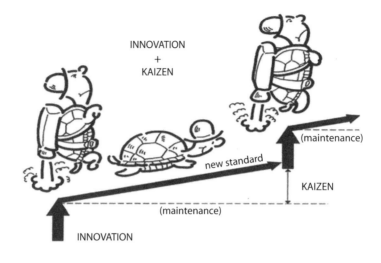

INNOVATION
+
KAIZEN

(maintenance)

new standard

KAIZEN

(maintenance)

INNOVATION

Figure 3.2 Innovation and kaizen, the journey of the turtle. Source: Japan Human Relations Association. (1997) *Kaizen Teian I: Developing Systems for Continuous Improvement Through Employee Suggestions*. Portland, OR: Productivity Press, Originally adapted from Imai M. (1986) Kaizen: *The Key to Japan's Competitive Success*. McGraw-Hill. (See chapter notes.)

which he provided several tools and methods for idea generation and development. Figure 3.2, adapted by the Japan Human Relations Association from Masaaki Imai's classic text, *Kaizen: The Key to Japan's Competitive Success,* is a further example of the integration of these two fields of thought. It shows the slow journey of the turtle, climbing up a slope of standardizing better performance through continuous, incremental improvement (the initial levels of the seven levels of change). However, from time to time, the turtle dons a rocket pack and zooms up to a new level of performance in a transformative, step change of innovation (the latter of the seven levels). This then creates a new standard from which the organization can practice maintenance and incremental improvement. Innovation and kaizen are simply different stages of the turtle's journey.

Integrating Lean and Innovation: Natural Overlaps in Tools and Methods

The natural fit of lean and innovation also extends to specific tools and methods. I will provide a brief overview here, and then give further illustrations through the more extended examples in the latter half of the chapter.

Lean tools raise awareness of and challenge specific mental valleys with respect to flow and waste, creativity tools extend this challenge to all types of mental valleys. The lean tool of 5S, for example, helps one reduce waste by inviting the user to sort, simplify, sweep, standardize, and practice self-discipline in work practices. One might apply the 5S method to a supply closet or exam room in a clinic, or use 5S thinking to redesign forms or documentation. In doing so, one confronts many common mental valleys in thinking about how we go about our work; for instance:

- It is good to keep things around just in case I need them some day.
- It is OK to know that something I need is "in there somewhere" because I can always find it when I need it.
- Standardization threatens creativity and autonomy.

These mental valleys become givens that we are rarely aware of, and even more rarely challenge. We tend to think of them as simply being *right;* no need for further thinking. The 5S tool forces thinking otherwise.

The creative thinking tool of *assumption busting* picks up where this leaves off in suggesting that *everything* we do has embedded assumptions and mental valleys that could be challenged. For example, an innovation frequently mentioned by Virginia Mason leaders is the practice of hospital nurses working in geographic cells. Previously, the assumption was that in order to present a reasonable workload, a nurse's care assignment for the day needed to be balanced in terms of patient acuity (degree of illness). This meant that a nurse might have, say, four patients, ranging from low to high acuity, but spread out over an entire nursing unit based on the random availability of beds when each patient arrived. Studies at Virginia Mason showed that nurses were spending most of their time walking around the unit, or at the central nursing station, and only about 35% of their time in direct patient contact.

Paying attention to and escaping the assumption that nursing assignments needed to be balanced based on acuity led to an alternative mental valley where the new concept is that a nurse could reasonably handle any four patients who happened to end up in adjacent rooms, if she or he had at hand the right equipment, supplies, information, and help (from a patient care technician teammate). This new assumption was reduced to practice and tested in a VMPS workshop in 2005. Nurses and their patient care technician partners now do almost all of the their work in patients' rooms, or in the hallway just outside the door. Nurses' time available for patient care rose to over 90%, while the average number of steps a nurse walks in a day fell nearly tenfold. The practice has since been standardized, where applicable, across the hospital. New patient care units are now designed without the traditional nursing station; it is simply not needed. By purposefully changing our assumptions we can change our practices, and the result can be an innovation. Virginia Mason was one of the first hospitals in the country to extensively use geographic nursing cells, a level 6 change (doing things no one else is doing).

Similarly, the design of the medical center's new Jones Pavilion busted many assumptions that were common at the time about space design. For example, instead of "someone must enter the room in order to stock the room," the design provides through-the-wall stocking. Instead of "the patient needs a portable support like a walker or a nurse's arm in order to get to the bathroom," there is a support system built into the room that extends seamlessly from the bed to the bathroom. These and many other ideas arose from deliberate assumption busting exercises in VMPS events. While some have since become common in healthcare space design as others hit upon the same ideas, the fact that they can be deliberately provoked through the use of simple group discussion tools is important. An organization that desired strategically to be an innovator need not wait for ideas to come from others, or by happenstance.

When they are written down for the first time by participants in the early stages of a lean workshop at Virginia Mason, assumptions such as those above seem like obvious statements of simple facts. "Well, of course, how else could it be?" is the usual reaction in these early sessions. That is simply the activation of the current mental valley speaking, ready for thought just to flow on through without pause. When the concepts of directed creativity are also explicitly drawn to mind, this natural instinct is replaced with an instinct to pause, pay attention, escape the mental valley, and move on to wonder how else it might be. It is at points like these in the workshop process that the integration of lean and innovation has its greatest value. Listing mental valleys and using assumption busting have now become standard features of VMPS workshops.

Lean thinking tools invite practitioners to see with new eyes, and directed creativity tools suggest hundreds of additional new eyes to look through. A KPO director was once pulled aside by a Japanese sensei who remarked that she had beautiful eyes. Rather than a comment on her physical appearance, this was the sensei's way of complimenting her skills at observation, a key tool in lean thinking. Prior to a workshop, leaders, front-line staff, and VMPS specialists typically spend many hours observing process flows and the experiences of patients, families, and staff. The goal is to *see* things in a new way, as a prelude to *thinking* about them in a new way.

The creative thinking tool of *be someone else* takes this idea a step further. VMPS workshop facilitators often ask teams to generate ideas as if they were a 10-year-old child, a titan of industry, a flight attendant, and so on. Facilitators use a long list of diverse personalities that they can select at random to spark creative thought. The goal is to explore potentially creative connections between the problem at hand and a selected perspective. For example, in a VMPS workshop aimed at redesigning the performance management framework, team members were asked to think about what the development and assessment of performance might mean to duos such as a professional athlete and coach, rock star and talent manager, CEO and board, and politician and campaign manager. These produced many fresh perspectives that went into the final design of a system. Compared to the traditional, once-a-year, written performance review with limited development discussion, the new system at Virginia Mason will be more continuous, staff member driven, active, transparent, exciting, and aligned to goals.

Lean not only encourages careful observation of the current process. Japanese experts, like Virginia Mason's sensei, Chihiro Nakao, also suggest looking reflectively to nature for analogies that can be used to improve a value stream. For example, the team creating the design vision for Virginia Mason's Kirkland Clinic studied ecosystems in a rainforest. Each level of a rainforest is a different ecosystem where species on the treetops do not compete for food or shelter with other layers, yet each layer is dependent upon the others' success in order for the whole forest to survive. This led to thinking about how different teams of specialists, internal medicine, and family medicine providers might optimize their designs to support their patients, yet have the whole clinic work together on core support services. As a result, the Mountain, Meadow, and Beach corridors in the Kirkland Clinic allow specialty and primary care teams to share resources when necessary, while operating autonomously at other times.

Through a tool called *mental benchmarking,* creativity experts suggest that potentially useful analogies might be spotted everywhere around us in the marketplace, provided we are willing to open our eyes to them. For example, in 2004, Virginia Mason was one of the first in the country to institute a drive-through influenza vaccination service, based on ideas generated by asking how fast-food restaurants might think of providing access to service.

However, to reiterate, the concepts and tools of both lean and creativity only work in a receptive culture. I have facilitated this quick exercise using fast-food restaurants in my directed creativity workshops with healthcare professionals around the world and am amazed at how many of them cannot get past their disdain for the health-harming practices of the fast-food industry in order to see useful concepts that can be put to good use. (For a secondary benefit associated with this idea and exercise, see the box titled, "We Laughed about It, but We Did It Anyway.")

WE LAUGHED ABOUT IT, BUT WE DID IT ANYWAY

One of the behaviors of creative individuals that is identified in the literature and practiced at Virginia Mason is the directed creativity heuristic to pause on ideas that make you laugh. The image of a drive-through window in a healthcare facility is one such idea. Virginia Mason Institute Faculty and Marketing Director Chris Backous reflected on this: "I think one of the things that we had all said and laughed about was the drive-through flu shot clinic. But now we've done it. I love the fact that we made something real that was initially so ridiculous sounding. Now it is something that we can point to and say, 'Yeah, it seemed pretty ridiculous at the time, but it worked. If we could do it there, where else could we do it?' It frees up our thinking every time we talk about it."

Lean thinking experts encourage the adoption of Japanese language terminology in order to highlight certain concepts for fresh attention, and creativity tools similarly encourage exploring all the language we use. Individuals are sometimes put off by the strange sounding terminology of lean methods that comes directly from the Japanese. For example, *nemawashi* is the process of laying the foundation for change with stakeholders, especially the operators in the process. Nemawashi literally translates as "going around the roots," as in digging around the roots of a tree to prepare it for transplantation. Senseis suggest that carefully preparing the soil is better than "throwing seeds on concrete."

The use of new terminology avoids the mental valleys that might be associated with more familiar terminology, forcing one to think more carefully. For example, to many organizational leaders, the phrase *preparing people for change* might immediately lead to thoughts of sending out an email announcement, or holding a meeting where the boss presents the changes in a rather hierarchical and mechanical way. The unfamiliar terminology of nemawashi, and its associated metaphor, conjures up more respectful and organic thinking about what might be truly needed to prepare the organizational soil for a transplanted, new idea. There are many such examples of unfamiliar Japanese terminology in lean thinking, deliberately there to spark unfamiliar thinking, and cut off the automatic flow into usual thinking.

Similarly, the creativity literature suggests that using different words can lead to different thoughts. For example, creativity expert and author Edward de Bono calls language "the graveyard of ideas" because the words we use to describe problems, processes, and activities puts us into usual mental valleys and results in the same thoughts we had the last time we passed through.

Wordplay is a directed creativity tool, based on de Bono's work, that is widely used by team leaders and facilitators in VMPS events to avoid this thinking trap. One variation of the method picks out key words in the problem statement and invites team members to explore what these mean in order to widen the search for ideas. An early example was a 2003 event looking for creative ideas to improve training and communication within Virginia Mason. When said in the context of an organization, *training* usually conjures up traditional images of individuals sitting in a classroom, or at their computer screens, receiving previously packaged input. Likewise, *communications* generally puts us in the mental valley of newsletters, staff meetings, and emails. Creative wordplay begins by asking what we really mean by training or communications, what we are trying to accomplish. When teams in the innovation event were then asked to come up with creative ways to inform and teach staff about new systems, they easily generated several dozen ideas such as using the rumor mill, creating a scavenger hunt with clues, creating systems that are so user-friendly that training is not needed, creating podcasts, and so on.

Another variant of wordplay is to take the time to select a word or phrase that sums up, metaphorically, the vision or goal one is seeking. This has become widely used at Virginia Mason because it has been suggested by both the lean senseis and me as chair of innovation. For example, the VMPS workshop team chartered to design a new clinic location in north Seattle selected the word *lagoon* to be its guiding keyword for the week. They noted that a lagoon, for example, provided a smooth transition, was flexible in that it supported both fresh and saltwater, looked calm and beautiful on the surface while teeming with activity below, was safe and nurturing, and so on. These concepts helped guide thinking in innovative ways throughout the week, resulting in a clinic design that is much more patient focused than the typical clinic.

A third variant of wordplay involves simply selecting a word at random and asking teams to use whatever comes to mind upon hearing the word to generate ideas for the topic at hand. An early example of the use of this variant of the tool came in a 2004 event looking for creative ways to implement a then-new healthcare patient-safety regulation. The regulation required organizations to establish a consistent practice to verify the patient's identity in *two ways* before providing information or services. The sticking point in thinking in those early days was around standardizing a way to do this that would apply to the wide variety of patients, conditions, and situations across the medical center. The facilitator asked one of the table groups in the event to generate ideas on this problem using whatever the randomly selected word *game* brought to mind. Someone mentioned *Bingo*, which led someone else to note that you did not need to cover all the numbers on your card to win the game, and that led someone else to suggest that maybe there could be a standardized menu of several different ways to identify patients and each unit could select the two that best suited them. This idea became the *It Takes Two* mantra that helped publicize the new requirement and assure conformance across the medical center.

Lean stretches thinking by aiming for perfection even when that seems impractical, and directed creativity methods can stimulate creative thinking by proposing seemingly impossible scenarios. Zero defects, no waiting, reduce by 50%, and so on are the only acceptable targets in lean thinking. Japanese lean expert Shigeo Shingo famously developed an entire methodology for thinking about changeover in manufacturing operations by challenging workers at an automobile plant to find ways to set up metal forming dies in less than 10 minutes, when the current status quo changeover process took hours or even days. He asked them to do the seemingly impossible, a level 7 change, and they did it. Similar breakthroughs in thinking have occurred in healthcare safety in recent years as clinicians have embraced the idea that things like zero hospital-acquired infections might be possible.

Cognitive scientists tell us that the mind often rises to seemingly impossible challenges in the most imaginative ways. At the same time, the mind is also quite happy to simply process the same thoughts over and over again in the absence of a challenge. Posing an extreme scenario, or setting an impossible sounding goal, has often been associated with innovation. President Kennedy's 1963 proclamation that the United States would send a man to the moon and return him safely by the end of the decade sparked dozens of innovations in the space program. Similarly, many of the ideas for technological advances in the telephone system came from a series of meetings at AT&T's Bell Laboratories in the 1960s based on an enacted scenario where a foreign government had supposedly wiped out the US telephone system and it had to be redesigned from the ground up.

The creative thinking tool of *leaping* involves making an outrageous statement and forcing the mind to make sense of it. Over the years, VMPS workshop teams have been asked to design processes that would provide service even after all the physicians have become infected with a serious virus, or to find ways to avoid paying newly enacted outrageous fines for waiting times or other patient dissatisfiers. The extreme nature of each scenario forces the mind out of comfortable mental valleys and causes it to entertain radical shifts in thinking. When the time for the scenario ends, the team is left with many new avenues of thinking about how to, for example, maximize the limited physician resource, or truly *wow* patients and families. These ideas can be scaled back with practical constraints to create innovations that transform the real-life situation.

These are but a few of the tools and methods from the fields of creative thinking and innovation that have been seamlessly integrated into the flow of VMPS workshops in order to stimulate thinking across the full spectrum of the seven levels of change. While the methods of creativity and lean came out of different literatures and traditions, all these tools can be seen as natural extensions of one another.

The Marriage of Lean and Innovation: A Careful Courtship

Before we move into more detailed examples, it is important to note that the integration described here has evolved slowly over time at Virginia Mason Medical Center. In the beginning, when the myth that creativity and lean formed a dichotomy was still active, the integration of these two fields was not so seamless. A brief review of the start-up and evolution of the relationship might be helpful to readers wondering how to help their own organizations move forward.

As noted in the previous chapter, the strategic emphasis on innovation and the birth of VMPS were contemporaneous events in the 2002–2004 time period. There was a great deal of change going on in the organization, with many new concepts, tools, and terms to be mastered. Executive sponsor for innovation, Lynne Chafetz, recalls how initially challenging this was. "We were trying to define what the innovation pillar meant and asking if we could integrate it into our Virginia Mason Production System work. There is only a certain amount of bandwidth for getting everyone engaged and we didn't want to inadvertently create the impression that these were two separate things." Current Virginia Mason Institute Executive Director Diane Miller, who was involved at the time in the setup of both the VMPS and innovation efforts, echoes this. "In the early days, we were trying to figure out how innovation and the Virginia Mason Production System could marry, be supportive of one other, and we were concerned that the language should not compete."

There is also a substantive difference in the scope of lean thinking and innovation as it potentially applies to organizational operations in healthcare service delivery. Lean thinking has the potential to be an organization's overarching management method. That is, it can become the way an organization fundamentally approaches *all* that it does, whether it is being innovative or simply doing reliably what it and others have traditionally done. Many healthcare organizations are missing the power of lean thinking because they only dabble in it, along with a variety of other methods, on a project-by-project basis. Lean can be helpful that way, but it is most powerful when it is seen as a pervasive approach to organizational management, as is the case at Virginia Mason.

In contrast, unless new ideas are an organization's principle output, for example, as in a design firm, advertising agency, or think tank, innovation is *not* a similarly pervasive approach to operations. Rather, innovation is a subset of operations, something that an organization needs to do from time to time.

In this sense, therefore, it was also necessary to assure in the early days that Virginia Mason leaders and team members saw VMPS as the preeminent focus, with creative thinking and innovation as a helpful complement in some cases. This is tricky to do because innovation is typically viewed as fun and sexy, while implementing lean is hard work. To pull it off, leaders may need to downplay the innovation initiative a bit, while staying on-message about the centrality of the lean effort.

For these reasons, early uses of the directed creativity and innovation tools were confined to selective training offerings and small events that were offline with respect to the mainline VMPS workshops. The goal was to stimulate creative thinking, but to then bring that new thinking into the context of the more formal VMPS workshops for development. Several of the examples above are cases in point. The original stimulus for the drive-through flu-shot clinic came from a mental benchmarking exercise in a training class, but the thinking was brought into a lean workshop for further development and testing by individuals who had attended the training. The wordplay on *game* that led to the It Takes Two patient safety campaign was done in an informal, two-hour meeting. An *idea notebook* from that event, another directed creativity tool, was then taken into one of the organization's formal workshops where the idea was selected and the campaign was actually developed.

Comfort levels increased as individuals saw successful creative ideas being generated to fuel VMPS workshops, alongside ideas generated using classic lean tools alone. At the same time, in connection with the capability-building strand in the evolution of the innovation strategy, the Center for Innovation was facilitating the use of creative thinking methods within workshops and training selected VMPS leaders on these tools for their use as they saw fit. In those early efforts, directed creativity tools were typically introduced not as specific techniques, but rather as simple prompts from the workshop leader when he or she saw idea generation flagging. How does a supermarket deal with peaks and valleys in demand at the check-out counter? When we say *access* to care, what are we really talking about, and what new ideas does that give us? Are we assuming that providers have to stay put and patients move around? What if we turned it the other way around? These are examples of the use of mental benchmarking, wordplay, and assumption busting as simple prompts from the facilitator, rather than another formal new tool that had to be mastered.

Over time, more and more leaders became familiar with these concepts and methods. Comfort with their integration into the structure of VMPS workshops naturally grew to the point that some elements are now explicitly listed in workshop planning documents. Workshop sponsors and leaders now routinely discuss their expectations of the output of a given workshop with respect to the seven levels of change, and plan for the use of specific innovation methods where necessary. As we will see in a subsequent chapter, training on directed creativity competencies—for use in workshops and in daily work—is also now standard for all leaders.

Competition and confusion were avoided. Integration was achieved. The key realization lay in seeing the distinction between lean as a pervasive management method, and directed creativity and innovation as potentially helpful tools. If those promoting innovation feel that they must be on equal footing and achieve equal recognition to those promoting lean, then integration of the two might be more difficult to achieve.

Innovation and Lean in Hospital Design

One of the earliest, large-scale, and systematic uses of directed creativity methods to support VMPS was in connection with efforts to design Virginia Mason's new hospital space, the Jones Pavilion, in accordance with lean thinking concepts.

Rethinking Hospital Design, 2006

Using the concepts behind the tool of assumption busting, a small group of leaders came together in an innovation planning session and identified over one hundred usual statements about what a hospital should look like and contain, along with alternative assumptions and provocations (see Table 3.1). The plan was to feed this thinking into a series of VMPS workshops planned over time to work out Jones Pavilion design details.

Following this meeting, the Center for Innovation and members of an emerging cadre of facilitators trained in directed creativity led a series of idea generation events to see what possibilities might emerge from deliberately challenging some of these assumptions. Using over a dozen leaping provocations and scenarios (see box), groups of leaders and front-line staff generated several dozen innovative ideas. The executive sponsors of the effort then reviewed the many ideas and used a *harvesting* methodology from the innovation literature to select the best and most innovative.

Table 3.1   Excerpt from Virginia Mason's Hospital Design Assumption Map (March 2006)

Usual	*Alternatives*
It has an emergency department.	• No emergency department • ED handles everything • ED is a really small space • Mobile ED units • Must place the patient before they arrive
Information gathering happens when patients get here; past information not trusted.	• Can't ask after arrival • Can't repeat any questions • Patients carry information with them • Can only get information from someone else (e.g., referral source)
Centralized lab, radiology, cardiac cath lab.	• No centralized staff or equipment • Radiology/lab equipment can't stay stationary; has to move • Can't have it in the hospital building—has to be at least 5 miles away
Patients are transported to each service (little privacy).	• Patient can't move • Staff must have same clothes as patients when transporting • No one else can see patient as they are transported (invisible)
This is our space—patients and families are guests.	• If patients/families not completely satisfied, no reimbursement • Patients/families customize their rooms • All services delivered in patient's homes
Tend to design space in the horizontal plane; don't think vertically.	• Nothing can go on the floor • No floors—tall building, hollow tube
Building divided into floors.	• Tall, hollow tube • Nothing above 1 floor • Patients only on one floor—other floors for other things
Some physicians need dedicated workspace.	• No dedicated space • Idea example: Box o' office—cargo pants and tool belts/no wheels
Care organized around traditional disciplines.	• Everyone part of a team; travel in teams • Traditional specialists are available in a call center

EXAMPLES OF CREATIVE LEAPING PROVOCATIONS USED BY VIRGINIA MASON HOSPITAL DESIGN GROUPS

PATIENT INTAKE SCENARIO

You have just been offered a great job as director of patient flow for a new hospital in Oregon that is scheduled to open next month. You couldn't believe the salary offer they made you—it was three times the salary you were earning before! The interview process was a little weird in that they came to your home to interview you, and now that you think about it, you don't really know that much about this new organization. But that salary offer was something that you couldn't refuse, and now that you think about it, maybe you shouldn't have signed that contract that locks you into working for them for 5 years, or else you have to pay back all the salary you have earned. But, hey, what could go wrong?

Well, now you have moved your family and you have shown up for day 1 at the new place and ... now you know what can go wrong. Some idiot designed the hospital without an Emergency Room! Oh, so that is why they wanted a director of patient flow—it is your job to figure out how patients who show up at the hospital as "unplanned admissions" will be handled. You find that there is a space the size of a small conference room that has not been dedicated for anything else and you can have that space, but that is it.

So, Mr. or Ms. high-paid director of patient flow, what are you going to do?

PATIENT INFORMATION GATHERING SCENARIO

A global terrorist group has released a chemical into the air that selectively attacks the vocal cords, rendering everyone speechless. At the same time, the Environmental Protection Agency (EPA) has discovered that chemicals in lead pencils, pens, crayons, markers, and (every writing implement known to man), cause cancer and must be immediately outlawed. If that wasn't bad enough, another terrorist group is reported to have perfected a deadly virus that grows extremely fast on paper fiber, and as a precaution, the Homeland Security Department has also outlawed paper, effective immediately. Here at the hospital, we note that 98% of the information that we gather from patients is gathered via interviews and paper forms. Clearly, we can't do that anymore. What are we going to do to gather and record the information we need to provide good care for our patients?

PATIENT MOVEMENT SCENARIO

Last year, Congress put in motion the economic reforms necessary to eliminate reimbursement barriers that were keeping hospitals from trying new ideas to cut costs and frustration with the healthcare system. Starting in six months, we will only be reimbursed if hospital patients stay in one location the whole time, from the minute they are admitted to the second they are discharged, and if we eliminate all waiting rooms, offices, nursing stations, and such. All space must be dedicated to patient care and all staff must be integrated into these patient care processes. What ideas do you have for creating a hospital in which the patient never travels and all space/staff are aligned directly with each patient's care?

These were assembled into an idea notebook for communication to the various VMPS workshop groups that would subsequently process the ideas, along with the other ideas they would generate in the context of the workshop.

The method by which the sponsors communicated this input to the various teams was also quite creative. Using the theme from the *Mission Impossible* television and movie series, the idea notebook was mocked up to resemble top secret plans and drawings. Photos of the executive sponsors, in disguise and with code names, were included. The teams' mission—should they decide to accept it—was to "topple the current approach to health services systems design," as identified by the assumption table included in the supposedly smuggled top secret document. This setup for the various VMPS workshops created an aspect of what innovation researcher Michael Schrage has called *serious play*. The explicit listing of assumptions in the document created attention, while the light-heartedness invited risk-free escape from tradition and freewheeling movement in thinking.

Example: Emergency Department Design, 2009

The group faced with the patient intake leaping provocation in the box above—*the emergency department is only the size of a small conference room*—illustrates the thinking that unfolded over the course of these events in a variety of design efforts. Faced with the improbable scenario, they designed a flow that brought an entire team of providers and all the diagnostic and treatment equipment needed in most cases into that small space, with the goal of processing the incoming patients onto other hospital floors, or back home, in only a few minutes. Attention to the patient's condition needed to be immediate, multidisciplinary teamwork was essential, access to a few critical pieces of diagnostic equipment was important, and detailed clinical workups would have to be performed elsewhere in the hospital. Over time, and through a series of VMPS activities that worked out the details, several of the innovative concepts derived from this scenario became elements of the new Emergency Department (ED) in the Jones Pavilion.

The first thing one notices upon entering the new ED is that the waiting area is small, comfortable looking, and not crowded; very much *unlike* many other hospital EDs. Patients are greeted by a clinician, and then assessed and assigned to one of three flows within minutes of arrival. Patients who do not need acute hospital care are treated by nurses and care team members utilizing *rapid medical examination* concepts and evidence-based guidelines embedded in standing orders. This ensures that this low-acuity population receives the right amount of care, in the right place, at the right time. These patients come into the ED space only a few dozen feet, never occupy a bed, receive personalized express treatment, and are rapidly discharged to home.

A second flow identifies patients who are not acutely ill, but can neither be immediately discharged (because they are not well), nor admitted (because the hospital unit they need to access is not ready to receive them). In most other hospitals, these patients are cared for in the ED as *observation* patients, creating a bottleneck and forcing more acutely ill patients to wait. At Virginia Mason, they go to an adjacent area called the Patient Accelerated Care Environment (PACE) unit. There they are stabilized, while processes are immediately put into action to quickly draw them onto an appropriate hospital patient care unit, away from the ED, for more detailed work up and treatment.

The final flow is for those patients who truly need the care of ED specialists, those with complex or hard-to-determine needs. They come into the main ED space and occupy one of the only seventeen beds in that area. This triaging of patients results in more focus and attention by the ED specialists on those few patients who are actually in the main portion of the ED.

In the end, all three groups of ED patients get rapid access to just the right level of care, in a more personally attentive environment. Time spent in the ED by patients who are eventually discharged to home has been reduced by 43%, and process times for receiving cardiac interventions and antibiotics have been cut by more than half. In addition, patient satisfaction is an impressive 90%. The process of getting to this design was a combination of:

- creative assumption busting;
- creative leaping in an obviously exaggerated scenario;
- the discipline of lean methods to assess, redesign, and test the various process flows that have to work in concert to make the innovative design possible; and
- an organizational culture and management method that created opportunities for diverse groups of leaders, clinicians, front-line staff, engineers, and architects to work together and take calculated risks to try something new.

Innovation Continues, 2012

In a similar manner, assumptions have been challenged, rules and traditions have been broken, and innovative design features have emerged in dozens of areas in the new Jones Pavilion. It is a showcase of what is possible when directed creativity, lean thinking, and the commitment and process to drive ideas through to innovation

---

A SURE SIGN THAT SOMETHING MIGHT BE INNOVATIVE

Regulatory agencies, by definition, are in the business of conservatively scrutinizing new practices in order to protect the public from potentially harmful ideas. They serve a necessary and important function in the overall marketplace for innovation, especially in healthcare where new practices can result in life or death. At the same time, the innovation literature is clear that most creative ideas sound a bit crazy when you first hear them, as they do not comfortably fit existing mental valleys.

The VMPS team designing the Lindeman Pavilion Surgery Center created a process for rapid room turnover supported by small sterile rooms adjacent to each operating suite. Each of these small rooms was effectively an operating room itself, in terms of airflow and air changes, and was connected to the operating suite by a door. The rooms were designed to support external setup of the sterile supplies and instruments needed for the next operation while another operation was being performed in the adjacent operating suite. New processes and systems, such as locking mechanisms, prevent shared airflow during an operations for infection prevention, but allow a complete back table setup to be wheeled in for the next operation as soon as the prior case is completed.

The design was so innovative that the state of Washington regulators initially said that they could not approve it. Basically, they had never seen anything like it! However, working in partnership to demonstrate and test the innovation, the Virginia Mason team and the state regulators came to agreement that it was an acceptable new practice.

---

come together. Further, the innovation in physical plant design is not confined to the Jones Pavilion alone. Similar innovation is happening throughout the medical center in areas undergoing redesign and movement of services (see the box, "A Sure Sign that Something Might Be Innovative," for another quick example).

Innovating in Primary Care

The area of the medical center with perhaps the most sustained use over time of directed creativity methods in concert with lean has been primary care. Virginia Mason Medical Center provides primary care in eight clinics dispersed around the Puget Sound, employing over 500 providers.

Flow Stations, 2003

Clinical and managerial leaders in primary care were among the earliest adopters of lean thinking and have historically been natural creative thinkers. Upon returning from one of the first study visits to Japan, clinic leaders set out to reduce the waste associated with so-called *indirect care*. This includes such things as documenting in the medical record, filling out forms, reviewing lab results, processing medication refill requests; in short, anything outside the provider–patient dialogue in the examination room. Typically, at that time, indirect care work was done in the provider's office during breaks in the schedule of patient appointments, or at the end of the day. Providers routinely spent several hours each day after the last patient went home doing this work. Lean thinking principles highlighted this practice as wasteful batching. The question was, what to do differently?

In a VMPS workshop, team members busted assumptions about the need for providers' offices and the accepted practice of batching indirect care work at the end of the day. Similarly, they questioned the wisdom of the provider prioritizing tasks versus a support person who might have a better awareness of the overall situation and the value of having the current number of exam rooms if the provider could only be in one of them at a time anyway. Escaping these assumptions led to movement that created the first clinic flow station. Providers left their offices, the middle exam room in a set of three was converted into a workspace, and the provider and his or her clinical support person went back and forth to see patients in the two adjacent exam rooms. In between patients, the provider would do as many in a series of waiting tasks that had been set up by the support person as was possible—document in the record, refill a prescription, review a lab result, and so on. The result was prompt and less error-prone patient care, *and* providers were able to leave for the day shortly after the last patient left. Flow stations, and associated flow managers (the term that evolved for the support person), have continuously evolved (no longer an old exam room, simply a countertop) and are now ubiquitous across the Virginia Mason primary care clinics. In 2003, these were an example of level 6 change (doing what no one else is doing). Today, this innovation is being further spread to other healthcare organizations through the work of the Virginia Mason's external education arm, the Virginia Mason Institute.

Team 5000, 2005

Primary care leadership wanted to stretch thinking about the ratio of providers to patients in the face of declining reimbursements for primary care. At that time, a provider typically cared for a panel of about 1800 to 2200 patients. To encourage radical thinking, leadership dubbed the new effort as Team 5000, with a charter to "develop a new healthcare delivery model that delivers high-quality care to a 5000-patient panel, without increasing the direct care resources needed."

Trained leaders facilitated a full-day innovation event that included exercises using mental benchmarking, assumption busting, and leaping provocations. The group of over 40 leaders, providers, and front-line staff realized that many of the barriers to effectively serving a larger panel had been overcome in other industries (for example, through the use of self-service when you check yourself in for an airline flight), or were simply artifacts of traditions that they themselves helped create (for example, what constitutes doctor-work, versus nurse-work, and so on). This is a common effect from the use of directed creativity tools. While resource constraints and legal boundaries are real, individuals often discover that the most significant barriers to change lie within their own patterns of thinking.

The event produced literally hundreds of ideas that groups then used as building blocks to produce six models for providing good care in panel sizes of up to 5000. These models were further distilled into a list of nine key concepts; for example, tiers of care based on needs, better education for self-management, use of technology to set up information prior to the visit, planned care, and so on. While the specific care model that grew out of Team 5000 and was eventually tested proved to be too resource-intensive with regard to the demand for nurses, the overall effort set the tone for taking reasonable risks to think outside the box and try new things.

Intensive Primary Care (IPC), 2007

Many of the key concepts brainstormed in Team 5000 have continued to live in new initiatives, such as Virginia Mason's Intensive Primary Care (IPC) service. IPC is an innovative effort, fueled by knowledge from initial research and design work conducted by the California Health Foundation and drawing from similar new primary care models advocated by the American College of Physicians and the American Academy of Family Practitioners. The work was done in partnership with large and small self-funded employers and insurance companies, and has the goal of reducing healthcare costs for employees with the most expensive health conditions, while improving their health status. Intensive primary care includes several of the same basic ideas from Team 5000, such as detailed patient education, personal care plans, intensive and appropriate use of proactive nurse care managers, 24/7 phone and email access to providers, and close coordination among primary care providers, specialists, and the hospital. In the initial pilot program, Virginia Mason reduced annual per capita claims by nearly 30% and reduced hospital admissions, despite the additional expense of nurse coaching. Quality also improved; for example, more patients with diabetes had healthier cholesterol levels (from 40% in 2000, to 68% in 2009). Patient satisfaction and functionality also improved. Virginia Mason is now making the same program available to its own staff and their families.

The Team 5000–IPC link illustrates another key aspect of innovation. If everything you try works perfectly the first time, then you probably are not pushing the envelope much and may only be doing incremental change. What others might call *failure* is actually just part of the learning process associated with innovation. Further, this provides another philosophical link between innovation and lean, as Virginia Mason's lean senseis often tell them to "fall down seven, get up eight times" in order to encourage risk taking and learning. Each innovation attempt teaches us something about what works and what does not. Components of the innovation may be reusable in future innovations. It is all just part of the process of creating the upward spiral of lean and innovation depicted in Figure 3.1.

Department of Primary Care Vision, 2012

The thread of linking innovation and lean has continued into the most recent efforts to create a future vision for primary care. Executive sponsors and workshop leaders reviewed the seven levels of change framework and made a conscious decision that they desired to redesign primary care for level 6 or 7 change (doing things that no one else is doing and doing things that cannot be done). They further reiterated their overarching theme as *better, faster, more affordable,* consistent with the mantra of Clayton Christensen's disruptive innovation.

In preparation for an upcoming VMPS workshop that would use lean thinking tools to design the primary care department's systems for the future, the leaders wanted to assure maximal creative thinking and desire for innovation among both staff and patients. The Center for Innovation worked with the Department of Primary Care leadership to design an open and inclusive process that ended up gathering over 650 ideas for change from staff and patients, with about an equal number from each group. Using the concept of the innovation funnel and the tools of harvesting from directed creativity, the planning team organized these into themes in order to feed them into the future VMPS workshop. Participants invited to the workshop were further assigned a *be someone else* role to research and play out in idea generation. These ranged from the traditional points of view of a current patient and a current provider, to that of a wildlife biologist, twelve year-old child, and an outside industry expert. When called upon to generate ideas in the natural

WE HAD BETTER THINK OF SOMETHING INNOVATIVE NOW!

As the Department of Primary Care visioning workshop teams were going into idea generation, a Virginia Mason security guard interrupted and asked to speak to Mike Ondracek and Catherine Potts, the administrative and medical leaders of Primary Care, respectively. Ondracek and Potts exited the room with the guard and returned looking solemn a few minutes later with Deb Madsen, Virginia Mason's associate general counsel and administrative director of the Legal Department. They informed the team of the news. "Our Legal Department has informed us that a local, unnamed major competitor has filed a cease-and-desist order related to delivery of our primary care. They claim that they patented the delivery method that we use and that we are in violation of federal patent law. We must rapidly redesign our Department of Primary Care with the stipulation that there is *nothing* we can do in the future that we are doing now."

flow of the workshop, participants were to think like these personalities in order to escape traditional mental valleys.

To encourage the workshop group to generate level 6 or 7 ideas, the planning team arranged an interesting provocation to be delivered just as the groups were going into idea generation (see the box entitled "We Had Better Think of Something Innovative Now!"). Provoked to truly think outside the traditional box, and with their *be someone else* role, the team generated over 300 ideas. They went on to theme, harvest, and evaluate the best of these using tools from the innovation literature. The process yielded a total of 37 key ideas across 5 themes: preventative care, acute care, chronic care, economic sustainability, and scheduling/access. The over 50-page report will now feed into multiple VMPS events over the next several years, where the various ideas will be further designed, tested, and implemented in an effort to transform primary healthcare.

Busting Assumptions about the Management of Medically Complex Surgical Patients

While the two previous examples illustrate the use of innovative thinking tools at a large-system level to generate ideas that are then filtered down to process-level VMPS workshops for refinement, Virginia Mason's work on medically complex surgical patients is influencing innovation in the opposite direction.

Chart reviews indicated that nearly 20% of Virginia Mason's general and thoracic surgery patients had two or more major comorbidities; for example, arrhythmia, diabetes, or hypertension. These patients also had average lengths of stay that were nearly 1.5 days longer than patients with less than two comorbidities, and there were concerns that they might also be more likely to require readmission. Workshop leaders, process owners, and sponsors noted several existing mental valleys associated with the current care process at Virginia Mason that might be ripe for reconsideration, for example:

■ Medically complex surgical patients will always have a longer length of stay (LOS).
■ Patients expect all their care to be provided by the surgeon.
■ Involving additional providers will make the system too complex and confuse patients.
■ General surgery residents must gain experience in managing complex medical patients through their surgical rotations.

Illustrating the deep knowledge that leaders have about the integration of innovation and lean, Chief of Surgery Dr. Fred Govier briefed the workshop team on the key concepts of innovation and challenged them to rethink all of the assumptions that were driving the process of care in order to "design a reliable standardized process to ensure medically complex surgical patients proactively receive the right level of medical management at the right time." The idea was to both move closer to a perfect patient experience *and* provide a good training experience for surgical residents.

The workshop team accepted the challenge of assumption busting and used the lean brainstorming technique of seven ways to come up with a variety of ideas on how to make the care and the training better. These included providing a navigator to oversee the patient experience; creating standard work to sort complex patients through standard protocols for a medical consult prior to surgery; developing standard work to signal medical providers to provide consults during the acute hospital stay; embedding evidence-based tools in the electronic medical record for clinical staff to identify risk factors; and provisioning of continuous information flow to a care team from the clinic visit, through hospital stay, and home.

The workshop leader also challenged the team to engage in creative wordplay by listing all the actions and functions that ideally needed to occur during the complete care process. The team then grouped these to create a new model of care comprising the six overarching functions of *communicate, oversee, prepare, cure, recover,* and *transition.* This model is now being reduced to practice for testing and implementation, using standard lean tools.

Interestingly, from the point of view of common barriers to innovation in healthcare, data showed that the surgical residents in the teaching program had an average of only about 3 minutes of interaction with the patients that they were supposed to manage, yet there was a significant reluctance to consider having a medical consultant help co-manage the patients. The residents' mental valley of "I have to do it all myself in order to learn" was a significant barrier to overcome. It is not uncommon in innovation efforts in healthcare to run up against such barriers of unrealistic self-expectations among clinicians. The direct involvement of those doing the work, and the small-scale tests of change methodology of lean, help work through these sorts of issues. Research suggests that this can result in significantly better sustainability of innovation, compared to ideas developed elsewhere and simply implemented by authority.

While this was an effort focused specifically on general and thoracic surgery patients, the leaders of the effort realized that the innovation of co-management of patients by surgical and medical specialists from initial clinic visit through the hospital stay and on to home was of more general applicability. This work is now merging with other lean improvement efforts around reduction of hospital-associated delirium, management of hypoglycemia, transitions out of the hospital, and others, to look at patients in a more holistic way, rather than the professional-discipline tradition of designating patients as either *surgical* or *medical* based solely on current admission diagnosis.

Once the mind conceives an innovation and creates a new mental valley for it, many new applications suddenly appear that can be candidates for changes in standard practices. This is becoming embedded in the Virginia Mason culture through the ritual of Friday report-outs on VMPS events of the week. Here, executives often challenge attendees to identify mental valleys that the teams that week have challenged, and consider whether they might need to do the same in their own areas. It is another benefit of the integration of innovation and lean.

Redesigning Surveillance of Healthcare-Acquired Infections

Lean thinking and innovation methods have also been applied to important patient safety issues at Virginia Mason. The It Takes Two campaign and the Patient Safety Alert (PSA) system are early examples that we have already touched on. Our final example will look briefly at a more recent lean workshop in this critically important topic area. It will also serve as a grand review of a typical flow of directed creativity tools in a lean project at Virginia Mason.

The Centers for Disease Control (CDC) reports that between 5% and 10% of hospital inpatients suffer one or more healthcare-acquired infections (HAIs) during their hospitalization, resulting in significant financial and human costs nationwide. Reduction in HAIs, with emphasis on redesign of the surveillance program, was one of Virginia Mason's 2011 organizational goals. This designation led to the planning of VMPS workshops, where the sponsors challenged the teams to think creatively.

The workshop leaders for the redesign of the surveillance system used a variety of directed creativity tools to stimulate thinking, along with classic lean thinking tools such as fishbone diagrams, value stream maps, and the seven ways.

- After mapping the current state of the organization's surveillance system, the team stepped back to list assumptions and mental valleys that gave rise to it (set up for assumption busting).
- The team brainstormed potentially useful keywords to describe their vision for the future state and selected the phrase "protect me" as an overarching theme to keep in mind throughout the workshop week (wordplay).
- Team members were asked to draw seven ways from nature that depict the phrase protect me (brainstorming).
- For homework between workshop days, subgroups were asked to research the key features of weather forecasting, air traffic control, and computer virus detection for ways in which they might be similar to infection prevention surveillance (mental benchmarking or be someone else).
- The team met with a patient who had experienced a severe HAI to discuss both his experience and ways it might have been prevented (be someone else).
- Teams were asked to explore the following provocation (leaping): There is a severe shortage of registered nurses (RNs) in Washington State. To protect the patients in our state, the legislature passed a law that RNs can only work in direct patient care jobs. At the same time, our infection rates have

increased from our normal level to up to 45% and 50%. There is no longer an Infection Prevention Department; the infection prevention RNs have been placed back into direct patient care work. How will Virginia Mason do infection surveillance now?

Using all these inputs and creative provocations, the team generated ideas and potential system models throughout the first three days of the weeklong workshop. They spent the final two days refining a model and developing an 18-month VMPS event schedule to design the details of the system. The vision was for a dynamic system that provides a common language and reliable information to support continuous learning about how to prevent, detect, analyze, and respond to HAIs.

A series of additional workshops was held over the next several months to design the details of the system that was envisioned. Breaking the mental model that a report to trigger an investigation had to come from a single system, infection prevention nurses now combine data from a variety of systems into a spreadsheet that has enabled them to reduce the time required to identify catheter-associated urinary tract infection (CAUTI) in hospital patients from over 7 hours to just over 11 minutes. Similarly, creatively condensing a 10-page policy down to a 1-page, at-a-glance, visual tool has improved staff compliance with the use of personal protective equipment from 50% to 85%.

Embedding Innovation Tools into the Structure of Lean Workshops

Throughout this chapter, I have used the general term *VMPS workshop* to refer to what is actually a variety of specific types of structured, lean thinking events and activities. At Virginia Mason, these are designated separately in order to specify the internal structure of the workshop, its length, and the level of sponsorship and resources. These also differ somewhat in the way innovation concepts and tools are used. The definitions and structures of these event types are constantly evolving. The following paragraphs describe the main VMPS event types, as they were defined during the time period of the examples in this chapter.

Production Preparation Process (3P) workshops are used to design new spaces or systems comprising multiple flows and processes. A 3P workshop is typically a weeklong event, sponsored at the executive level, whose main output is a system design on paper, with a multimonth plan for additional VMPS workshops to develop and test the pieces of the system. The aim of a 3P workshop is almost always at the more innovative levels of the seven levels of change; new thinking is strongly encouraged. Consequently, the concepts and tools of directed creativity are most extensively and explicitly used in 3Ps. The preceding stories about the development of the performance success framework, and the examples in the sections" Rethinking Hospital Design, 2006" and "Department of Primary Care, 2012," were 3P workshops.

Rapid Process Improvement Workshops (RPIWs) are also structured, weeklong events, typically with executive-level sponsorship and assignment of organizational resources. However, here the scope is more focused at the process or subsystem level. An important decision in the planning for an RPIW is the aim of the workshop with regard to the seven levels of change. Some RPIWs are aimed at better standardizing or incrementally improving existing processes, while in other cases, the sponsors challenge the team to innovate beyond the current process thinking. RPIW leaders may use directed creativity concepts and tools in a less explicit way by simply asking prompting questions—for example, about assumptions or how others might see it—when they see team members becoming stuck in their thinking. Flow stations in primary care and geographic nursing cells in the hospital were developed in RPIWs, as were the details of the ED and Jones Pavilion designs.

Innovation events are workshops ranging from one to three days, that may or may not have executive-level sponsorship, where fresh, new ideas are desired on a problem that has resisted solution, or where there is not enough of an existing process to incrementally improve. These are less formally structured events. Workshop leaders typically develop a customized plan based on the topic and the participants. Examples of innovation events in this chapter include the initial Team 5000 and hospital design assumption busting and idea generation events, and the effort associated with medically complex surgical patients.

Kaizen events are used when a possible solution has been identified, perhaps in a previous 3P workshop, RPIW, or innovation event, and it only needs detailed development and testing. Kaizen events are almost exclusively aimed at levels one through four on the seven levels of change (doing the right things, doing things right, doing things better, and doing away with things), although the basic ideas that they are now reducing to concrete application might have originally come from other levels. These events are typically one or two days in length and are sponsored at lower organizational levels.

Virginia Mason Medical Center conducts literally hundreds of these workshops annually. The examples described in this chapter are not isolated events. The practical integration of lean and innovation occurs on an ongoing, weekly basis, as these tools have been built into workshop plans and agendas. VMPS has evolved as a thoughtful combination of methods, quite likely unique among implementations of lean, across any industry, anywhere.

In addition to these formally designated workshops, in the Virginia Mason culture, innovation concepts and tools are also used in daily operational and project work by leaders, clinicians, and front-line staff. We will explore that topic in a subsequent chapter.

Transforming Healthcare: What Others Can Learn from Virginia Mason's Integration of Lean and Innovation Tools

Lean is not anti-innovation. Lean methodology and standardization do not stifle creativity. Innovation is directed creativity implemented, and therefore, innovative ideas need the follow-through that comes from a disciplined management method such as lean thinking. The tools of lean and innovation complement one another. Not only can these things coexist, they can work together synergistically to take things further than either could go alone. A decade of experience at Virginia Mason Medical Center proves it.

Integrating lean and innovation requires attention to underlying organizational culture, clarity, and constancy of leadership purpose, and a deep understanding of the practical synergy that one is trying to bring about. While lean and innovation might have separate terms, tools, and supportive infrastructures, if the two are competing for attention and recognition, the synergy is unlikely to emerge as powerfully as it could. Rather, the resources and organizational structures associated with each need to deeply value the other and seek collaboration for the purpose of achieving a higher, common goal. This collaboration has emerged wonderfully over time at Virginia Mason in its pursuit of the perfect patient experience.

Leaders in Other Healthcare Organizations Should …

Identify their organization's current management method. Whether it is explicit about it or not, every organization has a general approach to deciding what to pay attention to, organizing work, approaching problems, developing capability, and leading and managing on a day-to-day basis. Virginia Mason's management method can be summarized by the principles of lean thinking articulated in Chapter 1; they see these applying to everything they do.

- ◼ How would we characterize our current management method?
- ◼ Could we summarize our management method in a handful of principles, or is it more chaotic and diffuse?
- ◼ Do actions throughout our organization match our words?

Make thoughtful choices about where innovation might fit relative to their organization's management method and other initiatives. At Virginia Mason, innovation supports the overall organizational strategic goals and the management method of VMPS by further challenging status quo thinking. It is not a stand-alone function nor a competing set of priorities, goals, and methods. The aim is to create synergy in service to the overall goal of pursuing the perfect patient experience. This is not the only choice that an organization could make.

- What do we want out of an innovation effort?
- What priorities, goals, or lines of service do we want to be innovative in, or do we want to be innovative in everything we do?
- Do we want to distinguish innovation from other organizational initiatives and the way we usually do things, or do we want innovation to be a supportive part of these?
- Are those in our organization who are seen as the champions of innovation mostly competing with, collaborating with, or ignoring those who are champions of performance improvement and current operations?
- If we did generate some highly innovative ideas, would we be able to test, implement, and sustain them successfully, given our current management method?

Practice embracing impossible future scenarios, challenging current assumptions and mental valleys, and looking outward at how others see things and address opportunities. These are basic mental skills for creativity and innovation. The sooner one begins practicing them, the more natural they become. The more natural they become, the more likely they are to be used to coach others and make personal contributions to organization plans. At Virginia Mason, these skills are embedded in specific tools, but there is no magic in the tools. Learning to see and think differently is the key.

- What are some immediate opportunities for thinking differently on which we could practice some of these thinking skills?
- How can we better prompt and coach others to think differently?
- How might we get started on a more deliberate effort over time to embed creative thinking skills in our organization?
- How will we react when a seemingly innovative idea fails to work as we envisioned?

Chapter 4

Learning to Be Innovative

> It always starts and ends with leadership. If the leaders aren't understanding, embracing, and valuing innovation, why would anybody else in the organization?
>
> **—Sarah Patterson**
> *Executive Vice President and Chief Operating Officer,*
> *Virginia Mason Medical Center*

Knowing and doing are intimately linked. It is difficult to encourage innovation if the vast majority of individuals already think that they are doing their best, and they do not know how to come up with ideas to do better. Until they *know* different, they are unlikely to *do* different.

Further, while seeing is believing, the converse is also true. Numerous studies in the cognitive sciences show that humans tend to see what they already believe to be true. This is the basis for prejudice, for example. Training and years of experience subtly reinforce one's theories of how things work, creating what Thomas Kuhn called in his 1962 book on the sociology of science a *paradigm* that impedes scientific revolution. Leaders might be able to influence incremental change within the confines of an existing paradigm, but it is difficult to move further until new knowledge, new ways of seeing things, and new skills come onto the scene.

Learning is, therefore, a foundation for creating a transformation in healthcare. The innovation pillar in the Virginia Mason Medical Center strategic plan states the overall goal to "foster a culture of learning and innovation." The organization is passionate about learning—acquiring new knowledge, seeing things differently, thinking differently, and developing the skills and capabilities to behave differently.

I begin this chapter with an introduction to some key concepts regarding how professionals in organizations learn, or fail to do so. I will then describe Virginia Mason's systematic approach to learning with regards to both lean thinking and innovation. This will serve as the foundation to explore what it is that leaders of change at Virginia Mason know and do that enables the innovation it achieves.

Learning and Unlearning

Albert Einstein famously said, "You cannot solve a problem using the thinking that got you there in the first place." If healthcare is facing numerous challenges and calls for transformation, then replacement of the thinking that got us here is sorely needed.

Unlearning is the mental process of putting aside past thinking by overwriting it, pushing it to the background, or cutting off the pathway that triggers it. For example, most healthcare leaders learned somewhere in their experience that a waiting area is a good way to handle the unpredictable arrival of patients and the availability of providers. This has led to many well-intentioned incremental improvement initiatives associated with reducing waiting time, or somehow making it a better experience. Unlearning the concept of waiting areas might involve overwriting it with other concepts such as synchronizing supply to demand, pushing it to the background as an inferior approach that we are stuck with only until we find an alternative, or cutting off the pathway leading to it by wondering how one could better predict in advance the impending arrival of a patient so they could be taken in immediately (for example, a sensor system in the parking lot).

Unfortunately, unlearning is hard. What we already know has a long history of being acceptable. Even if we accept new concepts as valid, under pressure we might easily revert to the old thinking as being *good enough.* Herbert Simon, who won the Nobel Prize in 1978 for his research on decision making, noted this human tendency to *satisfice* rather than optimize. Further, we often fear that new concepts, even if they have been proven in other settings, might not work for us and could create even worse problems. Satisficing allows us to be comfortable holding onto past learning. Noting that the Toyota Production System had been successfully applied for over sixty years, immediate past board chair Carolyn Corvi, suggests, "It is still so difficult for leaders to wrap their minds around it because what they are not willing to do is throw out the old system and replace it with a new one." CEO Gary Kaplan echoes Corvi's point when he speaks of the transformation of healthcare: "I think you have to question lots of things in order to be liberated from the old tapes."

Paradoxically, traditional education may be one of the biggest barriers to the unlearning required for innovation and continuous learning. Harvard professor and researcher on the psychology of organizational learning, Chris Argyris, points

WHAT I LEARNED IN MEDICAL SCHOOL

I asked Virginia Mason neurosurgeon, Dr. Farrokh Farrokhi, if he found learning the Virginia Mason Production System easy and natural.

"It was not natural at all, because we're not trained that way in healthcare. For example, in my first lesson during internship, our chief resident pulled us aside and said, 'As you go through your career, the one thing that I want you to think about at every interaction, with any patient, is that everybody else in this building is trying to kill your patient. If you just think that way, from today forward, you will do the best job for your patients because you will always be on the defense, to protect them against any harm that can come to them.'

"That seemed like a brilliant concept to me at the time. Not only did I live that, I taught it to students and residents who have come under me. I would triple-check every single piece of work on a patient, because I was taught that I couldn't trust the system to take care of them. I didn't realize that kind of thinking by every member of the system generates the disaster of waste in healthcare that we have now.

"What was critical for me was getting that concept un-taught [in VMPS training]. I now understand that if we all work as a team and speak the same language, we can focus our energies on the piece that is our work, and we no longer have to worry that the work before us and the work after us is being done with the same level of quality. This enables us to do our work with much better efficiency, quality, outcome, and self-satisfaction because we now have the bandwidth to concentrate on how to make our little piece of the work better.

"That is the essence of the Virginia Mason Team Medicine℠ concept, but it didn't even exist in my framework before. It literally took me a couple of years of being here, where I would check the histories and physicals and the labs and all the other things that were the responsibilities of other people. I would still redo their work, just to make sure I didn't catch them in a mistake. And I didn't. After a couple of years, I said to myself, 'Oh! I don't have to go recheck because the system works!' And so, unlearning what my chief resident taught me, gaining trust, and letting go of control is a big leap of faith."

this out in his classic 1991 article, "Teaching Smart People How to Learn": Those members of the organization that many assume are the best at learning are, in fact, not very good at it. I am talking about the well-educated, high-powered, high-commitment professionals who occupy key leadership positions in the modern corporation." More than a century earlier, famed French scientist Claude Bernard had already summed it up by saying, "It is what we think we know already that often prevents us from learning."

Education and experience carve deep mental valleys in one's mind, making old thinking automatic and new ideas foreign (see the example in the box entitled "What I Learned in Medical School"). This leads to what Argyris calls *single-loop learning* in which problem solving becomes an exercise in trying to find a slightly better way to do things within the current mental valley (for example, shorter waits, or more entertaining television programs in the waiting areas). Transformation requires what Argyris calls *double-loop learning* where we question the basic valid-ity of our mental valleys and assumptions, and actively search for alternatives (for example, how would we handle patient flow if it were illegal to have a waiting area?).

Key Concepts: Pedagogy, Andragogy, and Reflective Practice

The issue of unlearning gives rise to an important distinction, best articulated in the 1950s by adult education authority Malcolm Knowles, between the approach to educating children (pedagogy) and that of developing the adult learner (andragogy). The child, or someone who is a complete novice on a particular topic, has little to unlearn. They are a blank canvas ready for an instructor to fill. Traditional forms of education, such as lecture, reading, or teacher–student hierarchal interaction work well in this situation.

The adult learner who already has some experience on the subject matter is entirely different, due primarily to the need for unlearning. As author Leo Tolstoy observed, "The most difficult subjects can be explained to the most slow-witted man if he has not formed any idea of them already; but the simplest thing cannot be made clear to the most intelligent man if he is firmly persuaded that he knows already, without a shadow of doubt, what is laid before him."

While lecture and reading are helpful to explain basic concepts, with the adult learner one must also deal with the processes of surfacing the old learning explicitly, helping the learner explore other ways of seeing things, and creating an emotionally safe environment to question what one has always believed to be true. In the 1980s, two books by Donald Schon, *The Reflective Practitioner* and *Educating the Reflective Practitioner,* laid much of the foundation for a more ideal approach to developing learning in professionals at work. Schon, and those who followed him, advocated the use of methods such as appreciative dialogue, guided reflection, coaching, net-working, job assignments outside one's field or comfort zone, and action learning. These approaches share the theme that integral to effective learning is the process of working together to apply learning to real challenges. When done correctly, the learner works through the cognitive and emotional processes of unlearning to the point where they come to see that what they used to believe was, at best, old-fashioned and, at worst, just plain wrong.

Creating a Learning Organization: There Are No Shortcuts

Success in both lean thinking and innovation requires significant unlearning and new learning. While the underlying principles of both become quite natural and easily apparent over time to the well-seasoned practitioner, they are quite foreign on first hearing. Helping an entire organization gain comfort with them requires a systematic and patient development effort. However, in a desire to get quickly to the outcome of higher-quality, safer, more satisfying, more efficient, and highly innovative healthcare delivery, some healthcare organizations seek to shortcut the process in one of several ways.

One enticing shortcut ignores the issue of unlearning completely and supposes that simply teaching everyone the principles and tools of lean thinking, creativity, or innovation will lead to sustainable application. Some healthcare organizations have invested money and time in such training, with typically little real impact, precisely because the force of habit or time pressure leads to the conclusion that the old way is still good enough (Simon's satisficing). Illustrating almost perfectly what Chris Argyris calls *fancy footwork* and *defensive reasoning,* the leaders who commissioned these training efforts often conclude either that their associates lacked the motivation to improve, or that lean (or creativity or innovation) simply does not work here because healthcare is different. In the end, these organizations learn very little and typically go on to embrace unsuccessfully the next big thing that comes along.

Another popular shortcut recognizes the slow and difficult journey of unlearning, but then concludes that the organization only has the resources and patience to see it through for a select group of individuals. This results in a cadre of experts, typically housed in a central support organization or given some special organizational designation, who do genuinely see and behave differently. The reasoning is that these individuals can then lead project teams to create and prototype innovative ways of working. The problem with this seemingly reasonable approach lies in the sustainability of the changes after the expert project leader moves on to the next effort. If the operational leader and front-line staff who are left to run the new process or service have not completely unlearned their old mental models, they are likely to revert to them when faced with the inevitable challenges that come along day to day. This is extremely frustrating to the expert who bemoans that they left it in a better state.

Peter Senge's concept of a learning organization goes beyond these shortcut approaches. In *The Fifth Discipline: The Art and Practice of the Learning Organization,* Senge describes the learning organization as one "where people continually expand their capacity to create results they truly desire, where new and expansive patterns of thinking are nurtured, where collective aspiration is set free, and where people are continually learning how to learn together." Pedler, Burgoyne, and Boydell sharpen the point when they describe the learning organization as one that "facilitates the learning *of all its members* and continuously transforms itself" (italics added for emphasis). Numerous studies demonstrate the link between indicators of a learning organization and high performance. In further fleshing out the practices of a learning organization, Senge and others describe, among other things, the importance of striving to better oneself (personal mastery), challenging mental models, sharing a vision or goal, and learning together as a team. Virginia Mason's lean and innovation capabilities development efforts leave no doubt that the organization is striving to become a learning organization.

A Quick Word about Leaders and Leadership

Because the goal is to establish a culture of innovation and learning, and because hierarchal leaders have a disproportionate impact on culture, the knowledge development efforts at Virginia Mason that I am about to describe have evolved through a process that generally started at the top of the organization's structure and worked its way down to the front lines. This is one sense of the words *leader* and *leadership*—that they are associated with position in a hierarchy—but it is not the only sense of the word at Virginia Mason.

Leadership also refers to the process by which some individuals influence others to change. This might involve goal-setting, communications, appeal to intrinsic motivation, insight, analytical and facilitative skills, the ability to work well with others, and so on. In this sense, leadership can be displayed by anyone, irrespective of her or his position in the hierarchy.

Of course, it is bad for the organization when someone who is in a hierarchal position of leadership lacks skill at the process of leadership. Further, the effectiveness of highly skilled leaders who are low in the hierarchy can be hampered by rigid policies that limit their access to resources and information critical to successful change. A learning organization seeks to develop skills in the process of leadership at all levels of the organization, *and* seeks to flatten hierarchy and eliminate rigid policies. Virginia Mason subscribes to this approach. Generally speaking, throughout this chapter I will use the term *leader* in the broad sense as one who is engaged the process of leadership, regardless of position in the hierarchy.

Virginia Mason's Systematic Approach to Skills Development for Leaders

Along with the story of the integration of lean and innovation in the previous chapter, the concepts of unlearning, andragogy, reflective practitioner, and learning organization form the threads for understanding the evolution and current state of education and skills development for the Virginia Mason Production System.

For example, the general educational effort on lean thinking for operational leaders began as a four-day course. "We batched all the learning," says Andy Baylor who, as director of Virginia Mason Production System (VMPS) operations, worked on the evolution of the learning curriculum. "It was hard for people to make it through the entire course and there was not much time to practice each tool, so we didn't have a good way to verify that they had learned anything."

The approach that has since evolved is much more consistent with adult learning theory. The four-day course has been replaced by a set of two- to three-hour modules that individuals can work through at their own pace. The module design also provides a better opportunity for unlearning and reflective practice in that they present the theory behind only one or two related concepts or tools, and then require the learner to go out and apply these to a real issue in their work setting. Further, this application phase requires the engagement of the learner's supervisor in the hierarchy, who is trained to focus, coach, and support learning as part of her or his job responsibilities. The learner returns several weeks later to report out to faculty on his or her small project. This gives faculty a chance to lead guided reflection that better solidifies learning, and provide coaching that clarifies points. Over time, participants build up a systematic base of knowledge and experience in VMPS through the process of action learning.

The scope and sequence of modules depends on the participant's role in the organization. The current structure has five levels.

Introduction to VMPS is a mandatory, two-hour orientation for all new hires that describes basic concepts. Lean thinking terminology is so embedded in the culture at Virginia Mason that this can be likened to the situation of someone moving to a foreign country and needing to learn at least some basic words and phrases in order to communicate with others.

VMPS General Education is an optional program to educate front-line staff (nonsupervisor) on basic terms, concepts and tools so they can independently apply these in daily work. Topics include history of the Toyota Production System and VMPS, waste, steps for change, respect for people, flows of medicine, time, value stream mapping, mistake proofing, setup reduction, and 5S. The course requires about thirteen hours of class time, with additional time for application in the work setting and report out. There is an optional two-hour module on creativity and innovation.

VMPS for Leaders covers all the topics in general education, and adds modules on promoting innovation and turning ideas into action. The goal is to give supervisors and above (managerial and clinical) the skill set needed to imbed VMPS into their unit's work. This requires about nineteen hours of class time, with additional time for application and report out. There is a formal organizational policy requiring completion of VMPS for Leaders within one year of hiring or promotion into any formal leadership position, supervisor, and above.

VMPS Certification is the next step on the education journey that is required for all administrative directors, vice presidents, medical chiefs, and above (others by invitation). At this level, the learning approach shifts from self-directed to that of a cohort whose members learn together at a faculty-directed pace. Certified leaders are expected to teach VMPS and lead various workshops and events. Certification covers sixteen content modules and provides additional in-depth materials on a variety of topics that build on the basic information contained in the VMPS for Leaders course, which is a prerequisite for certification.

The Kaizen Fellowship is a further level of development for those who have completed VMPS Certification. Its aims are to accelerate the implementation of VMPS, develop existing high-performing clinical and managerial leaders to be facile implementers of VMPS, build depth and knowledge among current and future leaders, and ensure strong succession planning. Over a sixteen-month period, participants learn from a variety of internal and external experts in twelve classroom sessions, travel to Japan to learn the Toyota Production System firsthand, get access to specialized knowledge, and work on special projects in their work setting. Selection to be a Kaizen Fellow is highly coveted. Upon completion of the development experience, most Kaizen Fellows are assigned to lead or support high-profile goals, initiatives, and projects.

Each of the three highest levels have formal sets of competencies and an evaluation process. At Virginia Mason, VMPS leadership development is not a casual effort. Rather, it is a serious endeavor and a basic job requirement for leaders in the hierarchy, supervisor to CEO, on both the clinical and managerial sides. Serious time and resources are allocated to it, both in high-profile ways, such as the ongoing series of two-week study tours to Japan, and also in the understanding that newly appointed supervisors need protected time in their days to learn. At the same time, it is not exclusive to positions in hierarchy. Front-line staff leaders, and those who aspire to be, are encouraged and supported at the VMPS General Education level. Such egalitarianism is characteristic of a true learning organization. While Virginia Mason leaders would not say that they have arrived at this lofty destination, these development programs certainly put them on the right path.

Structural Practices That Support Innovative Thinking in Leaders

In addition to educational content that encourages them to see and think differently, Virginia Mason also does several other things that encourage fresher, deeper thinking by leaders.

Job rotations. One such practice involves rotating leaders through a job in the Kaizen Promotion Office (KPO) for up to three years before placing them in other leadership roles in service lines. (Recall that job rotation was one of the practices advocated by proponents of Schon's reflective practitioner concept.) In each of the three KPO divisions—hospital, clinic, and corporate—there are two leaders in rotational positions leading the work alongside their operational service line counterparts. Additionally, each of the three KPO divisions has up to four KPO specialists, trained at the certified leader level. All these leaders become deeply immersed in the concepts, tools, and applications of lean thinking and innovation, and are then able to carry that knowledge and experience back into line management roles.

Director of the hospital's medical telemetry unit, Christin Gordanier, is an example. "I don't think that I could really do the job I have now if I hadn't had that time in KPO. It teaches you how to study and manage opportunities, make decisions, and guide a vision." So, while KPO might appear to an outsider to be a manifestation of the shortcuts to a learning organization previously described, because it creates a cadre of experts separate from operations, Virginia Mason uses it as a developmental ground for its service line leaders. After seven years with this organizational policy, an increasing number of leaders at the administrative director level or higher have served in a KPO rotation, where their horizons were broadened and they learned deeply about the application of lean and innovation.

Nontraditional role assignment. Another important practice that stimulates fresh thinking is that of assigning individuals to roles outside their formal backgrounds. Executive sponsor for the innovation strategic plan, Lynne Chafetz, describes the practice. "I think that one of the things that is different about Virginia Mason's approach to leadership is that we do not pigeon-hole leaders into roles [based on their training and background], but rather look at competencies and talent development that fosters innovation. We deliberately identify development needs of our leaders and place them in assignments that give them opportunities to get out of their traditional silos and understand value streams across the organization." Chafetz herself is a prime example. How many other healthcare organizations would give the role of strategic leadership of their care and service delivery innovation efforts to their chief legal counsel, a lawyer by training? However, she is not the only example.

Michael VanDerhoef, whose line-management job is that of president of the Virginia Mason Foundation, which raises over $15 million annually, is a similar example. "I've been in fundraising my whole, 20-plus year career," VanDerhoef recounts, "but for the last seven years I have also been involved with building service programs here. Most of my peers [in healthcare fundraising around the country] are envious that I have that connection because I have the ability to impact the patient experience that then becomes the gratitude that drives fundraising." Diane Miller, who now leads the Virginia Mason Institute, which provides training in lean to healthcare systems across the United States and Europe in service to Virginia Mason's mission to transform healthcare, is a another example as she began her career at Virginia Mason as director of the organization's employee child day-care center.

The policy applies to physician leaders as well. For example, Dr. Joyce Lammert began her career at Virginia Mason as an asthma and allergy specialist, became section head of internal medicine, then chief of medicine, and now medical director of the hospital. Pediatrician Dr. Donna Smith was an unlikely choice for director of the emergency department. She then went on to become the medical director of the hospital—a hospital that does not treat children. She currently serves as medical director of the clinics.

These are just a few of the many surprising examples I found in my interviews when I asked individuals to briefly describe their backgrounds and current roles. In addition to being consistent with the reflective practitioner concept, it is also the embodiment in an organizational human resources practice of the creativity tool of *be someone else.* When using this tool to stimulate creative thought and exploration of other mental valleys, a facilitator typically asks the group to spend a few minutes looking at an issue from the point of someone other than a healthcare professional. What ideas would a lawyer, fund raiser, or child day-care teacher have on this issue? How would they look at it? In these three cases, we do not have to speculate; we have those nontraditional points of view at the table with us. This is very different from the practice in most healthcare organizations where leaders rise through a silo; the executive in charge of a given area must also be a traditionally trained expert in that field. While the practice is not pervasive at Virginia Mason—the chief nursing officer is a nurse, the chief medical officer is a physician, and so on—there are enough examples like those above to send the message that nontraditional thinking is encouraged.

Physician–administrator dyads for learning. A third structural practice that supports innovative thinking is that of partnering clinical and managerial leaders for the purpose of learning together. Senior vice president for Clinic Operations, Jim Cote, provides an example:

> My first year here was about getting everybody on board and getting my VMPS education. I started to learn how to *lead* with this thinking, as opposed to looking at it as a stand-alone activity to do. It's just the way we do things around here. And my chief of surgery, Dr. Fred Govier, went through VMPS certification with me. It was great for us to do it together, the physician partner and the administrator, because I think we both learned together and supported one another and that was great. Now we have almost every manager and seventeen surgeons through the VMPS for Leaders training, or at least somewhere in the process.

Learning together, in order to *lead* together, is the kind of physician–management alignment that many healthcare organizations dream about. In terms of innovation, it has two critically important benefits. First, it means that when issues arise there is a more diverse set of mental valleys active in seeking an idea for a way forward. Second, it also means that implementation of creative ideas, the back half of the innovation process, is likely to go smoother because the ideas are already jointly sponsored by the managers and physicians. While the practice of joint training and operational leadership is not unique to Virginia Mason—Kaiser-Permanente and others have well-developed systems of physician–management partnerships throughout their organizational hierarchy—it is an important contributor to the organization's success at integrating lean and innovation.

Standard work for leaders. Another practice that supports innovative thinking is one that might seem counterintuitive. While further development and deployment is ongoing, departmental leaders are establishing standard work to guide what they do on a daily basis, just as it guides workers in the care delivery process. This includes updating visual production boards on units to show the status of key indicators of performance; working with a checklist that reminds them what they should be doing on a daily, weekly, and monthly basis to both run and improve their businesses; and holding daily huddles and rounding with staff to share information.

How does the implementation of standard work for leaders, which sounds regimental and restrictive, aid innovation? First, it supports transparency, free-flow of information, respectful relationships that suspend hierarchy, and forums for idea generation, all aspects of organizational culture that evidence shows are characteristic of highly innovative organizations. Second, it helps assure that normal operations remain stable, which then provides an excellent platform for testing innovative ideas to see their impact on key performance indicators. Third, standard work for leaders actually frees up the time and mental capacity of leaders to spend on innovative thinking. "It is hard to be innovative when you are constantly chasing down problems and fire-fighting" is a common complaint that I hear from healthcare leaders around the world. It is a problem that requires unlearning the traditional view of the manager's job, what Executive Vice President and Chief Operating Officer Sarah Patterson calls the *capes approach to management,* conjuring up the image of the cartoon superhero who swoops in to save the day. Standard work for leaders both helps preclude the fires from breaking out in the first place, and provides a forum for quicker resolution of those that do occur. Anecdotally, this is being validated by the experiences of front-line managers as standard work for leaders is becoming embedded in daily practice.

Institutionalized sharing of learning. *Report out* and *stand up* are phrases in the cultural language at Virginia Mason that describe a final example of the sorts of structural supports for innovation there. Because improvement and innovation are continuously occurring, there is almost always a VMPS workshop or event going on somewhere in the medical center. *Report out* is a cultural ritual that occurs on Friday afternoons in the organization's main auditorium. There, workshop and event teams who have been working throughout the week in improvement and innovation events share what they have learned. Over two hundred managerial and clinical leaders get their weekly demonstration of the practical application of concepts and methods that they have learned in classroom or self-paced learning settings.

Similarly, *stand up* is the name giving to the early Tuesday morning ritual that takes place in the KPO hallway in front of a large wall, upon which are VMPS event reports, target sheets, and other information relevant to the work of the hospital, clinic, and corporate KPO teams. Brief progress reports are given, as well as descriptions of barriers to improvement that are being encountered, in order to stimulate productive reflection. The narrow hallway is a standing-room-only event that routinely draws about fifty leaders.

Both of these rituals help stimulate ongoing dialogue about lean and innovation, and help spread the most innovative practices. They are hosted and actively led by the most senior leaders in the organization; CEO Kaplan and COO Patterson being the most frequent leaders.

These and other structures in the Virginia Mason Medical Center support ongoing application of knowledge about lean and innovation principles, sending clear messages about the expectation regarding education for all leaders.

Evolution of Training and Development for Innovation

As noted above, modules on creativity and innovation are now fully integrated into the four levels of VMPS education. This is the current state of an evolutionary path that developed alongside adoption of VMPS and the evolution of education on lean thinking. A brief history might help readers who would like to replicate Virginia Mason's approach, but could not imagine practically how they could do it in just one step.

As chair of innovation, I conducted the first training on creativity and innovation in 2003 at an all-day development retreat for over one hundred Virginia Mason leaders. This led to smaller, more intensive training sessions for a selection of individuals who were playing key roles in the emerging development of lean thinking. Later that year, I created the *DirectedCreativity™ Starter Kit,* a thirteen-page document describing the concepts of mental valleys; attention, escape, and movement; and six basic idea generation tools. This, along with other items, became take-away material from the small, intensive training sessions and allowed leaders to begin testing the application of these tools.

The desire to avoid introducing too many new terms and tools from the field of innovation while the organization was focusing on learning about lean led to a strategy of quiet deployment of directed creativity methods. This was accomplished via a series of invitation-only development programs that struck the balance between gaining experience with these methods and maintaining clarity of language around VMPS. These programs, variously labeled internally as mastery tracks, collaboratives, or training cohorts, were typically multisession efforts combining lecture, practice within the session, small-scale application back in the work setting, and reporting out for guided reflection. I led these sessions initially, but via a train-the-trainer approach, this quickly transitioned to Virginia Mason personnel as faculty. A similar train-the-trainer concept was employed to transfer teaching responsibility for lean thinking methods from the outside consultants to Virginia Mason personnel.

During the period from 2005 through 2007, invited participants included specialists from KPO, education, organizational development, and project management. (Many of the VMPS specialists trained on innovation have since rotated back out in the organization as line leaders.) We trained roughly ten to twelve new people in each year's cycle. The program content and length evolved, incorporating learning from previous sessions into the design, and reflecting the growing experience with the integration of innovation concepts and methods into VMPS. Typically, the total time spent in sessions was around eight to twelve hours over a year, with additional time for application work outside the sessions. Because participants were encouraged to test these tools in real problem areas where creative thinking was clearly needed—for example, access, patient safety, clinical quality, service—the application time was value-added for the organization and the individual.

The annual programs generated an evolving set of skills and self-assessment instruments, which were completed in a process of reflective dialogue with faculty and peers. This eventually grew into a formal set of innovation competencies, which are described in the next section.

In addition to these focused development efforts leading to a growing cadre of experienced individuals, over the years the Center for Innovation delivered many short sessions on focused topics at the regular meetings of the certified leaders collaborative, KPO staff meetings, all-managers monthly meeting, executive leadership meetings, and other such venues. Several guides and tools were also developed and placed on the organization's intranet for self-study and refresher.

In crafting an effective approach to education for innovation in any organization, it is important to return to the underlying concepts of unlearning, andragogy (adult learning versus teaching children or complete novices), reflective practice, and learning organization. The first three were designed into the various programs at Virginia Mason; for example, by doing modules over time and requiring reflective application in the work setting. The behind-the-scenes goal in all of this has been to create a learning organization, not simply a small cadre of highly skilled individuals who work separately from operations. By taking advantage of job rotations and other structures, and building a generalized set of competencies and supporting materials that have been field-tested, what might first appear to be efforts to create separate cadres can blossom into a true learning organization with thoughtful, strategic coordination.

Today, education to support innovation competencies is fully integrated into VMPS and the structures of Virginia Mason Medical Center. There is encouragement and opportunity for *everyone* to learn how to be more creative in their work; it is a requirement for managers. *Promoting Innovation* is a three-hour class offered monthly to leaders and staff who have completed their general VMPS education. All of these efforts tie back to Virginia Mason's strategic innovation plan evolution thread on creation of capacity and sustaining structures. Such widespread knowledge creates a powerful capacity for transforming healthcare and delivering on the promise of the perfect patient experience.

Virginia Mason's Innovation Competencies

What is it that Virginia Mason leaders across the organization are coming to know and do that enables innovation? In keeping with the organization's systematic and comprehensive approach to learning, it has identified fourteen specific innovation competencies (see Figure 4.1). As the notes at the bottom of the figure indicate, there are four potential levels of achievement for a given competency, and three tiers of expectations based on the role in the organization. While they are illustrated here as a separate list for clarity, these innovation competencies are fully integrated into the general VMPS set of competencies and expectations.

The long-term vision is for all Virginia Mason staff to at least be able to define creativity and innovation, and apply some basic concepts in their daily work and improvement efforts. There is quite a ways to go yet to reach this point. However, leaders at Virginia Mason Medical Center believe what decades of research in the field of creativity has already demonstrated, namely, that *anyone* can learn to be creative. This belief is not widely held. Many leaders of healthcare organizations, and staff within them, still seem to believe that creativity is a rare and special gift. Unlearning this belief is one of the keys to transforming healthcare. While believing that transformation is necessary in healthcare, too many leaders are waiting for someone else to figure it all out. Virginia Mason is building the capability to figure it out itself, and is reaching out to others through the Virginia Mason Institute to help them do the same.

Though far from pervasive, the early success at spreading these foundational competencies is evidenced by routine conversation within the organization. For example, the phrase *mental valley* is often used now when individuals describe how they are thinking about an issue, or how they need to *rethink* about it. Staff are exposed more deeply to such terms in the various VMPS events in which they participate, as the language and tools are now fully embedded in these. Executives further encourage spread through the use of creativity and innovation language in their communications; especially during organizational events such as the Friday afternoon report out, or the Tuesday morning *stand-up* review. While this might appear to an outsider as standoffish jargon and ceremony, we know from anthropologists that unique language and enshrinement of concepts in rituals are common

Summary of Innovation Competencies

Foundational Knowledge and Application	
#1: Definitions	Can explain Virginia Mason's definitions of innovation and creativity, and how they are helping achieve our mission.
#2: Concepts	Can explain and connect these concepts to my daily work and improvement projects: attention, escape and movement; mental valleys; parallel thinking; directed creativity cycle; innovation funnel.

Creating an Innovative Environment	
#3: Mental Benchmarking	Regularly explore and use what other industries do facing similar concepts and problems.
#4: Creativity Tools	Can effectively select and use the "starter kit" of creativity methods in improvement efforts with teams.
#5: PDSA	Can effectively use or teach Plan-Do-Study-Act (PDSA) cycles.
#6: Implementation	Can effectively take ideas to implementation and teach groups how to do so.
#7: Culture Dimensions	Understand the seven dimensions of an innovation culture and demonstrate use of supportive strategies with teams.

Setting Innovation Targets	
#8: Creative Reframing	Can effectively reframe a topic in ways that promotes creative thinking.
#9: Mental Valleys in Value Stream Maps	Can identify underlying concepts and mental valleys embedded in the value stream map for a process.
#10: Seven Levels of Change	Know how to use the Seven Levels of Change as part of target setting and idea generation.

Advanced Application	
#11: Breakthrough Innovation	Understand "breakthrough innovation" and can identify and integrate appropriate strategies into business and improvement plans.
#12: After-Action Reviews	Can effectively advise or instruct groups through reflection and an after-action review (AAR).
#13: Innovation Facilitation	Can effectively facilitate innovation through complex approaches, flexing based on group dynamics and needs. (Examples might include visioning sessions, innovation events or 3P workshops.)

Sponsorship	
#14: Innovation Sponsorship	Can effectively sponsor or work with a sponsor on innovation projects. (May include in the context of visioning sessions, innovation events or 3P workshops.)

Recommended Competency Levels by Group

All Staff, Providers & Leaders. Understand and can easily participate in use of creativity concepts. Achieve at least a level 3 on competencies 1-2.	**Levels of Achievement** 1 – Understands concept or method but has not yet actively demonstrated or taught
All Leaders. Add competencies 3-7. Recognize opportunities to apply creativity concepts and tools in a variety of situations, including target setting. Achieve at least a level 3 on all items.	2 – Has successfully demonstrated or taught this but needs more experience 3 – Has successfully demonstrated and taught this in more than one situation independently
VMPS Certified Leaders (post-certification). Add competencies 8-14. Achieve at least a level 2 on all items and level 3 in some.	4 – Demonstrates high levels of expertise; has mastered concepts or methods to the level that has taught or coached others

Details are available in the Creativity and Innovation Competency Guide and related links on the Kaizen Promotion Office/Innovation Resources page.
© 2011 Virginia Mason Medical Center

Figure 4.1   Virginia Mason's innovation competencies.

characteristics of a strong culture. Virginia Mason has come so far in integrating innovation into its lean culture that staff have to learn basic definitions and concepts in order to understand their conversations with coworkers. While this is by no means fully embedded, it does indicate how clear competencies, linked to a systematic approach to education, is beginning to fulfill the strategic plan's goal "to foster a culture of innovation and learning."

As indicated in Figure 4.1, all Virginia Mason leaders at the supervisor level and up are expected to be able to define creativity and innovation, and apply some basic concepts, as well as recognize and apply specific methods and tools for generating, testing, and implementing innovative ideas in their work areas. We will see examples of this in a later chapter on innovation in daily work. All leaders are also expected to be able to use an evidence-grounded framework for assessing and enhancing the culture for innovation in their workgroups (the subject of the next chapter).

Just as any manager would be expected to demonstrate basic competency at reading a budget or handling individual performance feedback conversations, Virginia Mason expects its managers to demonstrate a basic level of competency on key aspects of what it takes to be creative. While it is good that so many healthcare organizations today are calling out the need for innovation and transformation in vision statements, presentations by executives, and internal newsletter articles about occasional large projects, the demonstration of innovation on a daily basis by one's own supervisor is a perhaps a stronger message about its importance. The education effort associated with these innovation competencies for leaders is amplifying this message continually at Virginia Mason.

VMPS certified leaders are expected to demonstrate the remaining competencies in addition to these basic ones.

- *Creative reframing* is a set of techniques for restating the opportunity for innovation in ways that might stimulate diverse mental valleys. So, for example, instead of "We need ideas to improve access to clinical services," saying "We need ideas for how to link up people with a medical need or question with people who can help them" might stimulate a broader range of ideas. There are a variety of ways to approach reframing, and certified leaders learn to facilitate others through several of these to see where it might lead in idea generation.
- The competency of *identifying mental valleys in value stream maps* is a special application of the basic concept of mental valleys. It is natural integration of a lean thinking tool with a creativity tool. The basic technique involves stepping through each activity in a current-state value stream map and asking questions such as: What beliefs and assumptions drive us to create that step or activity? What are we thinking? What do we think is the point of that step? Who does that activity and why them? The dialogue that emerges identifies several long-standing assumptions and mental valleys that can be challenged, thus initiating the attention, escape, and movement flow of creativity. Many of the examples in the previous chapter involved the use of this skill.
- We have already introduced the *seven levels of change* and *breakthrough innovation*. The point here is that certified leaders know how to facilitate these tools and concepts to help stretch the thinking of teams to more transformational levels.
- *After-action reviews* are a technique for guided reflection. The reflective practitioner has more opportunity for innovation because he or she is pausing to

think, rather than simply racing down the same mental valleys as always. After-action reviews create attention, which can lead to the escape and movement required for creative ideas to emerge.

■ The *innovation facilitation* and *sponsorship* competencies cement the integration of innovation and lean as they focus on the roles of certified leaders as facilitators and sponsors of various workshops and events. The materials supporting these competencies provide checklists and numerous tips on how to be successful in these roles. For example, the chief of surgery in the improvement story about medically complex patients in the previous chapter used these materials to prepare his briefing for the team.

Recall that certification is required for *all* administrative directors, vice presidents, medical chiefs, and above. The fact that the entire upper half of the organization's hierarchy is competent to regularly demonstrate this level of expertise in creativity and innovation is a powerful capacity for innovation.

Transforming Healthcare: What Others Can Learn from Virginia Mason's Innovation Leadership Knowledge and Capability Efforts

When leaders, both formal and informal and at all levels, know better, they can do better to catalyze and support innovation. Anyone can learn to be more creative and innovative. However, this requires an adequately resourced, serious, systematic approach to learning and unlearning that takes into account what we know about the needs of adult learners. The pervasive language around innovation, daily actions of direct supervisors, and visible commitment of senior leaders at Virginia Mason work together to communicate a willingness to entertain creative ideas. The concepts and tools that have been integrated into VMPS education teach how to generate them. All of this is a product of Virginia Mason Medical Center's thoughtful approach to education and development at all levels. While leaders are quick to point out that it is a work in progress, at least it is a clearly recognized work that is underway.

Leaders in Other Healthcare Organizations Should …

Decide whether becoming a learning organization is a desirable goal worthy of full commitment. There is a vast literature on the learning organization and plenty of evidence of its relationship to overall performance. However, it requires hard work and constancy of purpose over time. There are enticing shortcuts that would seem to work, but don't. Virginia Mason's comprehensive and systematic leadership capability building and its supportive structures provide a vision of a learning organization in development.

- How does our effort to build capability and capacity for improvement and innovation compare and contrast with Virginia Mason's?
- Where are we doing similar things?
- Where might we be lacking?
- Are we happy with our current state and do we think it will get us to where we want to go?
- Do we want to commit to what it might take over time to begin the journey to becoming a learning organization?

Self-assess relative to the competencies for innovation. Figure 4.1 identifies what Virginia Mason has concluded are some of the key competencies needed to support innovation.

- How would we rate ourselves relative to these competencies?
- How would we rate the rest of the organization?
- To what extent are these competencies incorporated into our existing expectations of leaders—at all levels, both clinical and managerial—and our development programs for them?
- Where might we start, and what might we do, to enhance our competencies in the area of innovation?

Consider implementing structural practices that support innovative thinking. The section on this topic provided several examples of things that Virginia Mason does to create the mental space for innovation and diversity of thinking across discipline and hierarchy boundaries.

- What tends to happen when we assemble multidisciplinary groups to generate ideas or improvements; do they build on each other's thinking patterns naturally, or do they debate?
- To what extent are our promotion and task-assignment processes siloed in nature?
- Give evidence from the last several promotions or key project assignments to support your point of view.
- What examples could we give of structural supports that we believe support innovative thinking?
- What might we try in addition?

Examine their own personal willingness to reflect honestly and identify things that maybe it would be best to unlearn. Transformation requires new thinking. New thinking requires unlearning old ways that perhaps have served us well in the past. It is often easy to see the need for unlearning in others, but painful to face up to that same need in ourselves. Good leaders do not ask others to do what they are personally unwilling to do themselves.

- As we read the "What I Learned in Medical School" text box, did we think of similar examples in our own backgrounds where we have learned things that maybe are no longer the best things to think?
- When we hear new concepts that initially strike us as foreign or not applicable to healthcare, how do we react?
- Do we actively accept it as a potential invitation to unlearn something from our past, or do we just dismiss it?
- How will we address these needs for unlearning in ourselves?

Reflect on their organization's general approach to education and development relative to what we know from the literature on adult learning. Organizations tend to have patterns of thinking with regards to the need for and approach to education and development that transcends subject matter. Select three or four recent examples of training and development programs in your organization and look closely at how they were done.

- When trying to create new thinking, do we adequately attend to the cognitive and emotional processes of unlearning the old thinking?
- Do we tend to simply present new things and leave it up to participants to deal with application on their own, or do we build active, reflective practice with feedback over time into our programs?

Chapter 5

Supportive Culture for Innovation

> To me, an innovative culture is one where anyone can bring up new, creative, and sometimes even backwards ideas, without fear of being thought of as crazy, strange or funny … a culture where innovation is rewarded and celebrated.
>
> **—An anonymous Virginia Mason team member responding in 2002 to a survey asking "What does a culture of innovation mean to you?"**

Many healthcare organizations can cite a few *firsts* and showcase a clever idea or two, but do they have a deeply embedded culture that enables innovation throughout the organization on a daily basis? In their 1982 book that brought the term into common usage in business, *Corporate Cultures: The Rites and Rituals of Corporate Life,* Terrence Deal and Allan Kennedy define *organizational culture* simply as "the way we do things around here." More expansive definitions suggest that organizational culture is based in shared attitudes, beliefs, customs, and written and unwritten rules that evolve over time and are passed on to new members joining the organization. Culture is demonstrated in a variety of ways, including how the organization treats customers and employees, the extent to which freedom is allowed in decision making and the development of new ideas, how power and information flow, and how committed employees are to the organization's objectives.

Organizational culture either aids or hinders everything that an organization tries to do. There is no gray zone. Culture matters. It is the glue that holds everything together, but it is glue that can either keep an organization unified as it moves forward, or firmly fixed where it already is.

It has been cynically said that organizational culture is a lot like the weather—everyone talks about it, but no one can do anything about it. That is definitely *not* how Virginia Mason Medical Center approaches culture. Instead, as we saw in Chapter 2, it is an active focus of the organization's strategy. Culture is measured and actively worked on to make it ever more supportive of the organization's objectives.

In this chapter, I will describe an evidence-grounded framework that identifies and assesses the aspects of organizational culture that support innovation, and we will explore how these are being continuously developed within Virginia Mason.

Dimensions of Culture That Support Innovation

The characteristics of highly innovative organizations have been widely studied. While the bulk of the literature comes from outside healthcare, the few studies that do cover this context are consistent with the findings from other industries. People are people, and the cultural factors that they experience as supporting or hindering innovation are characteristic of a social system, regardless of industry. The bottom line is that literature supports the conclusion that organizational culture is a major factor affecting the speed, frequency, volume, and spread of innovation. It simply stands to reason that the two should be strongly linked. After all, culture is "the way we do things around here" and innovation arises from a challenge to the way we do things around here.

However, efforts to characterize the specific aspects of organizational cultures that support innovation are challenged by the nature of the subject. Different researchers tend to find somewhat different key aspects. Because organizations are complex, there are many variables to consider. What a researcher chooses to look at, and how she or he looks at it, will influence what is seen.

In 2001, I and British colleagues Helen Bevan and Lynne Maher (National Health Service, England) looked at the topic using a pragmatic approach. We conducted a literature search and identified seven dimensions of organizational culture that studies consistently showed made innovation more likely to occur. We worked with several healthcare organizations in the United Kingdom and other countries to confirm the face validity and usefulness of the model. A more extensive literature search conducted in 2008 reconfirmed the framework, while resulting in some enhancements. What we found is captured in Figure 5.1.

Risk taking is about an environment where people feel that it is permissible to try new things. While it is obviously important to avoid taking inappropriate risk, a healthy organizational culture seeks a balanced assessment that avoids prematurely rejecting ideas simply due to overestimation of risk. Leaders must provide emotional support to those willing to try something new, regardless of whether

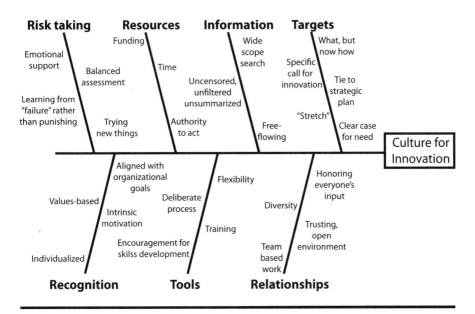

Figure 5.1   Elements of organizational culture that support innovation (© 2013 Paul E. Plsek).

the idea is eventually judged a success or failure. Leaders in innovative organizations demonstrate by their actions that they are interested in learning from failure, rather than punishing it. For example, Thomas Watson, founder of IBM, famously pointed out, "The fastest way to succeed is to double your failure rate."

Resources should be thought of in the broadest sense of the word. The climate for innovation is enhanced if people know that they have the resource of authority to act on innovative ideas. A 1991 meta-analysis by Damanpour showed that centralization of decision-making autonomy within an organization had a *negative* effect on innovation. Further, while innovative ideas do not necessarily need a lot of money or time to develop, staff members tend to back away if these traditional resources are not available, feeling that there is little point in putting forward a new idea. The presence of concrete resources signals that the organization is taking innovation seriously. Some industrial firms that rely heavily on innovation to survive in their industry—for example, Nike, Google, and 3M—have corporate policies giving employees permission to spend a certain amount of time working on new ideas.

Information is the fuel for innovation. It creates a richer set of mental valleys that one can draw upon when faced with a challenge. A systematic review, published in 2008, of over one-hundred papers found *knowledge management* to be a key factor in innovation management. Studies show that organizations create better conditions for innovation when information, both from inside and outside the organization, is widely gathered, easily accessible, rapidly transmitted, and honestly communicated. One recommendation from a 2008 Harvard Business School forum of innovation experts assembled to discuss how to improve an organization's innovation capacity was to "open your company to diverse perspectives." Since we cannot know in advance what knowledge might stimulate an innovative idea, censoring, filtering, or oversummarizing information detracts from this dimension.

Targets convey an important message in a healthcare organization. Leaders signal that innovation is highly desirable by setting aspirational goals in specific areas, and challenging others to find ways to realize the vision. In their 1994 best seller, *Built to Last: Successful Habits of Visionary Companies,* Collins and Porras studied eighteen companies that had survived as leaders over decades of change in their industries, and eighteen comparison companies that did not. One of their findings was the presence in the successful organizations of what they called "big, hairy, audacious goals" (BHAGs) that drive them to unimaginable levels of performance over long time horizons. Linking innovation targets to strategic priorities and being able to articulate a clear, multifaceted case of need, further signals the importance of the call for innovation. However, there is a caution. Innovative thinking is stifled when leaders go beyond statements of *what* needs to be achieved and also become prescriptive as to *how* it must be achieved. Harvard professor and innovation researcher Teresa Amabile sums it up this way, "Clearly specified strategic goals often enhance people's creativity. ... Creativity thrives when managers let people decide how to climb a mountain; they needn't, however, let employees choose which one."

Recognition refers to symbols and rituals in the culture whose main purpose is to reward innovative behavior. They signal how much value is given, or not, to the efforts of individuals and teams who come up with transformative new ways to help the organization achieve its strategic goals. Because it is all about encouraging more of this sort of behavior, the best recognition is that which appeals to individuals' intrinsic and personal motivation. The most successful recognition schemes avoid a one-size-fits-all approach and are instead based on a deeper understanding of what makes people do what they do. For example, research shows that frequent personal expression of appreciation is often more important to people than financial reward. The Harvard forum of innovation experts cited previously also observed that, "asking questions about a project and providing even a word of sincere recognition can be more motivating than money."

Tools usage tells us a lot about an organization's culture, just as it does when anthropologists study societal cultures. In high-performing organizations, innovation is the product of the deliberate use of facilitative processes and methods. Imagining that innovation will happen on its own would be as naive and irresponsible as imagining that financial controls would naturally emerge without some deliberate structures. While everyone is capable of innovative thinking, most of us have been socialized to be more conservative in our thinking in the work environment, especially in healthcare, where there are legitimate risks that must be managed. Leaders, therefore, need to consider how they build capability and capacity in deliberate methods for creative thinking.

> **BASIC IDEA BEHIND THE SEVEN DIMENSIONS OF CULTURE FOR INNOVATION**
>
> If you want innovative ideas from any collection of individuals, set aside the *resource* of time, nurture productive *relationships* among a diverse group of thinkers, *recognize* them in ways that they find intrinsically motivating, use good *tools* to stimulate group creativity, agree on an ambitious *target*, bring in new *information*, and be willing to take *risks*.

Relationships refer to the patterns of interaction between individuals in the organization. Innovative ideas are rarely the product of a lone genius. Even when they might appear to be, delving further into the story nearly always reveals that the idea was formed over time and through multiple interactions with others that fueled the process. Reviewing decades of research and experience, British innovation researcher John Bessant notes, "Studies of high performing organizations show that they place considerable emphasis on involvement in innovation … moving away from specialists and towards higher levels of participation from others in the workforce." Therefore, environments where individuals are routinely exposed to a wide range of different thinking—from a wide range of people, with a wide range of backgrounds, points of view, and mental valleys—provide rich soil for the growth of innovation. There must also be a sense of common purpose, of being *on a team* with others. This team environment must also enable those with different thinking to trust that their input will be honored and explored, rather than immediately argued against. For example, a study in two large aerospace firms showed a significant correlation between the degree of trust present in the environment, and the number of ideas submitted and implemented.

These seven dimensions of culture that support innovation apply at all levels: a meeting, a clinical team, a task group working overtime, a department, or an entire organization (see the "Basic Idea behind the Seven Dimensions of Culture for Innovation" box).

Innovation Culture Does Not Exist in a Vacuum

Before going further, it must be noted that constructs such as culture for innovation, safety culture, just culture, and so on are artificial and partial. An organization as a whole has an overall culture—the ways things are done around here—and one can never truly isolate some aspects from others. To be successful, an organization needs a culture that supports innovation, safety, justice, respect, diversity, performance, accountability, and a host of other positive qualities.

The good thing about the holistic nature of culture is that programmatic work on one topic can enhance aspects of culture that also support others. For example,

**VIRGINIA MASON FOUNDATIONAL
BEHAVIORS OF RESPECT FOR PEOPLE**

1. Listen to understand.
2. Keep your promises.
3. Be encouraging.
4. Connect with others.
5. Express gratitude.

6. Share information.
7. Speak up.
8. Walk in their shoes.
9. Grow and develop.
10. Be a team player.

most programs to encourage a culture for patient safety include something about a balanced assessment of risks, an aspect that is also included in Figure 5.1 as associated with the culture for innovation. Overlap and synergy between these two efforts is natural and should be exploited; competition between culture-development efforts is inherently unhealthy and wasteful.

A good Virginia Mason example of this general point comes from the organization's work to create a culture of *respect for people,* as advocated by leading patient safety experts. The ten Virginia Mason foundational behaviors of respect for people (see box) map nicely into the relationships, recognition, information, and tools dimensions of the culture for innovation in Figure 5.1. Similar mappings are possible with Virginia Mason's service, safety, talent management, and other similar efforts.

So, while the remainder of this chapter focuses on efforts aimed at assessing and improving dimensions of culture associated with innovation, one should not assume that the positive aspects of Virginia Mason's culture are solely the result of these efforts.

Examples of the Seven Dimensions of Culture at Virginia Mason

The dimensions of culture that support innovation are an underlying subtext in all the stories in this book. However, a few quick examples here to call out these dimensions explicitly will underscore the point.

Patient Safety Alerts. In addition to making the medical center safer, Virginia Mason's Patient Safety Alert (PSA) system is an organizational structure that reinforces several of the dimensions of culture in Figure 5.1. The fact that any team member can raise an alert bespeaks a culture where everyone has the *resource* of authority to act in order to make things better. The additional fact that peers and leaders immediately react positively upon the alert establishes a powerful *relationship* bond of being valued, trusted, and respected. Surgical and Procedural Services administrative director Denise Dubuque recalled a recent PSA in her area: "We escalated an issue and the senior leaders stood behind the team. The staff saw that they were listened to. It was pretty powerful." From the program's inception in 2002 through 2012, over 31,000 PSAs have been reported, giving a significant number of team members that same powerful message.

The presence of the system itself reminds everyone that Virginia Mason has a *target* of perfection in everything it does, and that the organization wants to learn, rather than punish, when things go wrong, or nearly so. Team members often take a risk when they report a PSA, but they receive immediate emotional support and *recognition* in one of several forms; for example, reassurance from their direct supervisor, a personal thank you from executives, or what the organization calls *applause points*. In addition, organizationwide, formal recognition can come in the form of the monthly Good Catch Program, which recognizes a PSA that led to significant improvement, or the annual Mary L. McClinton Patient Safety Award presented to the team that has done the most to improve patient safety in the organization. Staff focus groups have identified this award as the most meaningful and coveted recognition at Virginia Mason.

Finally, development is underway to create even better online systems to track *information* about PSAs and share the learning that come from them. "The mental valley that we are constantly breaking out of is that if something is wrong we need to be secretive about it," notes Cathie Furman, senior vice president, Quality and Compliance. "We say just the opposite. Let's be transparent about it."

Saturday opening. Services in most traditional medical centers are either not available, or are seriously limited, on weekends. Some executives would tell you that changing this tradition would be met with such severe push back from professional staff that it would not be worth the effort. Yet, in late 2012, Virginia Mason Medical Center began offering an extensive range of both primary and specialty care services on a Saturday, *with the active support of professional staff.* The culture at Virginia Mason facilitated this.

Virginia Mason's culture of sharing and clearly communicating *targets* creates a case for need that often stretches thinking beyond the usual mental valley of tradition; necessity is the mother of invention. Because of bad weather in early 2012, clinic visit volumes were behind target for the year, and the traditionally light-volume days around Thanksgiving, Christmas, and New Year's were approaching. In addition, the end of the year always brings some extra demand from patients—who, you will recall, are at the top of Virginia Mason's strategic pyramid—as they want services covered before the start of their new insurance deductible period. A Saturday opening in December was an idea that emerged out of the challenge to address both the patients' needs and the volume target issue.

Culturally, leaders at Virginia Mason tend to appeal to underlying values and intrinsic motivation—elements in the *recognition* dimension—in order to create an attraction for change, rather than using their position-power to dictate change. Leaders carefully communicated the idea of Saturday opening by noting foremost that it would serve patients better, an appeal to the values and intrinsic motivations of healthcare professionals. Further, since the coming light-volume days were on a Friday and two Mondays, if staff would volunteer to work some Saturdays, most could take the day off on these light-volume days and gain a four-day weekend. It was further suggested to surgeons, whose block time in the operating rooms (ORs) fell on these light-demand days, that Saturday operations could help them better serve all their patients.

A healthy *risk-taking* culture speaks often of trying new things, on a small scale, with willing volunteers, in order to assess and learn. This language permeates Virginia Mason. The idea of Saturday openings was presented as a test of change, rather than a new policy implementation. It was something that could be done to meet an immediate need, and if it didn't go well, there would be no requirement to keep doing it. "You can't get too far out or you will lose people," says Chief Medical Officer Dr. Michael Glenn. "We'd rather say, 'How can we make it work for you?' and 'What if we just try it and see how it goes?' It gets people outside the tradition, outside the mental valley, but not so far out that they stop listening to you."

The careful communication of the idea left plenty of room for everyone's input to shape the final operational details. The trusting, open, *Team Medicine* environment of Virginia Mason—the *relationships* dimension—is something that most team members have learned to count on. They know that they will be heard when they have ideas, concerns, and suggestions—nearly 85% responded favorably to the staff partnership survey item "my direct supervisor recognizes my ideas or suggestions for improvement." Clinic Operations senior vice president Jim Cote says that when he tells colleagues in other healthcare organizations about the Saturday opening they say, "'Wow! What did you have to do to force the physicians to do that?' But there was no forcing. We put the idea out there and everyone had tweaks to it."

By all accounts, the test of Saturday opening was a success. Clinic volumes for 2012 were increased by several thousand visits, and 19 of the 90 Virginia Mason surgeons performed operations in 9 fully functioning ORs. The Saturday opening statistics also included 221 new-patient visits. Importantly, the process succeeded in creating an attractive pull from the medical staff. CEO Dr. Gary Kaplan recalls the comments at the professional staff meeting shortly after the test. "People were talking about how successful it is, and we need to do this all the time. Somebody said, 'It's all about the patient, as opposed to about *us*. It's not about our weekends. It's about meeting the patients' needs. We showed that we could find ways to manage that, *and* be respectful to our people and our work–life balance." The pull of the patient at the top of the strategic pyramid, combined with the elements of culture that support adoption of innovation, have enabled Virginia Mason to rapidly scale up a test that some healthcare executives would have shied away from, to an implemented policy of offering a complete range of medical center services on selected Saturdays each month. Both the medical staff and the patients love it.

The culture around target setting. A final example involves the way Virginia Mason typically sets its *targets*. Toyota Production System founder Taiichi Ohno stressed *relentless pursuit of perfection* and *zero defects* as core concepts in lean thinking. These traditions of lean thinking, which are reflected in Virginia Mason Production System (VMPS), are very much in line with Collins and Porras's *BHAGs*, or *stretch goals*, from the innovation literature. Challenging the mind to attempt to do what seems to be impossible is a technique for stimulating creative thought at level 7 of the seven levels of change. Stretch goals also heighten the clarity and urgency around an issue.

The standard target sheet for Rapid Process Improvement Workshops calls for at least 50% reductions in indicators such as lead time, space, and travel distance. At Virginia Mason, defect targets related to safety practices are routinely set at zero or 100%, without argument. As described earlier, a 2005 innovation effort in primary care asked team members to create a model that would allow a physician practice to care for a panel of 5000 patients, when the typical panel size at the time was 1800. The 2009 innovation strategic plan had goals calling for "100% staff satisfaction," a completely "waste-free pipeline" of ideas, and "100,000 ideas per year." These are only a few examples of what those in other healthcare organizations might say are *impossible* targets.

It takes courage and sophistication in leadership to set stretch goals effectively. The sophistication lies in accepting the concept of *relentless pursuit* of a goal, even if actual achievement of it never comes. In my experience, working with healthcare systems across the United States and Europe, some organizations tend to set timid goals, and only after a conservative sanity check to assure themselves that they can meet them, because they fear failure. So, where another organization might aim for a 10% improvement on a given issue and succeed in getting that, Virginia Mason would approach the same issue with a very different philosophy. Virginia Mason would rather set itself the *impossible* challenge to meet a 50% improvement goal. While it might "fail" to achieve this aggressive target, the invitation to stretch thinking outside the current mental valleys might result in a 30% improvement, compared to the timid organization's 10%. In addition, Center for Innovation director Jennifer Phillips points out, "Teams often surprise themselves and actually hit the target or go beyond." She goes on to note the synergy between innovation and lean that this aspect of culture supports. "Such targets no longer seem so much a stretch once you're deeper into lean. The ability to innovate on this front is very connected to where we are culturally with VMPS."

A not-yet-perfect culture. While there are many examples of how the seven dimensions that support innovation play out in the Virginia Mason culture, it would be wrong to suggest that all is perfect. As in any large organization, there are pockets of microcultures at the team or work-group level where the picture is less rosy. Both leaders and staff are imperfect, because people in general are imperfect.

Leaders at Virginia Mason noted that some dimensions had further to go to catch up with others. As in most healthcare organizations, there never seem to be enough resources (time and money) to think about and execute on all the innovative things one could do. Assessments of the culture for innovation at Virginia Mason consistently show that the information dimension is the weakest of the seven. Members of staff do not always feel that they know enough about what is going on both within and outside the organization. However, lean thinking is an inherently optimistic mindset. While perfection is the goal, the pursuit of perfection is the ongoing and never-ending process.

Describing Organizational Culture for Innovation: Portal Charts

Identifying the seven dimensions and the specific constructs under each makes assessing the culture possible. We can go beyond anecdotal evidence and say something in a more rigorous way about the cultural elements that support an innovative organization.

It is useful to think of the seven dimensions of culture as a sort of window, or portal, through which innovative ideas either flow freely, or are blocked. The more supportive the culture, the wider the opening of the portal, the more innovation flows through. Thus, a portal chart, like the one shown in Figure 5.2, is used to display the results of an innovation culture assessment.

The lines coming out from the center correspond to each of the seven dimensions and provide a scale of negative and positive numbers, anchored at zero in the middle. A value of zero indicates that the behaviors and practices corresponding to that dimension neither aid nor hinder innovation. Negative and positive scores indicate the presence of behaviors and practices that tend to hinder or support innovation, respectively. Larger values, further from the anchor at zero, indicate more aid or hindrance. The scores are plotted on each scale and then connected with

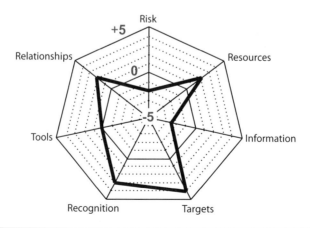

Figure 5.2   Example of a portal chart for assessing cultural dimensions that support innovation.

**ASSESSING CONDITIONS FOR INNOVATION: HOW
TO READ THE PORTAL CHART IN FIGURE 5.2**

Figure 5.2 depicts a culture where there are strong targets for innovation (+4), fairly strong recognition (+3), pretty good resources for innovation (+2), and supportive relationships (+2). So far, it sounds good. The tools, processes, and methods of the organization neither hinder nor aid innovation (0), which may be OK, but is not very assertive for innovation. Of even more concern, risk taking is somewhat discouraged (–2) and the lack of free flow of information somewhat hinders innovation (–2.5).

We conclude, based on our seven dimensions framework, that despite the strong targets and recognition for innovation, other factors in the culture will limit innovative output. To put it another way, the portal is not exactly wide open for the free flow of ideas. The leaders of this organization clearly have some work to do to create better conditions for innovation. Stronger language about targets and more recognition will have only limited impact if risk taking and information sharing are not also addressed.

lines to create a "portal," as shown in the example. The box provides a narrative interpretation of the diagram.

The metaphor of the portal through which innovation either flows or is impeded helps us understand the common phenomenon that I call the *ideas-to-action problem*. Many healthcare organizations experience getting wonderfully creative ideas from an improvement team, but having great difficulty implementing them in the workplace (see Figure 5.3). When we charter improvement teams, we often pay attention to the elements of culture that support innovation *when the group comes together to do its work*. For example, we give them time to think creatively, facilitate them with tools, tell them it is OK to challenge current ways of thinking, and so on. In other words, the portal chart of the project-team meeting environment

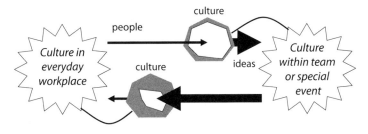

Lots of great vision and ideas generated...
...few are translated into reality across the organization

Figure 5.3   The ideas-to-action problem (© 2007 Paul E. Plsek).

is wide open and many great ideas flow. Unfortunately, this is often remarkably *unlike* the portal chart of the everyday workplace from which we have taken the team members. So, when we try to get those new ideas to flow through the culture of the everyday workplace, we encounter significant impediments because staff do not want to take the risk, have not been exposed to the tools for change, do not feel appreciated, do not trust their leaders, and so on. The key point is that it is not enough to attend to the culture for innovation in improvement teams only. *The culture must support innovation throughout the organization if transformation is the ultimate goal.*

Assessing Organizational Culture for Innovation

The final piece of theoretical work undertaken in the United Kingdom around the dimensions of culture that support innovation is associated with creating the scores that are plotted on a portal chart. This can be accomplished via either a nominal group dialogue process or a survey.

Nominal group dialogue method. This is a straightforward approach involving a meeting of a representative cross section of organizational leaders and staff to rate each dimension. A facilitator describes each of the seven dimensions and asks table groups to come to consensus on a score for each. These are compiled, leading to large group discussion and consensus building. The group then agrees on dimensions needing attention and compiles a preliminary list of action items to enhance the culture for innovation. This might also be supplemented by further, offline discussion to do a more in-depth analysis and identification of actions.

This method provides a quick assessment of the culture of the organization as perceived by the attendees, typically in a one- to two-hour meeting. The dialogue around and across table groups provides a rich depth of understanding. Bringing people together also creates an environment of cross-organizational learning (relationship dimension) and signals that creating a supporting culture for innovation is seen as important (targets dimension). However, there are some considerations to take into account when using this method. Small groups might not be representative of the larger organization. The approach results in a highly subjective rating that is difficult to compare over time. It also may be subject to the bias associated with discussion-oriented group-consensus processes; for example, it can be dominated by a few outspoken individuals if not properly facilitated.

Survey method. To create a more reliable assessment process, the English National Health Service's Institute for Innovation and Improvement created and tested a twenty-nine-item survey instrument that has been used in many health-care organizations in England, and some abroad. The survey consists of a set of initial demographic items (for example, profession, department, length of service); four items for each of the seven dimensions; plus an overall culture rating. Leaders reviewing the results can see if physicians, nurses, and managers perceive the climate differently, or if the assessment varies across departments in an organization. This leads to action planning and feedback to the organization.

Particularly when administered online, the survey is an efficient and effective way to get input from a large number of staff. Compared to the nominal-group dialogue method, the survey provides a more consistent measure over time. With a thoughtful set of demographic items, results can be segmented in a variety of ways to provide even greater insight. However, it does require a survey administrator to manage the process and associated logistics and communications efforts. (Although, as we will see below, Virginia Mason has found a clever way to address this issue.)

Virginia Mason's Assessment of the Dimensions of Culture That Support Innovation

The Innovation pillar in Virginia Mason's strategic pyramid calls for it to create a culture of learning and innovation. The culture of lean thinking emphasizes measurement. Integrating innovation and lean, therefore, led naturally to interest in the work that had been done in the United Kingdom to measure the culture for innovation.

On my first visit to Virginia Mason in February 2003, I introduced the seven dimensions framework and led a group of over one hundred executives, managers, and clinical leaders in an assessment of the culture of innovation using the nominal-group dialogue method. The portal chart from that initial assessment is shown in Figure 5.4. This marked the first time that an American healthcare

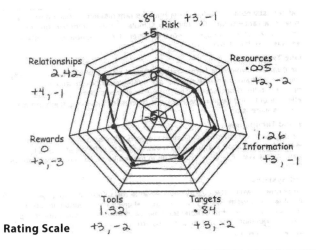

Figure 5.4 Initial assessment of elements of culture that support innovation at Virginia Mason Medical Center (February 2003. The numbers give the average and ranges of scores on each dimension.)

organization had used the framework to assess itself regarding how its culture supported innovation.

Consistent with where Virginia Mason was on its innovation journey in 2003, most of the average scores were near zero, indicating that the culture neither strongly supported nor strongly hindered innovation. Virginia Mason's long history of team medicine was perhaps reflected in the rather positive score on the relationships dimension, and the then-recent introduction of lean thinking methods probably accounts for the positive score on the tools dimension. As we will see momentarily, the relative good score on the information dimension is interesting.

It is important to note that this was a group of leaders only; it did not include frontline staff. Further, each dimension featured a four- to five-point spread across the reports from table groups, indicating a lack of full consensus. The assessment might have been quite different if more of an organizational cross section had been involved, using a more rigorous method. Nevertheless, this initial assessment did make the idea of *culture for innovation* from the strategic pyramid more concrete, and led executive sponsor Lynne Chafetz and me to recommend that the organization explore the use of it as one of its measures of innovation.

To begin to explore potential differences between the perspectives of leaders and frontline staff, the innovation team did a cross-walk between these culture assessment scores and items on the organizationwide staff satisfaction survey that were at least loosely related to each of the seven dimensions. Staff survey results strongly supported the high score on the relationship dimension, but only as it applied to teamwork *within* a workgroup, not necessarily *across* workgroups. For example, the survey item "There is a spirit of teamwork in my immediate workgroup" received a rating of 73.8 (out of 100), while the statement "There is a spirit of teamwork at Virginia Mason" received a rating of only 47.9. Frontline staff also seemed to see the information dimension differently. The staff survey item "We are generally kept informed of activities in other departments that affect our work" received a tepid score of only 53.5, while it was highly rated by the leaders. In any event, these early explorations piqued curiosity and suggested that assessing the culture was both important and useful.

In the period 2004–2005, Virginia Mason continued to use the existing items from the staff survey to assess the culture, while prototyping a separate, more specific survey, based on the tool developed in the United Kingdom. However, there were serious concerns with implementing yet another staff survey due to fears that it might create survey fatigue among staff. At the same time, the Center for Innovation had produced a guide for leaders giving suggestions for actions they could take to improve scores in each of the dimensions. Given all this, and the fact that the initial assessment indicated that work was needed across all seven dimensions, the idea of doing a more rigorous, survey-based assessment was put on hold. Managers and clinical leaders were asked to reflect on the seven dimensions framework and suggestions for improvement as they applied to their workgroups, and

VIRGINIA MASON'S SURVEY TO ASSESS ELEMENTS
OF CULTURE THAT SUPPORT INNOVATION

Method: Statements below are presented in random order, mixed in with other staff partnership survey questions. Respondents read each statement and indicate agreement on a four-point scale.

Risk-taking
> My work provides me an opportunity to be creative and innovative.
> It is easy to talk to my direct supervisor about things that go wrong on my job.

Resources
> My workgroup finds the resources we need to try out innovative ways of doing things.
> My direct supervisor provides me the time to work on promising new ideas.

Information
> My workgroup is kept informed of activities in other departments that affect our work.
> I have sufficient information about what other organizations are doing to meet the challenges we face.

Targets
> I know what the priority goals are in my workgroup.
> My direct supervisor makes it clear that innovative new ideas are highly desirable.

Recognition
> Employees in my workgroup have a strong sense of connection to their work.
> My direct manager recognizes my ideas and suggestions for improvement.

Tools
> I know how to generate creative ideas.
> My workgroup uses specific methods to generate creative ideas to meet the challenges we face.

Relationships
> The teams that I work on have people with a diverse mix of skills/styles.
> Members of my workgroup treat one another with dignity and respect.

the item "continue to develop the culture for innovation" was added to the strategic innovation plan in 2006.

In 2008, the innovation team began working with the human resources team overseeing the organization's annual staff survey in an effort get a more rigorous measure of the seven dimensions, while avoiding survey fatigue. This was being done in concert with a proposal to further strengthen the focus on the culture for innovation by adding the goal "achieve 100% staff satisfaction on key indicators of an innovative workplace" to the innovation strategic plan for 2009.

The survey vendor had recently dramatically pared down its set of standard questions, from 69 to 39, and was allowing client organizations to add items back in, or suggest new ones, on a customized basis. This provided an opening to add 9 custom items to the survey with little impact on the perceived length. Combined with selected standard items, this created a 14-item subscale within the survey results that could indicate staff perceptions of the seven dimensions (2 items per dimension, see box), while still dramatically reducing the overall length of the survey compared to previous years. While the 14 items are not optimal to cover all the constructs on the fishbone diagram in Figure 5.1, they represent a pragmatic compromise. The win-win opportunity was too good to pass up. The 2009 survey provided Virginia Mason its first-ever survey-based assessment of the elements of organizational culture that support innovation in a healthcare organization.

Consistent with lean thinking's insistence on measurement and visual controls that indicate performance at a glance, the final piece of development required translating the survey instrument's rating scale into scores on a portal chart, along with red, yellow, green indicators. Based on the way the survey vendor assigns numerical values to responses, Virginia Mason uses a green indicator for scores above 66.7 (out of possible score of 100 if everyone strongly agreed). This corresponds to a high level of agreement with the survey item, leaning toward strong agreement. Correspondingly, values below 33.3 are assigned a red indicator, as they indicate general disagreement, leaning toward strong disagreement. A yellow indicator is used for scores falling between these values.

Using demographic information provided by participants as they log into the online survey system, managers and clinical leaders get culture for innovation portal charts, along with the overall staff engagement results, for each of their workgroups. These are rolled up to cover the entire medical center. In 2012, the medical center–wide indicator was in the green zone for 6 of the 7 dimensions, with scores ranging from 72.5 to 77.6. Only the Information dimension was in the yellow zone, with an overall score of 62.6 (above 66.7 is required for green).

Figure 5.5 provides two example workgroup portal charts illustrating differences on the dimensions of culture that support innovation. As I pointed out in the discussion associated with Figure 5.3 and the ideas to action problem, workgroup A is likely to struggle to produce or implement innovative ideas, while workgroup B is likely to be more successful. The reasons for these differences are many, but the important point is that workgroup cultures vary and are most influenced by workgroup

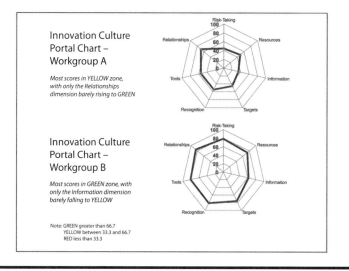

Figure 5.5 Examples of Virginia Mason work group portal charts illustrating contrasting cultures that support innovation.

peers and direct supervisors. There is only so much that very senior leaders and centralized programs can do. This is why it is so important to make support and training for innovation available pervasively, to all leaders throughout an organization. Further, where value streams span multiple workgroups, the possibility for innovation is likely to be constrained by the weakest link. At Virginia Mason, assessing, feeding back, and continuously improving workgroup culture is key to the organization's overall success in innovation.

The final organizational culture indicator is the one that is reported to the board. Consistent with the lean principle of pursuing perfection, this indicator is defined with an aggressive stretch goal—percentage of workgroups that are green on *all* seven dimensions. In the period 2009–2012, this indicator hovered around 30%, with many workgroups just missing the cutoff point by falling into the yellow zone on only one of the seven dimensions.

While the strategic goal of developing a culture that supports innovation is a constant, the approach to assessing it is always open to improvement. In 2013, Virginia Mason leaders are actively investigating other options in search of even better ways to measure, report, and support line management efforts to improve aspects of the organization's culture.

Innovation Culture Kaizen

While some believe that organizational culture is a given that cannot be altered, Virginia Mason leaders know different. Because culture can be assessed and is primarily the result of actions by leaders and peers, it is no different from any other organizational or process performance characteristic. It can be continuously improved. In other words, what I would call *culture kaizen* is possible, using many of the same methods applicable to care processes.

Initial, ad-hoc efforts to improve culture. In 2004 the Center for Innovation produced a short guide for managers and leaders that provided practical things to try for each of the seven dimensions. For example, to improve on the information dimension, the guide recommended:

- Ask your team to identify what knowledge or information they wish was more readily available to spark ideas and help them innovate. Develop an action plan to tackle one of these needs at a time.
- Start a *Not Invented Here* effort. Encourage staff to seek out ideas from elsewhere to import for use in their work. Have fun with it.
- Send scouts out to other departments with the goal that they are to bring back at least one good idea that you can test in your department.

These practical ideas were designed to be tested on a small scale using the VMPS tool of plan, do, study, act (PDSA) cycles in just the same way that one might test a process or clinical protocol change. This is another example of the integration of lean and innovation. Lean methods can be used to improve the culture for innovation, which in turn can support even better, more transformative ideas for ways to provide value to customers and eliminate waste. It is a virtuous cycle.

The guide was also meant to show what organizational culture experts have known for a long time. Culture is the accumulation of many small actions, rituals, and practices that send messages about what is valued and desired in the organization. By themselves, the formal statements of organizational values and the big fanfare launch events that most organizations use to feed a campaign to change the culture do very little in the end. What matters most to members of staff is what they see, do, and feel on a daily basis, *within their local workgroup and in connection with their direct line manager.* This message, along with the guide and its updates, was shared with managers and clinical leaders at Virginia Mason in forums over several years. While there was no formal assessment of these efforts, these sessions raised awareness of the seven dimensions and gave leaders some useful tools.

Formalizing the effort. The 2009 implementation of the more rigorous assessment via the staff survey sharpened the focus on the elements of culture that support innovation, and on efforts to improve scores at the workgroup level. Integrating with the organization's vendor-supplied staff engagement survey created the need to update the short culture improvement guide to a format that was more consistent with a corresponding guide supplied by the vendor for the other items on the survey. The *Virginia Mason's Guide to Creating the Culture for Innovation* is a 39-page resource that gives background on the seven dimensions, describes how to interpret responses on the two survey items associated with each dimension, provides ten or more tips for raising scores on that dimension that can be tested via PDSA cycles, and identifies resources for further information. It is available to all managers and clinical leaders via the organization's intranet.

Culture improvement collaboratives. In July 2010, the Center for Innovation met with managers whose culture of innovation workgroup reports showed strength in all or most of the seven dimensions in order to identify additional potentially better practices that could be shared with others. This, along with the emerging recognition of the parallels with any other topic for improvement, led to the establishment of a culture of innovation collaborative. Collaboratives—where individuals, teams, or organizations come to share, learn, and improve together—are a well-known element of the improvement landscape in healthcare. However, their application to aspects of organizational culture is somewhat novel.

The 2011 pilot collaborative was small, but successful. It comprised ten monthly meetings of ten managers who wanted to improve their culture portal scores, along with coaches from the Center for Innovation, Human Resources, and Organizational Development. Six of the ten participant workgroups improved their scores from 2010 to 2011, four improved in all seven dimensions. The risk-taking and information dimensions saw the biggest overall gains. The participating leaders said they found the collaborative useful and hoped that other leaders and their workgroups would be given the chance to participate in a similar effort.

Executive chef Jeff Anderson was one of those participants. He said with a laugh, "It was suggested that I join the collaborative because I had poor staff satisfaction survey results. But I really enjoyed it. I learned a lot from sitting with the other managers, learning some of the tools and tips they used. I'm usually buried in work and put my nose to the grindstone." Emergency Department director Sharon Mann echoed a similar sentiment. "[As a manager] you don't always get to hear from others, you just go, go, go all the time. In the collaborative, you could hear what others were doing and borrow from them."

What each learned was simple but powerful in terms of changing their workgroup's culture. Anderson borrowed the idea of a comments jar that staff could contribute to anonymously to allow him to demonstrate that he was taking them seriously and would respond to ideas. This built trust and communication, key elements in the relationships dimension. Mann heard about how a manager in Finance let team members design many of their processes and job aids, and it got her thinking about how much more involvement she could get from her team members. Letting go of things and letting others do them contributes to the risk-taking and recognition dimensions. In addition, she sent her team members out to scout around in other areas of the hospital to look at how they did things before they finalized their own approach to common issues. This helped build the information dimension. Little things, done consistently as a management practice, can add up to a lot when one is trying to build organizational culture (see the "Walking in Anotherr's Shoes "box).

**WALKING IN ANOTHER'S SHOES: BUILDING
UNDERSTANDING AND RESPECT INTO THE CULTURE**

Cheryllynn Waymack of the Virginia Mason laboratory tried a creative twist as part of the 2012 Innovation Culture Collaborative. She helped her team focus on building relationships and respect for people by writing their names on surgical booties and then walking in each other's shoes as part of an exercise to learn about each other's jobs and challenges.

Another innovation culture collaborative was launched in 2012, involving ten managers accountable for twelve workgroups. In this collaborative, innovation mean scores were up in seven of the twelve workgroups, with many managers reporting that staff members were bringing up more ideas to work on as a result of their efforts.

While these two collaboratives represent small samples, many confounding variables, and somewhat inconclusive results, they suggest that elements of organizational culture can indeed be improved using the same lean thinking methods that can be applied to processes and services. Anecdotal reports from collaborative participants further underscore the point about an organization having an overall culture, not a separate culture for this and that. Participants noted that things they were doing as part of Virginia Mason's initiatives on Respect for People and standard work for leaders were also helping boost their culture for innovation and vice versa.

Partnering with a Human Resources initiative, Virginia Mason's 2013 focus is called *go wide and go deep*. The plan is to continue efforts encouraging all leaders to attend to culture on a daily basis (go wide), while providing targeted support and a series of learning labs for leaders of workgroups with big drops in scores, or sustained low scores (go deep). At Virginia Mason, the lean principle of *pursue perfection* applies to the culture of innovation in just the same way it applies to everything they do.

Transforming Healthcare: What Others Can Learn from Virginia Mason's Innovation Culture Efforts

Organizational culture is key to success in both lean and innovation. Change cannot be sustained unless the culture supports it. Excellence has to be a cultural value before it can be an enduring statement about performance. The Virginia Mason Medical Center experience shows that aspects of culture that support innovation can be measured and continuously improved through deliberate and systematic effort.

I asked immediate-past board chair, Carolyn Corvi, whether the culture at Virginia Mason was fragile in that it might not sustain itself if a few key leaders left. Her reply speaks volumes for what Virginia Mason has accomplished over the last ten years. "It is like a tree. The roots go down and keep getting deeper. That tree isn't going to blow over. The roots are strong enough now."

Leaders in Other Healthcare Organizations Should ...

Reflect on whether their organizational culture aids or hinders innovation. The seven dimensions, and their associated subelements, as described in Figure 5.1, provide an evidence-grounded framework for reflection.

- Are we content to showcase a few innovative things, or do we want to create a culture that enables innovation in all parts of the organization, every day?
- How are we currently doing in each of the seven dimensions?
- Which are our strongest and weakest dimensions?
- How do we know?
- How might we gain momentum through synergy with other cultural improvement initiatives in our organization?
- Is our organizational culture relatively uniform, or do we have pockets of microcultures?
- Do we suffer from the *ideas to action problem?*

Seek out the views of a cross section of the organization. With culture, perception is reality. For example, if frontline staff perceive that they will not be supported if they try new ideas and do not succeed in the traditional sense of the word, then they will be unlikely to take the risk. It does not matter that senior leaders feel that they will be supportive. Therefore, it is not enough for leaders to assess the culture and plan actions alone. It is necessary to ask around.

- Would middle managers, physicians, and frontline members of staff agree with our assessment?
- How would we know?
- How should we engage them in dialogue to understand their perceptions?
- Do we have any data from existing indictors (for example, staff surveys) to help us reflect further?

Take some high-profile actions to signal the desire to create a culture that stimulates innovation. While each dimension is important and everything that leaders do has impact, some actions have the potential to create strong signals that spread quickly through the social structure of the organization.

- Should we consider putting in place some high-profile, organizationwide system around patient safety or the experience of care that empowers every member of staff to *stop the line* and get immediate attention from senior leaders if something is not right in order to signal a major shift in our culture?
- Should we examine our high-profile organizational goals and targets and perhaps set some aggressive stretch goals to indicate that we are willing to think outside the usual mental valleys?

Set up structures and processes to enable leaders to learn from one another about what works in establishing a supportive culture. Healthcare organizations are often quite siloed and leaders have little knowledge of what others are doing. Virginia Mason Medical Center captured best practices from well-performing leaders and set up collaboratives to support culture improvement.

- If we do have pockets of microcultures where some are better than others, how can we learn from the positive deviants?
- What forums do we have for clinical and managerial leaders to share honestly, without fear of judgment, their struggles and triumphs in leading their workgroups?
- How are these forums doing? Should we have more or different ones?
- How do senior leaders communicate the importance of creating great team cultures that support innovation in workgroups?
- Is the culture of a leader's workgroup taken into account explicitly in promotion and recognition decisions?

Chapter 6

Supportive Infrastructure for Innovation

The innovation team has always seen itself as owning very little operationally. Instead, we've seen our role as catalyzing innovative thinking and capabilities within the organization. The freedom to innovate is everyone's privilege, not just that of a separate workgroup.

—Jennifer Phillips
Director, Virginia Mason Center for Innovation

Culture and infrastructure are intimately linked. If culture is the way we do things around here, then infrastructure is what aims to make it easy to do the right things. If leaders desire a culture where information flows freely to stimulate innovation, then it is helpful to have systems that facilitate information flow. If they desire a culture where everyone is facile using methods that generate creative thought, then it is important to put structures in place that efficiently educate and coach on these.

Infrastructure should support operational functions, while avoiding becoming a function of its own. Functions deliver beneficial outcomes or results; infrastructures make that process easier and more efficient. The Internet is infrastructure; banking, publishing blogs, or purchasing products are functions. When infrastructure designers do and control too much, they stifle creativity and limit the emergence of future functionality.

Therefore, the infrastructure questions for any healthcare organization desiring to be innovative boil down to two:

1. What aspects of culture are we trying to support with our infrastructure?
2. Where do we draw the line between infrastructure that supports, and the function or outcome that it is supporting?

One of the threads in the evolution of the strategic innovation plan has been the effort to create sustaining structures. Virginia Mason Medical Center has chosen to create a minimalist infrastructure that focuses on enhancing certain dimensions of culture, and sends a clear message that the function of creative thinking and innovation is a daily responsibility for everyone. After a quick review of illustrative innovation infrastructures in other leading healthcare organizations, I will describe the principles that lie behind Virginia Mason's approach and show how these have translated into practice over time.

Examples of Innovation Infrastructures in Leading Healthcare Institutions

Infrastructures to support innovation in healthcare delivery organizations come in a wide variety. While dozens of innovation centers have emerged in healthcare, a brief review of three of the most well known will illustrate some of the contrast between how Virginia Mason and other leading healthcare organizations have addressed the two key infrastructure questions.

Kaiser Permanente. California-based Kaiser Permanente maintains two formally designated national structures to support the innovation that occurs across all its regions and functions. The Innovation Consultancy is a ten-person team, called in on high-profile projects to "work with frontline staff, management and patients to design and implement solutions that improve the care experience for our patients and the work experience for our care providers." Consultancy team members bring special skills in design thinking and idea generation, having been trained by industrial-design leader IDEO. The Sydney R. Garfield Healthcare Innovation Center is a 37,000 square-foot laboratory of mocked-up clinical environments, where new ways of delivering healthcare can be simulated and tested by teams drawn from the frontline, using rapid prototyping methodologies. Importantly, the realistic environment allows for the simultaneous testing of innovations in process flows, equipment, and technology. The Center supports coaching and education to spread creative thinking competency, and actively seeks "to bring together disciplines, people and ideas to maximize innovation potential."

Mayo Clinic. The Mayo Clinic Center for Innovation describes itself as "a bridge between the medical practice and human-centered design thinking." With a full-time equivalent staff of over fifty, it is the largest in both square footage and staff, and claims to be "the first to be integrated into a world-class medical practice setting." The Center includes an outpatient lab that allows for the observation of patients while they interact with providers in the clinical setting; a lab for healthy aging and independent living housed within a continuing care retirement community; and spaces for low-fidelity and high-fidelity prototyping, workshops, and classes. Mayo maintains an impressive list of external partners, comprising academia, technology vendors, payers, and other healthcare delivery institutions. The expert teams within the Center "develop ground-breaking solutions and facilitate the application of these discoveries in the practice of medicine." The Center holds conferences and provides a variety of educational outreach efforts.

Boston's Center for the Integration of Medicine and Innovative Technology (CIMIT). CIMIT is a nonprofit consortium of Boston's leading teaching hospitals and universities, with additional strategic affiliations and partnerships. Employing over 50 central program staff, while cultivating a host of other investigators and specific project leaders, CIMIT's mission is to "improve patient care by facilitating collaboration among scientists, engineers and clinicians to catalyze the discovery, development and implementation of innovative technologies, emphasizing minimally invasive approaches." CIMIT professionals play four key roles in the consortium. *Site miners* "penetrate the multiple isolated member institutions, and connect people and ideas across the cultural walls of these institutions." They literally "mine" the institutions for projects and people deserving CIMIT's attention and help. *Program leaders* are eminent clinician scientists and technologists who can either judge viability and coach effectively proposed programs of innovation, or know the experts who can. *Clinical systems innovation managers* help tie together multiple innovations with the major administrative commitment and institutional operational resources required to change care processes, aiding the translation of ideas into innovation. Projects and grants managers handle the substantial administrative leadership burden associated with a grant portfolio that averages around 75 active projects at a time. Over a 12-year period, CIMIT has supported over 550 projects, generating over 500 peer-reviewed publications, 200 patent applications, 30 issued patents, and over 15 spin-off companies.

In each of these three cases, the infrastructures described clearly support the resources, information-sharing, tools, and relationships dimensions of culture for innovation. Each obviously supports risk taking, targets, and recognition, *but mainly in the context of specific projects, not necessarily in the organization as a whole.* The capital costs and staff expense associated with each are not insignificant, although each is associated with organizations with substantial revenue bases. The visibility of these efforts clearly signals that the senior leadership of these organizations aims for the type of transformation that healthcare needs. The resource commitment, link to targets, and visibility assure a strong focus on delivering innovative ideas that have been at least tested through prototype and are ready to spread.

At the same time, there is a potential downside to these infrastructures in terms of the embedding of skills *across the whole organization*. In each case, the unintended, subtle message might easily come across as saying that the knowledge, skills, and practices of innovation are something that happens outside of daily work, by specially trained or gifted people working in a different environment. While content knowledge in design thinking, creativity, and innovation will no doubt spread through contact with these elements of infrastructure, that spread is likely to be slow. To sum it up, the infrastructures described above not only support the innovation function, but they may actually perform quite a bit of the innovation function *because they house the experts who know how to innovate.* Their challenge is to avoid inadvertently disempowering operational leaders and staff by separating innovation from daily work.

Does this matter? We do not know yet. Only time will tell what yields the quickest and most sustainable path to healthcare transformation. However, research on the sustainability of change indicates that the level of frontline leader and staff engagement in designing change is correlated to the quality of execution *and the durability of that change.* The advantage of a more minimalist and decentralized infrastructure—in the presence of full, executive-level, strategic commitment to innovation—is that it virtually guarantees the involvement and commitment of others from the very beginning of the innovation process. In response to the second key infrastructure question about enabling others versus doing centrally, this is the strategic choice that Virginia Mason has made in its approach to supporting innovation.

Infrastructure Evolves in Context

Like nearly everything else in a complex system, infrastructure needs to evolve over time and adapt to setting. While it is useful to design what one thinks might be a good infrastructure, and then set about putting that in place, it is best to be flexible and learn as you go. Research for this book uncovered past structural models for the innovation work at Virginia Mason that brought smiles and reflections of "Oh yeah, that's what we thought at the time, but things evolved differently." This is not an indication of a failure of planning or forethought; it is simply an artifact of a complex organizational system. It is hard to know exactly what you need until you get into it.

Rather than sticking steadfastly to rigid design plans, complex organizational systems evolve best when a few general principles—what complex systems scientists would call *simple rules*—are kept in focus, allowing details to work themselves out over time. In practice, these principles are often only clearly visible in hindsight. When written down, they represent explicitly what were the implicit intuitions and preferences of those involved in guiding the way forward. The dimensions of culture that support innovation provide principles to address the first infrastructure question about what it is aimed at supporting. The principles outlined in the "Principles Guiding Innovation Infrastructure Evolution at Virginia Mason Medical Center" box have guided Virginia Mason decisions on the second infrastructure question about where to draw the line between supporting and doing.

**PRINCIPLES GUIDING INNOVATION INFRASTRUCTURE
EVOLUTION AT VIRGINIA MASON MEDICAL CENTER**

- Focus on the pursuit of the perfect patient experience (rather than on tools and methods for their own sake).
- Integrate seamlessly into the Virginia Mason Production System as our management method.
- Reinforce line-leadership responsibility for improvement and innovation. (Corollary: Infrastructure should align to operational goals and work, not the other way around.)
- Coach and teach others (rather than do for them).
- Use infrastructure to cultivate future operational leaders (rather than have infrastructure units become a staff bureaucracy).
- Keep it minimal.

These principles have led to substantial changes in infrastructure over time at Virginia Mason. For example, in the early days of implementation of VMPS, a small team of specialists in what was then called the Office for Process Improvement oversaw education on lean methods and tools. However, an audit of the first 275 Rapid Process Improvement Workshops (RPIWs) revealed that change was not being sustained, a violation of the first principle. This led to the formation of the Kaizen Promotion Office to go beyond simply educating about tools and to provide more hands-on coaching support for operational leaders through the entire VMPS process. Similarly, Virginia Mason's Center for Innovation was initially set up as a stand-alone entity. But, in order to do a better job on the principle of integrating seamlessly into VMPS, the Center was eventually integrated into the Kaizen Promotion Office (KPO).

The following descriptions provide a snapshot of some of the major infrastructure elements that support innovation at Virginia Mason, circa 2013. Additional elements are covered in the next chapter. These descriptions will naturally one day be out of date as the systems will continue to evolve and change in ways that are consistent with a living organism. The simple rules that guide this evolution are not likely to change much over time.

The Kaizen Promotion Office (KPO): Supporting the Implementation of the Virginia Mason Production System

The main, and most visible, infrastructure element supporting improvement and innovation at Virginia Mason is the KPO. Its core function is to accelerate the adoption of VMPS as a means to pursue the perfect patient experience throughout the organization, and to cultivate VMPS specialists assigned to coach improvement and innovation on high-priority organizational goals. Structurally, it consists of a central KPO and three divisional KPOs, supporting hospital, clinic, and corporate functions.

Central KPO responsibilities include providing training and education in VMPS, setting the standards for deployment of VMPS, and developing and implementing new strategies as part of VMPS. It is in fulfillment of this latter responsibility that Central KPO plays a key role in leading the innovation effort in Virginia Mason. KPO administrative director Linda Hebish, sits on the Innovation Leadership Team, and the Virginia Mason Center for Innovation reports to her, elements of infrastructure that we will describe momentarily. She reports directly to executive vice president and chief operating officer Sarah Patterson, assuring that improvement and innovation concerns receive the highest attention.

The three divisional KPOs dual-report to both the respective divisional executives and Central KPO. This arrangement both reinforces the concepts that improvement and innovation are line-leadership responsibilities, and ensures that KPO remains aligned with operational work. Further, leadership positions in the divisional KPOs serve as development grounds and are staffed on a rotational basis by leaders who serve a time in KPO and then go out better prepared to lead an operational unit.

Hebish describes the work of the divisional KPOs as very hands-on. "Our KPO team is in there working with frontline managers and staff side by side to learn and implement changes and figure out what works and what doesn't." Years of such helpful support work, says Hebish, means "We communicate much better and more effectively throughout the organization at all levels, and our sustainment rate has improved dramatically. We are definitely getting further along every day, although we are not there yet."

Although VMPS is the organization's management method, and KPO is the main infrastructure element supporting it, KPO is an example of the principle of minimalist infrastructure. Toyota Production System guidelines recommend that between 1% to 5% of an organization's nonmanagement full-time equivalents (FTEs) be dedicated to the KPO function. Virginia Mason's KPO weighs in at just 0.6% (28 FTEs). Nonetheless, the impact of the KPO team is felt throughout the organization because of its structural links to operating divisions and its focused involvement in high-profile initiatives.

In my experience with a variety of healthcare organizations, I see a subtle, but profound, difference in the approach of Virginia Mason's KPO coaches compared to improvement advisors in some other organizations. Too often, advisors take on accountability for improvement efforts and end up leading the improvement themselves instead of coaching the line-leaders on how to do so. While I have no doubt that this also occurs from time to time at Virginia Mason, I find that there is a much more conscious effort to avoid this problem compared to what I see in some other places. I believe this as a direct result of the Virginia Mason decision to keep its infrastructure minimal.

Innovation Leadership Team (ILT): Providing Board and Executive Level Guidance for Innovation

The Innovation Leadership Team (ILT) was formed in 2003 along with the initial strategic innovation plan. It comprises CEO Dr. Gary Kaplan, innovation executive sponsor Lynne Chafetz, board members and representative administrative and clinical executives who serve on a rotating basis, KPO administrative director Hebish; Center for Innovation director Phillips, and me as the chair of innovation. Amy London from the Center for Innovation serves as staff to the team. ILT conducts its work primarily through quarterly meetings and monthly email updates.

Details of the ILT's role have flexed over time to match the evolution of Virginia Mason's understanding of innovation and its integration into VMPS, but core responsibilities have remained consistent. It is an advisory group—not an executive decision-making body—that helps identify strategies for fostering a culture of learning and innovation. It provides strategic oversight regarding the continued integration of innovation into VMPS, and reviews plans for processes by which innovative ideas are proposed, triaged, funded, and incubated. Because of their senior position in the organization, its members are also asked to serve as ambassadors for the innovation work, fostering strategic discussion in other forums and contributing new knowledge and thinking. Executive sponsor Chafetz and innovation center director Phillips are quick to point out the many contributions of the ILT over the years; notably in pushing further integration of innovation and lean, planning for other infrastructure elements, constructing innovation metrics for the board, and defining breakthrough innovation.

The ILT provides a forum for educating key senior leaders about innovation and its integration into VMPS, while at the same time tapping the organizational wisdom of these seasoned leaders in terms of how to get things done. Importantly, it does not take the responsibility for the detailed guidance of innovation efforts in the areas within their scope away from operational line-leaders. At Virginia Mason, innovation is not a separate strategic initiative with its own decision-making and power structure; it is an embedded strategic initiative that is woven into the culture and existing structures across the organization.

The ILT is also a forum where board members can contribute directly to the innovation effort. Board members contribute wisdom and insights from their experiences outside healthcare. For example, ILT member Lonnie Edelheit was the executive leader over research and development at GE, while fellow ILT member Bob Lemon was a partner at consulting giant Accenture. These board members also see their role as one of constructive challenge. "We are a very outspoken board,"

Lemon reflected. Edelheit expressed similar thoughts. "I think it's our job to keep pushing." Innovation becomes less of a risk for executives when they have such strong, board-level support.

Center for Innovation: The Small Team behind the Scenes

CEO Kaplan and executive sponsor Chafetz cite the establishment of the Center for Innovation in early 2003 as a major milestone in Virginia Mason's journey to integrate innovation and lean. The Center's mission is to "serve as a catalyst for innovation efforts at Virginia Mason, working with responsible and account- able operations leadership to support the entire innovation cycle, from creativity to design to prototyping and piloting to full implementation in operations. It will provide support to build a culture of innovation." It was initially a stand-alone center, but consistent with the principle of integrating into VMPS, it has since been reorganized to be part of the Central KPO.

Since its inception, the Center for Innovation has been led by Jennifer Phillips. Chafetz provides ever-present executive support and direction; I provide content knowledge via several multiday visits annually and telephone and email contact between visits, while the executive and board members on the ILT provide high- level strategic oversight on a quarterly basis. As mentioned before, Phillips and Chafetz have been directly involved, most often behind the scenes, and almost always in partnership working with others, in nearly all of the work described in this book.

The Center for Innovation serves in a variety of ways. It staffs the ILT, pre- paring the agendas, and framing plans and work for review and advice. It leads on the development of the strategic plan for innovation, and provides support to the strategic plans for people, service, and quality that helps to integrate innova- tion into each of these. The innovation training and leadership development work described in Chapter 4 was developed directly by, or under the supervision of, the Center for Innovation. Phillips personally facilitates events where innovation tools and methods are needed, and has trained and coached a cadre of others among the VMPS specialists and certified lean leaders to do the same. Finally, the Center for Innovation led the development of, and now operates, the information technology elements of infrastructure described in the next section.

The Center for Innovation primarily supports the cultural dimensions of tools, information, and resources for innovation. Consistent with the principles of mini- malism, reinforcing line-leadership's responsibility for innovation, and coaching and teaching others rather than doing for them, the Center for Innovation has always been a very small group. It has never been more than two full-time equiva- lent positions and, at times, has been Phillips alone. However, thanks to the focus on educating and supporting others, in a very real sense the Center for Innovation at Virginia Mason is quite large. Many other leaders play an active role as partners in achieving the Center's mission to catalyze innovation.

Information Technology Supports for Innovation: Browsing for Knowledge and Ideas

Information technology (IT) greatly expands the reach of the small Center for Innovation, making the knowledge and ideas it has acquired widely available to anyone in Virginia Mason. There are two main structural supports in this area.

Center for Innovation intranet web pages. All of the materials produced by the Center are available for browsing or downloading by any Virginia Mason team member via the KPO website on what the organization calls *V-Net*. The major sections of the Center's web pages are:

- Culture boosters: Tips and guidance for assessing and improving the culture for innovation in one's work unit.
- Competency guide: Materials supporting the development of the skills on innovation, including case studies that demonstrate how others have used directed creativity concepts and tools at Virginia Mason.
- Tools and references: Easy-to-use guides on specific tools for generating, harvesting, and developing creative ideas.
- Innovation training: Information about the availability of training on innovation, as well as the training materials and handouts used in these sessions.

Idea Supermarket. This is a place for online shopping for ideas that have been tested and proven effective within Virginia Mason. Originally set up to house ideas generated and tested through the organization's Everyday Lean Idea (ELI) system (described fully in a subsequent chapter), it now also has the capability to store ideas generated in VMPS workshops. Phillips describes it as "a personalized, web-based toolkit where Virginia Mason team members can work on and store ideas from start to finish, and where managers can easily track and support ideas within their teams." While the vast majority of the ideas are incremental improvements at levels one through four on the seven levels of change, the system supports the risk-taking dimension of culture and supports an environment where change is the norm in daily work.

A simple click of the *Start an Idea* button on the site leads individuals through a process of thinking to clarify and document the issue, the idea, how it was tested, what was learned, and how the idea has been shared and spread. The online form can be saved for entries to be made over time as the idea is developed, tested, and shared. Leaders receive email alerts when a plan to test an idea is ready, and when the results are in, to allow them to have an active role in coaching and helping decide how the idea should progress.

A 2009 audit of 20% of the ideas published in the Idea Supermarket between January and June of that year—32 ideas from 19 departments—indicated a 100% sustainability rate. These are not mere suggestions; they are implemented ideas that work so well that they become embedded in the process.

The system is also a hit among those who use it. In a survey of staff who had used the system, 87% reported a positive experience. Comments included:

■ "My supervisor's excitement and encouragement make me confident in bringing up ideas."
■ "That Virginia Mason would want my idea out there for others to see and maybe use made me excited."
■ "I love the fact that anyone that works here can impact savings, patient safety, and worker safety."

Unfortunately, usage to date has not been universal with only 10% of workgroups actively using the supermarket to submit 213 ideas in 2012. This does not mean that only 10% are actively improving things on a daily basis, only that documentation of improvement on this particular system is far from universal. Consistent with the infrastructure principles cited earlier, the Center is providing more training to managers on how to coach on idea development and supermarket use, and is working with the organization's Standard Work for Leaders, Respect for People, and Patient Safety initiatives to more fully integrate use of the supermarket into these elements of Virginia Mason culture.

Emerging Infrastructures: Innovation Grants and Moonshine

A drawback to the minimalist approach is that one cannot do everything one would like to do, as rapidly as one would like to do it. This is illustrated in two additional infrastructure elements that are only recently taking form (circa 2013).

Some of the earliest strategic innovation plans called for the establishment of an internal fund to support promising innovative ideas. However, the small size of the Center for Innovation, other organizational priorities, and basic organizational readiness to embrace such a concept kept pushing this idea to the proverbial back burner. However, in 2012, the concept was finally realized with the establishment of the first innovation grants. I will describe this effort in much more detail in the next chapter, but briefly, the infrastructure that supports it consists of a committee to screen proposals and a budget category that can allocate up to $25,000 to an individual to support early stage idea generation that might lead to break-through innovation.

Similarly, Virginia Mason is also now exploring more formal support for the lean concept of *moonshine*—creating physical prototypes and mock-up solutions to problems in an offline laboratory. Moonshine labs, with supplies, equipment, and engineers who can convert a concept or sketch into a working model, are common in lean manufacturing companies like Toyota or Boeing. Such capability rarely exists in a healthcare organization, but Virginia Mason is working to create it. The current state of this work, and some practical examples, are described in more detail in the next chapter.

Time will tell whether these emerging infrastructures add value or not. Both are under the strategic oversight of the ILT and their evolution will be governed by the simple rules for infrastructure cited earlier.

Communications Infrastructure: Getting the Word Out about Innovation

The Center for Innovation has worked closely over the years with Virginia Mason's Communications Department to get the word out internally about the organization's innovation strategy, and developments associated with the integration of innovation and lean. Annual innovation communications plans formally state objectives, key message threads, key strategies, and a monthly schedule of activities. The "Excerpt from 2011 Innovation Communications Plan" box provides an example from the 2011 plan. Note how it covers a range of themes that we have explored in previous chapters associated with Virginia Mason's integration of innovation into VMPS. Again, the ILT provides overall strategic guidance on this.

Working through the Communications Department, rather than communicating as a separate entity, assures that messages on innovation are coordinated with similar plans on VMPS overall, as well as other organizational initiatives such as Respect for People, Patient Safety, and so on. This coordination is yet another side benefit of the strategic decision to keep infrastructure small; the Center for Innovation does not have the resources and time to communicate across the organization on its own.

The Center has developed a quarterly Innovations Insights column that is distributed electronically via the organization's intranet. Video interviews of staff highlighting leadership practices that have helped improve work group culture, descriptions of innovative projects and practices, and profiles of teams who are highly successful at idea generation have also been produced and distributed through various internal communications channels. "And," points out Phillips, "it's not just about traditional channels. I think what has given us the most traction is

EXCERPT FROM 2011 INNOVATION COMMUNICATIONS PLAN

OBJECTIVES

- Increase comfort with and understanding of innovation concepts and strategies; make them real and accessible so managers and their teams see benefits and uses.
- Managers and their teams know the 7 dimensions of an innovative culture, their team's strengths, and how to improve where needed for the 14 items included in the staff satisfaction survey.
- Staff, managers, and providers know that Virginia Mason now has a set of innovation/creativity competencies, are building familiarity with the details, and know how to access development opportunities.
- We observe increased participation in various aspects of the lean idea system.

KEY MESSAGES TO USE AS THREADS FOR THE YEAR

- Innovation is directed creativity implemented, and we can tap the innovation "rocket pack" toolkit to boost the level of creativity on everything from small-scale ELIs up to large-scale projects.
- Having a strong culture for innovation is as important as having methods. That's why we're heavily focused on the details of the 7 culture dimensions and leadership/team practices.
- There are lots of ways to learn and practice: classes, daily use, workshops.

people starting to talk about their use of innovation and creativity, and executives like Gary [Kaplan, CEO] and Sarah [Patterson, COO] deliberately calling out examples in forums such as Tuesday stand-up and Friday report-outs."

Organizational leaders often neglect communication. Change management guru and Harvard professor John Kotter famously stated that, in his extensive experience, most leaders "under-communicate by a factor of ten." Executive director of Virginia Mason's educational and coaching external outreach arm, the Virginia Mason Institute, Diane Miller, echoes Kotter's observation. "I think communications is a critical piece of infrastructure as it reinforces what staff believe is important to leaders. Almost all of our clients thus far have not considered the importance of communications as a regular component of their strategy to shape a new culture, such that we now require the guiding teams to have it as a regular agenda item at every meeting so they intentionally discuss what and how they are communicating." This infrastructure element is an indication that Virginia Mason practices what it preaches.

Center for Health Care Solutions: Catalyzing Breakthrough Innovations in Care by Supporting Uncommon Conversations

The Center for Health Care Solutions is a final piece of infrastructure that also faces outward into the marketplace. Established in 2004, the Center was created to offer employers, health plans, and policy makers the opportunity to work collaboratively with Virginia Mason leaders and frontline clinical providers to reduce unnecessary healthcare costs. The Center's formal budget line is only 0.7 FTE, but like the other minimalist elements of Virginia Mason infrastructure, it works through partnerships with others.

The Center's main function is to facilitate the coming together of these diverse stakeholders in what are called *marketplace collaboratives* to address the most costly medical conditions for purchasers. These efforts integrate and leverage concepts from evidence-based medicine, lean thinking, and transparent cost accounting to create models of better, more reliable, and more affordable healthcare. The Spine Clinic case study in Chapter 2 was a project supported by the Center.

As a piece of infrastructure, the Center and its collaboratives provide an unprecedented forum of communication with payers and employers in a relentless focus on pursuit of the perfect patient experience. In these marketplace collaboratives, frontline providers get to work directly with benefits managers and others they would rarely have access to, and see detailed cost accounting that colleagues in other organizations rarely see. This supports the information-flow and relationships dimensions of culture for innovation, and provides the mental valley challenge needed to spark creativity. The Center's success in collaborating with employers to improve quality and rapid access to care while reducing cost has been featured in the *Wall Street Journal,* and in peer-reviewed journals such as *Health Affairs.*

Transforming Healthcare: What Others Can Learn from Virginia Mason's Innovation Infrastructure Efforts

Good infrastructure feeds the culture for innovation and keeps it alive. Too sparse or too fragile an infrastructure can result in innovation becoming lost amid the day-to-day urgencies and issues. Too much or overly centralized infrastructure can inadvertently signal that innovation is a function separate from day-to-day operation and thereby stifle the innovative potential of frontline leaders and staff. Getting the balance right is tricky.

The Virginia Mason Medical Center infrastructure for innovation has evolved over time, guided by a few principles that have remained stable. At Virginia Mason, the freedom to innovate is everyone's privilege, not just that of a separate workgroup. Only time will tell if Virginia Mason's answer, which is quite different from that of some other leading healthcare organizations, is the best way to transform healthcare.

Leaders in Other Healthcare Organizations Should ...

Review the reflections from the previous chapter regarding cultural aids or hindrances to innovation, and add to these elements of infrastructure that work for or against each dimension. The seven dimensions of culture that support innovation provide the framework for answering the first question in planning for infrastructure for innovation: "What are we aiming to support?"

- What structures and processes make it easy for us to positively build our culture for innovation?
- What are we lacking?
- What might we need to dismantle or redesign?
- What would it take to build even better elements of infrastructure?
- Where should we begin?

Dialogue thoughtfully about the difference between infrastructure that supports innovation across the organization, versus structural elements that perform the function of innovation offline from day-to-day operations. This second infrastructure question is key. There is no one-size-fits-all answer to it. The approach taken needs to be consistent with the organization's values, history, style, and goals. However, it is important to be clear to avoid sending mixed messages.

- In our organization, who do we want to be responsible for innovating on a ongoing basis?
- What do we see as the major differences between the infrastructures briefly outlined from the three other leading healthcare organizations and that of Virginia Mason?
- What do we, as leaders who know our organizations, think of these differences?
- In what ways do we want to emulate the Virginia Mason approach, and in what ways do we favor aspects of the other approaches?
- What is our history with regard to setting up infrastructure to support change and do we want to do more of the same or something different now?
- What might constitute an initial set of principles to guide our way forward in creating infrastructure to support innovation?

Chapter 7

Bringing Innovation to Daily Work

Our leaders say to everybody, "We want you to keep thinking every day, to have daily ideas. Wherever you are in the organization, you are just as important as anybody else." And so, small, everyday contributions make a difference. I think there is a culture here that says, everything matters.

—Francis Salinas, MD
Anesthesiologist, Virginia Mason Medical Center

The integration of innovation and lean is not confined to the formal events of the Virginia Mason Production System (VMPS). Everyone in the Virginia Mason culture, from executives to frontline staff, is encouraged to apply the concepts and tools of lean and innovation to their day-to-day work. This is a natural consequence of the lean principle of pursuing perfection and the strategic goal of achieving the perfect patient experience. At Virginia Mason, *everything* matters and *everything* can be done differently and better. Everything is a candidate for change at any of the seven levels of change.

The concept of everyone producing ideas to make things better is a foundational part of the Toyota Production System, dating back to its roots in the 1950s. In *40 Years, 20 Million Ideas: The Toyota Suggestion System,* author Yuzo Yasuda documents how Kiichiro Toyoda learned about employee suggestion systems from a 1951 visit to Ford Motor Company's River Rouge Plant in Detroit. Since then, Toyota has created a culture and supporting infrastructure that now generates, *and implements,* over 100,000 ideas annually.

While nowhere near Toyota in this regard yet, Virginia Mason aspires to this level of natural creativity, involvement, and commitment in its culture. That effort is off to a good start.

I will begin with several examples illustrating a range of efforts by individuals and work teams to think creatively about the challenges and opportunities they see in their daily work. Some of the individuals involved were simply being naturally creative, while others learned concepts of directed creativity in training events or through involvement in VMPS workshops. As the language of both lean and directed creativity have become embedded in the culture, it is difficult to trace the origin of any specific idea, and in the end, it does not really matter. I have purposefully selected the examples to illustrate how innovation in daily work is happening across the spectrum of organizational levels, professional disciplines, and settings (hospital, clinic, and corporate functions).

Then, building on these ad hoc examples and the infrastructure discussion in the previous chapter, I will describe four structures at Virginia Mason that more formally support innovation in daily work—the Everyday Lean Idea (ELI) system, moonshine projects, clinical informatics practitioners, and the Virginia Mason innovation grants process. While these specific structures may not be right for every organization, in the absence of some sort of supportive structure, calls for innovation in daily work can come across to staff as empty rhetoric.

"I Swore I Was Going to Find a Way to Make That Never Happen Again"

Kaizen Fellows receive the highest level of VMPS training and are, therefore, often at the forefront of innovation in daily work. Roger Woolf, administrative director, Pharmaceutical Services, is a typical example. Woolf focuses his Kaizen Fellowship work on the medication use value stream. This process comprises everything from the time a provider orders a medication, through filling in the hospital's pharmacy and administration by a nurse on a unit, and on to monitoring by the nurse for therapeutic response and reactions. Various portions of this value stream have been the topics for formal VMPS events over a ten-year period.

Virginia Mason has been among the innovators in healthcare in applying bar code scanning technology to multiple steps in the medication use process. For example, all medications leaving the pharmacy are labeled with a bar code and then scanned on the nursing unit as they are loaded onto automated medication cabinets to assure that the correct medication is in the right place and will be given to the right patient.

Generally speaking, there is high confidence in manufacturer-supplied medications because of the extremely strict quality control and regulatory processes in place in the pharmaceutical industry. However, medications mixed uniquely per a physician's order in the hospital pharmacy present a slightly higher risk. The nurse administering the mixed medication must simply trust that the preparation and labeling process in the pharmacy is accurate.

This pharmacy process relies on the technician who mixes the medication doing a self-check, and then getting a pharmacist to do a successive check. The complexity of achieving perfection in this work is illustrated by data from a study at Virginia Mason that indicated that pharmacists caught an average of two errors per day in the successive check. Unfortunately, one day an error made it all the way through to the patient.

"It was New Year's Day," recalls Woolf, "and I got a phone call because we discovered an error where we had given a young lady a chemotherapy drug rather than an immune modulator as had been ordered. They look and sound somewhat similar. She had beautiful dark black hair, but she had to cut it because she was concerned of losing it due to the chemotherapy. Fortunately, she didn't have any long-term or serious effects, but it was one of those things that resonate with you. I swore to myself that I was going to figure out a way to make that never happen again."

The idea that Woolf and his team have developed to improve their daily work is the application of bar coding technology to the preparation process. Each *component* in a mixture is first individually bar coded, and then scanned so that the computer can check that the ingredients match what was ordered. "There are very few people who have done this," notes Woolf. "Nobody has quite done it the way we have approached it. I got the idea during a site visit to Duke University because they were experimenting with this but had really not designed a complete system. So, we took that idea and our learning as a team from applying bar coding to other aspects of the value stream, and now we are doing level 6 change—doing something no one else is doing."

The innovation principle here is again around connecting mental valleys in novel ways. In this case, the mental valleys are not far apart in a conceptual sense; bar coding for error-proofing was being used in other portions of the medication use process, it had just not been applied to the preparation of mixtures in the pharmacy. An outsider might ask, "Why not? It seems so obvious?" The answer has to do with the mental act of attention. In this case, Woolf and his colleagues needed to pay attention to the need to question the ingredients in a pharmacy-prepared mixture and escape the assumption that it is correct, as one can reasonably assume with a medication coming directly from a pharmaceutical company. This then leads easily to mental movement that links up this situation with the bar coding technology being applied elsewhere in the value stream. Innovation in daily work often involves simply pausing to pay attention, escape assumptions, and think.

"We're Throwing Everything, Including the Kitchen Sink, at You"

The need for innovation—challenging the notion that the way we do things now is the only way—applies just as well to daily clinical practice as to the flows of medications. Anesthesiologist Dr. Francis Salinas, and his work on multimodal pathway pain management, provide a good illustration.

During hip and knee replacement surgery, pain signals are generated at the surgical site, transmitted through the peripheral nerve to the spinal cord, and then on to the brain. There had been a long-standing history of using regional anesthesia to block the pain signals as they try to move along the peripheral nerve (this is called a *continuous peripheral nerve block*). In fact, one of the innovators in the development of regional anesthesia, Dr. Daniel C. Moore, did much of his pioneering work at Virginia Mason during his tenure from 1947 to 1983. Care must be taken, however, to use only the minimum effective amount of anesthesia in order to avoid leg weakness that could result in a fall during the postoperative period. Further, the blocking effect wears off over time, allowing pain signals through eventually. Because of this, Dr. Salinas points out, "We used to think that pain was a necessary part of surgery. But that is archaic thinking."

Applying better thinking to this almost daily practice for anesthesiologists, Dr. Salinas recommended giving these patients a combination of medications to target multiple sites along the *whole* pain pathway. This *cocktail* of medications could begin before surgery, and then continue through the surgery and after, allowing them to work synergistically to decrease the patient's pain and inflammation. Says Dr. Salinas, "I tell the patients, we're throwing everything, including the kitchen sink, at you, but we are just trying to target as many ways as possible to interrupt the pain."

The VMPS infrastructure of *kaizen* events and Rapid Process Improvement Workshops (RPIWs) helped turn these creative thoughts into standard work that is now practiced on all hip and knee replacement patients, and is also being applied to many other types of surgery. Benefits of this approach include reducing the risk of falls, earlier mobilization following surgery, and reduced lengths of stay.

Dr. Salinas points out that the mechanisms of the various pain medications have been well known for quite some time. The innovation lies in combining them all, thinking about the *entire* patient journey (pre-, during, and postoperation), and having the disciplined infrastructure to get agreement and practice change among all of the clinical disciplines involved. This provides yet another example of how evidence-based practice, creative thinking, and standard work can be mutually supportive.

Since daily work never stops, thinking about how to innovate in daily work should never stop. Having rethought pain management in the case of *elective* hip and knee surgery, Salinas and his colleagues pressed on in their thinking.

Every year, Virginia Mason takes care of close to three hundred, mostly elderly, patients who fall and need *urgent* surgery for a hip fracture. These patients come to the Emergency Department, get admitted to the floor, and then get worked up by medicine, surgery, and anesthesia clinicians prior to surgery. Many of these elderly patients have multiple comorbid medical conditions, and are at particular risk for the respiratory depressant effects of narcotic-based pain medications, which are often not fully effective for hip fractures anyway. As a consequence, they often get inadequate pain control in the hours prior to their surgical procedure.

Salinas and his colleagues reasoned, "We know that the hip joint is supplied by three main nerves, and the easiest to get to is the femoral nerve. A continuous femoral nerve block is a well-known, well-validated technical procedure that we're all good at now. So, we asked the question, 'What if we did a femoral nerve block as soon as the patient was stabilized in the Emergency Department, and then continue that block through whenever they get their procedure, and into the next day or two beyond that?'" The infrastructure of VMPS again helped turned this idea from a provocative question in daily work into vastly improved pain control for hip fracture patients, via the establishment of the standard work across the multiple departments and clinical disciplines needed to make it happen.

Bringing Fresh Ideas to the Daily Practice of Surgery

Many staff members, like surgical technician Jolanta Jankowski, innovate daily by constantly being on the lookout for ideas to share and ways to make things better. Jankowski has brought new insights and ideas to the operating rooms at Virginia Mason. For example, along with surgeon Dr. Jeffrey Hunter, she modified a surgical retractor for moving the liver out of the way in laparoscopic gastric bypass surgery. The old retractor was a straight rod that got in the way of other instruments. Jankowski and Hunter bent a few rods at different angles and now the retractor is no longer in the way. In another instance, she recommended to a surgeon doing laparoscopic surgery that an instrument used in brain surgery might be helpful, eliminating the need to invest in two instruments. The combination of creative thinking, thoughtful observation in daily work, and a respectful culture that supports a surgical technician making practice change recommendations directly to a surgeon, is quite powerful.

KVM Radio

Doctors Kim Pittenger and Ted Johnson found a way to take one of the most basic and mundane aspects of organizational life and spice it up a bit with a little creativity. These physician leaders were looking to communicate to their colleagues in a way that would cut through the background noise of the normal flow of organizational memos and meetings. A brainstorm about novel communication methods led them to the idea of producing a talk-show format that they dubbed *KVM Radio*. It is a five-minute, biweekly voicemail that is delivered to all Virginia Mason providers, administrators, managers, and supervisors.

"The show grew out of the feeling that communications to clinicians wasn't as comprehensive as it could be," says Johnson. "We are at many different sites and have grown into a large group. We also thought that people would benefit from hearing the information in an auditory format. It makes Virginia Mason more personal and helps us bond as a group."

"We use humor, music, and a quick pace to get our points across and make the show enjoyable," says Pittenger. "Our goal is to increase common understanding, while supporting the cultural direction of Virginia Mason. We do segments on clinical innovations, VMPS improvement projects, administrative initiatives, and financial and quality challenges and accomplishments. We also introduce new doctors and say goodbye to retiring doctors."

The multiple mental valley escapes that this idea provides led one respondent to an internal communications survey to write, "KVM is a unique and innovative way to communicate!" It has been a hit for over a decade now.

"I'm Doing It Today, and Never Again"

As Virginia Mason sleep disorders specialist Dr. William DePaso discovered, sometimes innovation in daily work follows the old maxim, "Necessity is the mother of invention."

DePaso recalls the day the Sleep Center was having some staffing issues, leaving him without an assistant. The manager told him that he would have to room his own patients. (Rooming is the process, usually done by a nurse or assistant, of escorting the patient from the waiting area to the exam room and doing the initial interview to set up the visit for the doctor.) "We wanted to keep the schedule going, so I said, 'OK. That's what has to happen. But I'm doing it today and never again.' I just remember saying those words," recalls DePaso.

"I saw about twenty-five patients that day, and by about the tenth patient I started to say, 'There's something interesting about this.' So, I said the next day I would do it again. By the end of the second day I realized I had discovered a whole different way of thinking about what we did."

"If you're a patient," DePaso explains, "you spend a lot of time in a room waiting for somebody to come talk to you. But the visit cannot really start until I am available, so why should they wait in the exam room? And if I'm ready, why should I wait for somebody else to go get the patient? Why can't I just go and meet them myself, when I am ready?"

Escaping these mental valleys led DePaso to insights that have further improved care, reduced the potential for error, and increased productivity. Escorting the patient to the exam room allowed him to initially assess the patient and have "a little chit-chat," so that by the time they reached the room, both were ready to start the visit. DePaso also recalls several occasions where escorting the patient back out to the front desk allowed time for things that either he or the patient forgot to bring up; things that might have otherwise led to errors of omission or misunderstanding.

DePaso continues, "I then realized that if I was rooming the patient when I was ready, I only needed one room instead of the three rooms I had. Patients do not need to sit in a room and wait for anything else, they only needed time with me. So that allowed us to triple the size of our practice in the same three rooms. I no longer need multiple rooms to run just my practice. I could have one doc and one patient in each room, and have a three-person practice in the same space.

"Lots of these small things ended up leading to the completely different way that we do our work today. I think it [being forced to room his own patients that one day] was one of the best things that has ever happened to me."

The Sleep Center team is also a good example of how innovation in daily work can contribute to organizational culture. Recall that one of the aspects of culture that supports innovation is the risk-taking practice of trying new things. Lean thinking provides the plan, do, study, act (PDSA) cycle as a method for this. However, it is not always easy to get people to be willing to go beyond their emotional barriers to try new things.

DePaso recalls a personal epiphany in a 2003 RPIW where he was asked to test the practice of dictating the medical record notes from a visit *in front of the patient*. "I said, 'Over my dead body! I have been doing this for twenty years, and I am just not doing *that*.'" Workshop leader, Dr. Joyce Lammert, currently the hospital's medical director, persisted and convinced him to at least try it. "By the end of a week," DePaso recalls, "once we had worked out a few details, I made a complete turnaround." DePaso saw the benefits of assuring that he and his patient were clear on what was discussed, and what the plan was.

"So, you have a couple of those kinds of things and soon you are willing to try anything. My mantra now is: *You try it.* You don't say a word until you have done it ten times. At the end of ten times, you get to have an opinion. If it is not the right thing to do, then do something different. But, if on the tenth time you think, 'There's something here,' then work out the details and move on with it. That is literally how we do it now, every day. We might do four or five PDSAs in a day. Sleep Center team members are empowered to *just do it*; 'Try it ten times and see how it works.'"

These examples of ad hoc, individually driven change in daily work illustrate how, at Virginia Mason, everyone—executives, managers, clinicians, and frontline staff, across the hospital, clinic, and corporate divisions—gets involved in thinking differently about day-to-day work. The individual ideas here and in subsequent examples span the spectrum from improvement to innovation; that is, they range across the seven levels of change. As we noted in Chapter 2 in the discussion about Everett Rogers' definition of innovation, there is a danger in mislabeling everything as innovation. However, as we also saw in the discussion around the risk-taking dimension of the culture of innovation in Chapter 5, creating an environment where change is the norm is good for innovation. Virginia Mason leaders, therefore, see no need for debate and strict classification. Several of the examples above also illustrate how VMPS encourages and accelerates the implementation of innovative ideas. Let us now look at the more formal structures that make this even more systematic, visible, and paradigm stretching.

The Everyday Lean Idea System

Virginia Mason's Everyday Lean Idea (ELI) system provides a structured way for all staff to apply lean thinking and try new things in their daily work, one of the hallmarks of an organizational culture that supports innovation. The vision is to involve *all staff* in reducing waste in their work areas *all of the time,* and then share what they do so others can learn and good ideas can spread. Not only does this bring immediate, tangible benefits to the organization, it also provides ongoing development of future leaders who have been steeped in lean and innovation thinking.

What is an ELI? Many issues do not need a workshop or big project in order to get to a solution. ELIs are meant to be small, quick-to-implement improvements, typically falling into levels 1 through 4 on the seven levels of change, tackled by staff involved in the particular process and impacting only an immediate, local work unit. These are ideas that do not need the cross-functional collaboration of a formal VMPS workshop. The solution or idea can be evaluated, tested, and implemented immediately as part of daily work. The typical focus of ideas is around improving safety, reducing defects, organizing materials or information, saving time and money, and supporting the organization's environmental initiatives.

An organizational communication about the system suggested that ELIs are intended to "kick-start your thinking; inspire your brain to think about doing your work differently." So, while the individual ideas themselves are not necessarily always a great stretch in terms of creative content, the ELI system promotes a general culture of challenging the way things are and doing something concrete to bring about change.

It is important to distinguish ELIs from the old-fashioned employee suggestion system, where staff typically offered up ideas to managers, who were often too busy or too disinterested to act upon them. In stark contrast, ideas in the Toyota Production System, or ELIs in VMPS, are fully tested and proven effective ideas that have been implemented by staff, with the support of leaders. As Chris Stewart, a supervisor in the Patient Financial Services Department put it, "It's a way for somebody to say, 'That process bothers me, but instead of letting it bother me, I'm going to improve it.' I don't know many organizations that will allow you to

> Ideas are like rabbits. You get a couple and learn how to handle them, and pretty soon you have a dozen.
>
> **—Author John Steinbeck**

make changes and implement ideas without having to go through management or jump through hoops. Virginia Mason not only allows it, it encourages it." In the period 2009–2012, Stewart's team of sixteen individuals has submitted an average of forty-four ELIs annually.

The leader's role. As noted in a previous chapter, an ELI template to guide thinking is available online in Virginia Mason's Idea Supermarket, and leaders are trained to coach staff in testing and putting ideas in place. If a team member's idea falls outside their scope to fix, they are encouraged to ask their leader for help in contacting the appropriate work team to see if it is possible to collaborate on a solution.

Jennifer Phillips, director of the Center for Innovation, says the ELI system "works best when departments incorporate it into their regular processes, such as staff meetings or huddles." The Inpatient Physical Medicine and Rehabilitation Department is a good example. Leaders Catherine LeViseur and Brenda Molina have communicated the expectation that all staff (except per diems) should contribute at least two ELIs per year. In various huddles and check-in opportunities, the team uses their high-level value stream to identify ELI opportunities. The leaders have a structured coaching process and have further developed others as idea mentors who can partner with peers to help them learn how to use the tools and test ideas. Similarly, when the ELI process was rolled out in Human Resource's Recruitment team, time in the monthly staff meeting was devoted to having everyone review the idea template and fill them out during the meeting. This multitasking has now become a ritual in the Recruitment team's culture. Examples like these reinforce the expectation that everyone should be on the lookout for ways to make things better, and that leaders support a culture of constant, staff-driven change.

Leaders at Virginia Mason also encourage a healthy, fun mix of competition and collaboration with ELIs. While numbers of ideas are counted, and individuals and groups with the most, or most widely copied, ELIs are recognized, leaders also encourage teaming up with coworkers. For example, an ELI might be initiated by an individual, but have other names added as others get involved in testing the idea. This allows individuals with burning ideas to team up with those who might be a little less confident, but do not mind contributing. Another form of collaboration involves shopping for ideas in the online Idea Supermarket and then repurposing these ideas to create a new ELI in one's own work situation.

Examples of ELIs. There are literally hundreds of ELIs posted in the Idea Supermarket, and countless other anecdotal reports that have not been documented. Collectively, these have eliminated a huge amount of waste throughout the medical center and made things better for patients, team members, and visitors. I have selected just a few examples to once again illustrate pervasiveness of application.

Tammy Davis, a staff member in the Kirkland Ophthalmology clinic, noted a safety issue in that used needles were not being capped because staff were often too busy to unlock the medication drawer to get the caps. Using "a small cup, rubber band, and small metal ring" she created a holder for the safety caps to hang on the sharps container. She tested the idea by simply hanging one on the sharps container in one exam room, without fanfare, and then went back at the end of the day to examine the contents. She noted in her ELI description, "All the needles placed in that sharps container had safety caps." She and her colleagues outfitted the rest of the clinic.

The application of simple visual controls to create situational awareness—a key concept in lean thinking—has also been the subject of many ELIs. For example, Kym Brune in the Inpatient Rehab Unit created a visual flag to alert nurses on a unit when a patient's bed alarm should be activated. Manj Randhawa in Pharmacy created a stop sign that can be velcroed to a computer reading "No Interruptions during Chemo Reviews" to eliminate a potential source of error during that critical process. Ilir Cerekja in Hospital Clinical Decision Support embedded the standard process for the sepsis prevention bundle into the form used by nurses to document care, as an immediate visual reference aid. Kristen Falk at the Issaquah clinic placed a simple, bright-colored dot on the chart of patients who had missing health history data elements so that these could be collected easily by the medical assistants as they roomed the patients.

As a new HR benefits manager, Tom Cranney watched benefits presentations to employees and saw how varied the content could be. The lack of standard work led Tom to develop PowerPoint-style benefits presentations, along with standardized speaker notes, to enable multiple team members to step in and give the same presentation, ensuring the right information is consistently delivered to Virginia Mason staff.

A staff member in the Patient Financial Services Department, Raquel C. Pagaduan, believed there was too much paperwork related to clinical referrals. "We seldom need to go back to this paperwork," Raquel wrote in her idea summary. "It takes up space and it takes time to copy and file." Instead, she proposed scanning the referrals immediately upon receipt, and then shredding the documents. This reduced delays in patient care, while saving approximately thirty minutes a day for the initial preparation that was being done to save the documents, and another two hours per week going through to clean out old files.

ELIs can be team efforts as well. A group of three staff members in the hospital's Physical Medicine Department took the initiative to set up a system with a local supplier of durable medical equipment (DME) to assure that patients always left the hospital with the critical things they needed for care at home. The result was an improvement from sending eight patients home without the DME they needed in December 2012, to only one in March and none at all in April 2013. Supervisors and managers in the Patient Financial Services Department noticed that they were often attending the same meetings, when, in fact, it would have been fine to have only one member of the team representing the department. Their ELI was the simple idea of huddling quickly every Monday morning to review calendars and discuss meeting attendance. The first month, they saved twenty-six person-hours. A group of five individuals from clinics and the call center worked together to dramatically reduce the practice of community pharmacies requesting refills for medications that were no longer needed. This effort reduced the number of such calls to the Kirkland clinic from ten per week to zero. This partnership was so successful that the same ad hoc group also created another ELI that took advantage of a patient's phone call for a medication refill to offer them appointments for needed preventive screening tests.

All of these examples are at levels 3 and 4 on the seven levels of change (doing things better and doing away with things). They are more properly called *improvements*, rather than *innovations*. The key point is that by making change the norm, through publicity about the ELI system, Virginia Mason is fostering a culture that enables more impactful and paradigm-altering innovation.

ELIs and standard work. ELIs are another example that change and standard work are mutually supportive at Virginia Mason. As Chris Stewart puts it, "I have always told people that writing standard work initially is actually doing an ELI. If you are putting standard work in place where there wasn't any before, you are making the daily work process better so that there is not as much variation. But that standard work is just a base, a jumping-off point. There could be better ways of doing it, and those would be the subject of future ELIs." Standard work also sustains the numerous improvements found in ELIs, thereby enabling these many small efforts to add up to something big.

ELI kaizen. Like everything else at Virginia Mason, the ELI system and Idea Supermarket have been the subject of continuous improvement over the years. Feedback on surveys indicating that staff and managers were experiencing frustrations with the Idea Supermarket resulted in a redesign of the web tools in 2012. Data collected in 2011 indicating that only 19% of departments had finished ideas posted in the Idea Supermarket has led to efforts to better educate and communicate about ELIs, and to build it into standard work for leaders. The organization's innovation strategy makes it clear that Virginia Mason is firmly committed to promoting a culture of learning and innovation that aspires to match Toyota's output of 100,000 ideas per year.

Making Things Better While the Moon Is Shining

Virginia Mason Medical Center has an area that is signposted *Moonshine Lab,* but what they do there is not what you might be thinking (see the box "Why Do They Call It Moonshine?" for the origin of the term). While not a fancy place, the moonshine lab is a space for what lean sensei Chihiro Nakao calls *trystorming.* While brainstorming is the process of letting the mind freewheel in the creation of ideas, trystorming lets the hands in on the fun as individuals and teams create new objects out of inexpensive, easy-to-use materials. The concept of reducing an idea to a series of ever-better, rapidly produced prototypes is a staple in design thinking and a common practice in innovation in other industries. Toyota Production System founder, Taiichi Ohno, put it this way, "Quick and dirty is better than slow and fancy."

As practitioners of lean thinking become more skilled at spotting waste and impediments to flow, they sometimes find that equipment and tools generally available in the marketplace are inadequate. Corporate KPO director Theresa Craw cites

WHY DO THEY CALL IT MOONSHINE?

In the Japanese organizations that pioneered lean thinking, the culture of pursuing perfection created a dedication in the workforce that often resulted in frontline workers and engineers staying on after the shutdown of the production line at the end of the day in order to find ways to make things better. They would often create new work tools and production process fixtures, using whatever they could get their hands on, that were then incorporated into the process the following day. These individuals were, quite literally, practicing kaizen while the moon was shining.

the example of shelving. "Current shelving designs perpetuate excess inventory. When you have a space that is larger than that needed to stock a supply or piece of equipment at a lean par level, you naturally tend to fill that space with excess inventory. That adds to inventory carrying costs. It is wasteful of space, processing, and transportation effort. If there is an expiration date on the supply there can be quality issues as well."

Working in the moonshine lab, and using techniques from Virginia Mason's *Moonshine Playbook,* a small team took on the challenge of designing something new. They began with some creative wordplay to escape the mental valley of *storage* to instead think about the concept of *dispensing.* Team members brainstormed seven ways of dispensing, based on common approaches seen in other settings such as a lazy Susan, a paper towel holder, or the dispenser for soft drink cans that comes in most refrigerators these days. (This is an example of the use of the directed creativity tool of mental benchmarking.) They then moved on to trystorming, creating a variety of mock-ups of dispensing devices for common supplies and equipment, first as tabletop models and then at full scale. Some ideas could be immediately built and implemented, while others would require working with a partner-vendor or specialty manufacturing shop to produce. The team envisioned that as the various dispensing devices are implemented to transform what used to be called *storage areas* into *dispensaries*, cartloads of excess inventory could be hauled away and space freed up for other uses.

In 2013, the team succeeded in implementing two of the concepts from the dispensary vision. Available shelving space is now restricted by means of dividers and bins to only that required to maintain par levels. They have also been able to create some gravity-fed dispensers for certain objects, much like the soft drink can dispenser in some refrigerators. The other items in the vision await arrangements with outside vendors because the team lacks the time, skills, and equipment to go beyond the mock-ups from the moonshine lab to durable equipment that can be permanently and safely installed.

The dispensary moonshine effort illustrates several key points. First, moonshine often sits at the overlap of innovation in daily work and the more structured workshops of VMPS. The individual ideas produced are reminiscent of those cited in the previous section on ELIs; for example, the clinic nurse who created a holder for the caps for used needles. However, because what was needed was a system of items that were a bit more substantial, this moonshine work was done in the context of a kaizen event by a small team of frontline staff who stocked or used the storage areas as part of daily work. This conceptual overlap is characteristic of most of Virginia Mason's moonshine efforts. Second, concepts and tools from directed creativity can stimulate thinking that leads to radically different prototypes. Third, while internal Virginia Mason staff can sometimes produce working prototypes, as a healthcare organization it does not have a cadre of engineers, machinists, carpenters, and others, such as would be found naturally in a manufacturing company like Boeing, who can build things at a moment's notice or create permanently installable items. There are limits to the moonshine lab's current capabilities. The Center for Innovation is actively partnering with others to fill the gaps.

A good example of innovative moonshining that has gone all the way to producing a product usable in daily patient care is the Virginia Mason therapy car. Getting into a car is a significant challenge for the hundreds of patients annually at Virginia Mason who have had total hip or total knee replacements and are discharged home. The Physical Medicine and Rehab (PM&R) department owned a mock-up car purchased from a vendor, but it was located far from the patient care unit, nearly impossible to move due to its weight and size, and could not replicate the varying heights of today's automobiles. Consequently, few patients were able to practice this critically important skill before discharge. Their first car ride home following surgery was literally placing them at risk. A kaizen event was convened to moonshine a better way.

First, work was done to get the team out of the mental valleys associated with a car. These would likely impede their thinking in trying to produce a streamlined simulator that could be more easily moved, but still retained the important physical challenges presented by a car to an orthopedic surgery patient.

Mental Valley of a Car	Alternatives/Escapes
Seat has to move.	Perhaps the dash and something to simulate the constraint of the floorboard moves instead.
Door has to open and close.	Maybe we just need to reproduce the angle of an open door.
Must have a full front seat, steering wheel, and pedals.	Only the passenger half is really needed.
Must have a dashboard.	But it doesn't have to be solid.
Etc. …	Etc. …

The team then set some stretch goals for its product to further provoke thinking. They specified that the simulator must mimic the physical constrains of anything from a sedan to an SUV, fit into a 52-inch space, be able to be changed over in less than a minute, and have fewer than five moving parts. The team then set about creating tabletop models out of wooden tongue depressors, building blocks, cardboard, and other materials, and sharing these prototypes and successively creating new ones from the best ideas. They moved on to build a full-scale version that they were able to test themselves and with staff on the orthopedic surgery unit and PM&R. However, this prototype still needed further development in order to be safe for use with patients; for example, the seat cushion needed to be of material that had appropriate infection control properties. Each successive test led to improvements in the design.

Five months after the kaizen event, the team had a plastic-coated steel-pipe *therapy car* simulator, approved for use with patients. It does not *look* anything like a car, but still presents all the challenges that someone with a new hip or knee will face in getting in and out of one. It is compact and easy to adjust to the dimensions of the type of car in which the patient will be transported, via the use of a gauge that provides settings for all common makes and models. Standard work incorporates its use into daily work in PM&R and on the orthopedic surgery nursing unit.

Data collection indicates that the target of having 100% of eligible patients receive car transfer training before discharge has been achieved. Patients and staff love it. PM&R supervisor Catherine LeViseur commented, "The therapists *love* the car. It's so great to have this equipment available to our patients and I am so proud to work here, where innovation is one of the key strategies in putting patients at the top." Virginia Mason has been issued a provisional patent for this idea and is looking into partnering with a vendor to produce the product so that patients in other healthcare facilities can also benefit from it.

Over the past several years, moonshine has been applied to a variety of challenges, including better tools for use in sterile processing, preventing patient falls, tracking available hospital beds, designing clinic workstations and new hospital spaces, and creating a platform for standing x-rays. Moonshine building materials and coaches are available, and the *Virginia Mason Moonshine Playbook* provides helpful tips and tools to take ideas through a process that includes initial brainstorming, tabletop trystorming, full-scale trystorming, testing in the actual work environment, and decision making on whether to pursue further development. Moonshine is yet another way that Virginia Mason demonstrates that it wants creative ideas for putting in place the elements of the perfect patient experience from every corner of the medical center, *and that the organization is prepared to act.*

Informatics Practitioners: Making Better Use of Information in Daily Clinical Work

Healthcare is awash in complex data. However, trying to extract useful information from all that data is often a challenge in daily work. Virginia Mason supports a small, mostly informally organized group of individuals who are constantly on the lookout for better ways to process information to support better, safer care.

Informatics for better hospital care. Hospitalist Dr. Barry Aaronson serves half time as a clinical informatics practitioner, and is passionate about the computer's role in helping medical care get to perfection. "We cannot get to 100 percent without the computer, because so much in patient care and safety depends on diligence. The computer is the ultimate in diligence; it doesn't take a nap or look the other way. But, it has to know what we are trying to do in order to be able to help us by checking it." Getting the computer to know what a clinician is trying to do in the complex flow of daily work, and feeding information about that back in a meaningful way to support that daily work, is now part of Aaronson's daily work.

Mimicking the old paper medical record, most electronic medical records support physicians' notes in free-form text. This is fine and traditional, but it robs the computer of its potential power to help the clinician achieve 100% compliance with good clinical practice. For example, in order for the computer to recommend ACE inhibitors for patients with heart failure, it must first know which patients have heart failure. If that information is only contained in a free text note, which it traditionally is, the computer becomes what Aaronson calls "a $46 million word processor."

Aaronson and colleagues began by identifying a software tool, readily available from Virginia Mason's medical record vendor, that physicians can type free text into and get back the more specific codes that the computer can recognize. "So, we say to clinicians, instead of typing 'CHF' [congestive heart failure] into your note, you type CHF into this tool and it says, 'Oh, you mean congestive heart failure, code 982.4.'" In other healthcare organizations, tools such as these are not widely used by physicians because they do not see added value from them; it is extra work to bring up the tool and populate the diagnosis code field. Aaronson and colleagues' innovation was to integrate this tool into the physician's work flow in a meaningful and useful way to help physicians achieve 100% compliance with good practice, something that they deeply want to do. They realized that once the computer knows the patient's specific conditions, it can then provide reminders and feedback linked to evidence and best practice on a variety of clinical topics. For example, it can question the physician as to why a patient is still on a certain medication, or why she or he has not yet been put on one.

Another essential piece of the information loop that clinicians need to support daily work in the hospital is an overview that focuses their attention on what needs to be done. Virginia Mason has created a *clinical andon board* for this. *Andon* is the Japanese term for a lantern or signal light. The use of signboards incorporating signal lights showing key performance indicators for the various workstations or processes in a factory is a principle element of the Toyota Production System. It provides, at a glance, an overview of quality or process flow problems, and focuses the attention and effort of managers and engineers. Similarly, Virginia Mason's clinical *andon* boards give real-time situational awareness to a team of clinicians in, say, a critical care unit, about the status of the care of each and every patient, based on evidence and recognized guidelines. For example, if the guideline says that a patient should be on a certain medication and there is no order for it in the medical record, a box in a grid for that patient glows red on a screen for all care team members to see until either the order is placed, or a note documenting a clinically valid exception is written. This is quite different from the practice of retrospective chart reviews and subsequent feedback to clinicians that most other healthcare organizations use in trying to achieve 100% compliance with guidelines. It is another example of level 6 change, doing what no one else is doing (or only few are doing).

Informatics in primary care. Internist Dr. Keith Dipboye is Aaronson's counterpart in clinical informatics on the primary care side. Like Aaronson, a good portion of his daily work involves innovating with the electronic medical record to support the daily work of other primary care physicians. One of his relatively simple ideas, a software program called SmaRTE™, now has over 3,000 users within the medical center and is making a big impact on physician productivity.

A common complaint among clinicians using currently available electronic medical record systems is that many daily clinical tasks, such as reviewing PAP test results and notifying the patient, often require clicks through multiple screens of the record. A data collection effort at Virginia Mason showed that it took 20 clicks and 2 minutes to go from a PAP result to a letter to the patient. Over time and hundreds of clinicians, the waste of physician productivity for this task alone in the clinics is staggering. Written in a language designed to automate Windows applications, SmaRTE creates a single button to initiate the process, reads the test result in order to alert the clinician about possible high-risk findings, and sets up an appropriately worded letter for the physician to approve, all in a matter of seconds.

SmaRTE has been similarly applied to automate many other common tasks in the daily work of busy clinicians. For example, it now provides a floating button that provides a one-click process for printing a chart note, or portion thereof, on Virginia Mason letterhead. Initially developed to print letters to patients, this feature was adapted through later kaizen events to produce a variety of point-of-care documents; for example, a care summary for the elderly or eyeglasses prescriptions.

A second example of innovation in informatics applied to the daily work of primary care involves what Virginia Mason calls the *health maintenance module.* These are a set of guidelines for screening and preventive tests that most adults should receive at various stages of life, for example, mammograms or colonoscopies. Information about such tests are often in the medical record, but data collection at Virginia Mason indicated that it could take as much as ten minutes of a medical assistant's time manually searching through the record to find it. It was simply not feasible to do this for every patient, and hence, it would be unlikely to achieve 100% compliance with the health maintenance module guidelines relying on this work process. "The electronic medical record was not really designed to do the kind of searching and aggregating of data that we needed," notes Dipboye. "But, after a lot of work among a lot of very bright people, we figured out how to make it do what we wanted it to do." The anecdote that began this book about the patient who was advised to have the routine colonoscopy screening that saved her life illustrates the benefit of convening a lot of very bright people to figure something out.

Again, once the data elements were identified and aggregated, the power of the computer to be more than just an expensive file cabinet could be tapped to apply further intelligence to the information. For example, the computer can tell the difference between a thirty-year-old man with low risk who does not need to have his cholesterol checked every year, and someone who has had a heart attack before, where the clinician should not only want to check it, but also make sure it is at a certain level.

Dipboye and colleagues developed sophisticated algorithms for a variety of these prevention and health maintenance indicators. "We were the first institution in the world, as far as I know, to calculate the Framingham heart attack risk index every time some relevant data element hit the chart. Every time blood pressure was checked or we clicked off whether the patient smoked or not, it would recalculate the Framingham score and assign a target cholesterol level that drove the system to tell us whether the patient was due for a check. We got a lot of positive feedback from around the country on this. We are still one of the most innovative users of this particular tool to have our electronic medical record help us manage chronic conditions."

These are only a few of the examples of how the innovative daily work of clinical informatics and information technology practitioners are creating tools to improve the daily work of other team members at Virginia Mason. However, there is an important side note to these efforts. In relating their stories, the work of nearly all of these individuals illustrated a key character trait shared by most true innovators—perseverance. Innovators in health IT must contend with numerous issues regarding data quality, privacy, multiple systems that do not talk to one another easily, and so on. While initial success makes future success a bit easier, the challenges of persevering through a web of complex issues to achieve innovation in the healthcare IT space seems to come with the territory.

Innovation Grants Process: Supporting Those with Potential Breakthrough Ideas

While the ELI system supports *many* individuals with *small* ideas to create a culture where change is the norm, Virginia Mason's innovation grants process is aimed at supporting a *few* individuals with *big* ideas to create a culture where breakthrough thinking is also the norm. The grants process supports the innovation plan goal to "differentiate Virginia Mason as a breakthrough innovator" by providing up to $25,000—to an individual, outside the normal departmental budgeting process— to support the early idea generation and harvesting that could potentially lead to new approaches that transform healthcare.

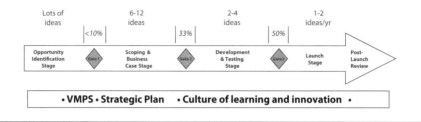

Figure 7.1   Stage-gate model for breakthrough innovation development process.

Virginia Mason defines breakthrough innovation as an idea that breaks out of current mental valleys and creates a significant and rapid jump on some important performance indicator. (The formal definition and more about the evolution of breakthrough innovation was covered in Chapter 2 on Virginia Mason's strategy.) The organization conceptualizes breakthrough innovation as occurring in a value stream with four stages and three decision-making gates (see Figure 7.1).

Stage-gate models are based on empirical research into what discriminates new product development success and failure in general industry. Over the years, the basic concept of progressing creative ideas through a disciplined process of development and critical review has been adapted to fit a variety of situations, yielding innovation process models with three to six stages and two to five gates, depending on the level of rigor and structure desired. The numbers across the top of the model recall the innovation funnel concept (Figure 1.3); it generally takes many brainstormed ideas, and learning from several early prototype failures, to produce a few true innovations. The gates are checkpoints where the innovators present ideas and plans to a panel of sponsors for guidance, and to solicit additional resources and supports to move some ideas on to the next stage. It is expected that only a percentage of ideas make it through each gate. This ensures that the organization is both always trying new things, while also always focusing its innovation investments on ideas with the most promise. It provides a balance between being so risk-averse that the organization will only invest in sure things, and the risk of diluting the potential for success by trying to resource everything.

At Virginia Mason, the tools and workshops of VMPS provide the structural supports for stages 3 and 4, while the annual organizational goal setting and planning processes provide a formal mechanism for stages 1 and 2. The innovation grants process is an additional, less formal approach that aims to engage frontline individuals in also feeding the pipeline with ideas in stages 1 and 2 of development. It creates the conditions for *anyone* at Virginia Mason, regardless of formal position, to tap into the organization's resources to work on an idea that might transform healthcare. Similar processes exist at many innovative organizations in general industry, but are rarely seen in a healthcare organization.

The first call for proposals for the Virginia Mason Innovation Grants process was issued in December 2011. The provocative, opening line of the communication read, "Do you want to fundamentally transform how Virginia Mason delivers a certain product or service to our patients or staff, and could you use a booster of resources to ensure progress?" Potential grantees were asked to enlist the support of a leadership sponsor. The template further asked them to explain their proposed breakthrough innovation topic, its potential transformative impact, and how they planned to generate a host of paradigm-altering ideas and develop initial business cases for a few of these. The Center for Innovation offered coaching on the proposal process, and completed applications generally ran from three to five pages. The process was intended to signal the seriousness of the organization in wanting to fund only thoughtful proposals, while making the process accessible in the course of the daily work of busy, frontline staff.

The call attracted eleven proposals, six from physicians. These were evaluated by a panel of Virginia Mason executives using a set of criteria that considered the stage of development represented by the thinking, breakthrough potential, fit with organizational goals and resources, and the likelihood that ideas could be moved into stage 3 (initial testing) in 12 to 18 months of effort. Half of the original proposals were already well-formed ideas ready for stage 3 development and testing, not the early stage thinking that was the target of the grants process. These individuals were counseled to pursue their ideas through other organizational processes. Four finalists eventually made it through the proposal review process and were interviewed in March 2012 by the grants committee. One was funded immediately, another was deemed to be more suitable for another development path, and the other two were asked to do more research and resubmit their proposals. These two were eventually funded later in the year.

Sports medicine physician, Dr. Jordan Chun, was awarded the first innovation grant for his proposal "The Modern Healthcare Interface: Innovating Communication in Medicine" (see box). He is using the funding to cover some of his time and to engage a part-time project manager and research assistant for literature review. He has formed an ad hoc team of advisors from across the organization to think along with him, and to offer challenge from a variety of mindsets. Chun displayed one of the qualities that is often found in innovators and entrepreneurs—being open to challenge—as he described one of his team members, "I actually got her involved mostly because she disagreed with just about everything I used to bring up in terms of these ideas."

Chun's research and brainstorming with colleagues has led to identification of what he calls "ten main paths and ideas for exploration," which he is further fleshing out through a road show to engage a variety of others. His aim is to package several ideas for development and testing as input to the organization's goal-setting and budget-planning process in fall 2013. That process will serve as the second gate in the breakthrough innovation process model in Figure 7.1. Chun is receiving ongoing coaching support, and is regularly reviewing his work with the innovation grants committee, who are performing the function of the first gate in the model.

The other two grants are several months behind Chun, but are proceeding along a similar path. Occupational therapist Ron Porter was awarded a grant to rethink

THE MODERN HEALTHCARE INTERFACE:
INNOVATING COMMUNICATION IN MEDICINE

I asked Dr. Jordan Chun to explain the opportunity he is pursuing with the innovation grant that he was awarded. He has a big idea in the early stages of thinking that might lead to transformative, breakthrough innovation.

"The idea is really to redefine the modern, currently dyadic, patient–provider interface. I'm using the word *interface* because it is no longer just the one-to-one, face-to-face conversation it used to be. Today, it's email, it's telephone, it's reading something on the Internet. There are so many different ways in which that interaction can happen.

"Our *social* world outside of medicine has changed. We interact through social media and texting versus phone calls and face-to-face time. So, the big question is, how should our communication strategies within medicine change? It behooves us to be prepared, and to figure out how to leverage these new ways of interacting for positive benefit. No one has really yet defined what impact these new forms of interaction are going to have on the traditional provider–patient relationship. Nobody really knows. It could go really well, or it could go poorly.

"What I want to do is to get at least a theory or construct on which one can build and evaluate innovations. My concern is that we do things, like creating a web portal, but we are making grand assumptions that it will help, without really understanding what effect it might have on our relationship with patients. So I thought it might help future innovation to have a better construct of the interface among the patient, provider, and computer, or at least an honesty about what we know, and what we don't know."

the process that unfolds in the life of a person and his or her family when they must face the fact that they are no longer fit to drive. Currently, patients are referred to occupational therapy for assessment by primary care providers who have concerns, or as a result of a driving incident. The assessment and counseling all happens in a one-hour appointment that is often highly emotional and leaves the person angry and anxious about his or her future. The third grant was awarded to Kristoffer Rhoads, a PhD in Virginia Mason's pain clinic. He and his colleagues will explore breakthrough ideas for making access to multidisciplinary care and development of self-management skills available to more than the 2% of chronic pain sufferers in the United States who currently have such access.

Only time will tell if these three grants result in transforming some aspects of healthcare. However, each illustrates the passion for change and frustration with current thinking that many frontline providers have in their daily work of caring for others. While these three individuals, and their team members, are doing great work, I have met many others just like them in healthcare organizations around the world. While such passionate individuals seem evenly distributed across healthcare organizations, what is different here, and at a handful of others, is that Virginia Mason is establishing a supportive process by which these passionate individuals can potentially make a real difference.

Transforming Healthcare: What Others Can Learn from Virginia Mason's Innovation in Daily Work Efforts

Taiichi Ohno once said that the Toyota Production System is "a system that says that there is no limit to people's creativity. People don't go to Toyota to *work,* they go there to *think.*" Virginia Mason Medical Center's structural supports and examples of success in promoting innovation in the daily work of all members of staff are consistent with Ohno's worldview. Staff who have participated in any of the systems described in this chapter know from firsthand experience that their ideas are valued and supported. They know that the organization allows them to make a difference on a daily basis, in both small and large ways. Virginia Mason frontline staff regularly take advantage of this opportunity.

Being able to make a difference provides *meaning in work,* a quality that noted creativity researcher Teresa Amabile called "the single most important" factor contributing to an organization's success in executing any strategy. It is also one of the concepts in Virginia Mason's Respect for People initiative. Creating such a level of meaning and engagement of frontline staff is obviously important to a healthcare organization that aspires to innovate and create the perfect patient experience. While leaders at Virginia Mason would say that they still have a long way to go, the organization has made great strides and is set up well to continue its momentum.

Leaders in Other Healthcare Organizations Should …

Reflect on their mental models about what staff are seeking when they come to work. Toyota Production System founder Taiichi Ohno believed that individuals came to work to be challenged and engaged to think. By their actions in setting up the various systems and cultural supports described in this chapter, it is safe to infer that Virginia Mason leaders believe the same thing.

- As leaders, what do we each individually believe about the motivations that those we work with daily?
- What do we think they really want?
- Is meaningful work really that important?
- In what ways, honestly, are our actions and infrastructures consistent or inconsistent with our answers to these questions?
- Are we constantly creating an environment where our staff finds meaning in their work?

Wonder how individuals in their organizational culture would react to some of the situations described by team members at Virginia Mason in this chapter. The first half of the chapter presented several stories of individuals and small work teams reacting to the daily occurrences of life in a typical healthcare organization.

- How do we tend to react to untoward safety events in our organization and how does that compare to the story of Roger Woolf?
- To what extent do we have examples of challenging the accepted wisdom, comparable to the story of Francis Salinas?
- What would happen in our organization if a member of staff suggested changes in practice to a surgeon, as in the case of Jolanta Janakowski?
- Do we find ways to break through the noise of organizational communications and training, like Drs. Pittenger and Johnson, or do we stick with the same old methods?
- What would happen in our organization if we had a situation such as the one experienced by Dr. DePaso where he was forced to do a job that was normally done by another team member of lesser traditional status?
- What does all this tell us about our organizational culture with regards to change, safety, improvement, and innovation?

Consider putting in place organizational infrastructure supports that signal that innovation in daily work is desired. I have described four such structures at Virginia Mason here. They may or may not be the ones that are right for you. However, the absence of such structures sends a strong message that may be drowning out your statement of values or other rhetoric.

- What are the pros and cons of the four structures from Virginia Mason that are described in this chapter from the point of view of where we are as an organization?
- What similar systems do we have in place?
- How do they compare to Virginia Mason's?
- What actions should we take, what goals should we set, and who should do what by when?

Chapter 8

Using Patient Experience to Drive Innovation

> I would say that we have a culture that is really about our patients; doing everything that we can for them and being willing to change our ways of doing our daily work for their benefit. We have a lot of staff members who are really engaged in that work; willing to try new things and be creative and innovative.
>
> **—Jennifer Richards**
> *Administrative Director, Virginia Mason Medical Center*

A misconception about lean thinking that may have slowed its acceptance in healthcare is the belief that lean's focus on efficiency, flow, and standardization is so mechanistic that it ignores the customer and the human elements of care. Nothing could be further from the truth. Lean is a production method that considers as *wasteful* the expenditure of resources for anything other than the purpose of creating value for the end customer. Indeed, lean practitioners often define the word *value* as something for which a customer would be willing to pay.

At Virginia Mason Medical Center everything begins and ends with the goal of providing ever-increasing value for patients and families. CEO Dr. Gary Kaplan puts it succinctly. "The critical first step in the Virginia Mason Production System process was recognizing that the patient had to come first in everything. It is the patient who drives the Virginia Mason aspiration to be the quality leader."

Having begun the story of innovation at Virginia Mason with the 2001 strategic decision to put the patient at the top of the strategic pyramid, I will now conclude with a description of how a deliberate focus on patients and families is used to drive innovation throughout the organization in ways that are thoroughly consistent with the principles of lean thinking.

The Customers' Role in Innovation

The importance of the customer's point of view is as clear in the innovation literature as it is in the literature on lean. While there is no single, generally accepted definition of innovation, experts agree that it implicitly involves acceptance of an idea in some sort of marketplace, where the customers, users, or beneficiaries are the ones making the final judgment.

However, the customers' role in innovation is not only as one passively awaiting the opportunity to judge. In *The Sources of Innovation,* Professor Eric von Hipple, who has thirty years of research to his credit, was among the first to note the prevalence of *user-initiated* innovation across many industries. Users naturally experience products and services in a wider variety of contexts than producers could ever imagine. They also bring a wider variety of points of view and preferences than could ever have been taken into account by designers. Therefore, users are often the first to spot an unmet need—the seed of all successful innovations. In *Democratizing Innovation,* von Hipple further documents the trend toward users as innovators in software and information products (for example, apps for smartphones), and goes on to cite additional examples of user innovation in physical products ranging from surgical equipment to surfboards. He argues convincingly that producers would be well advised to incorporate methods for capturing customers' experiences, wants, preferences, and ideas directly into their innovation efforts.

Another modern thread in innovation thinking, led by C. K. Prahlad and Venkatram Ramaswamy, revolves around what they call *experience innovation.* They note that technology increasingly enables users to co-create with producers unique packages of products and services that provide the user with just what he or she needs, on a very personal level, drawing on the user's own willingness to be involved. In experience innovation, the producer's role is to understand the potential scope of these individualized needs and create an environment for easy access to choices that allow the user to craft what is best for him or her, in the moment.

These and other ideas from the innovation literature have found application at Virginia Mason Medical Center. Integrating innovation into the Virginia Mason Production System (VMPS) magnifies the already intense desire from lean thinking to let the customer's voice drive change at all seven levels (see the box "The Shame of Waiting"). We will look first at how Virginia Mason has evolved and focused this desire through work associated with its strategic plan for service, then explore another body of literature and experience from the field of design science,

THE SHAME OF WAITING

Lean thinking's passionate devotion to labeling bluntly as *waste* anything that does not add value for the customer often provokes the attention and escape required for creativity. For example, the very first team of Virginia Mason leaders who traveled to Japan in 2002 experienced the sometimes uncomfortable creative provocation of lean thinking when a sensei asked if they were not ashamed to have so many areas in the medical center where patients waited an average of forty-five minutes for a doctor. It was a natural question to ask if you believe, as the sensei did, that anything that a customer would be unlikely to be willing to pay for is waste. It was quite an unnatural question to be asked if you are steeped in the traditions of healthcare, deep in the mental valley that accepts waiting areas as a necessary, naturally occurring phenomenon in a healthcare facility. Asking unnatural questions often provokes innovative thought, provided that the ones hearing the question take it as an invitation to think differently, rather than something to be simply dismissed, or be defensive about.

In this case, that simple provocation led to creative thoughts that have manifested themselves in countless ways over the decade since its first delivery. In 2009 the new Virginia Mason Kirkland primary care clinic opened *without a waiting room*. In the context of healthcare, this certainly qualifies as level 6 or 7 change; it is something very few in healthcare are doing and something that most in healthcare might say would be impossible. However, at Virginia Mason it was made possible because the flows in the clinic have been so beautifully planned and continuously improved over the years that there is no need for a waiting room. Patients who prefer to arrive early and relax before seeing the provider have the option to do so, but the *necessity* to wait is no longer *forced* upon them by uncoordinated and poorly flowing processes, as it is so often in so many healthcare facilities around the world.

and finally describe how the organization's innovation efforts have built further on these foundations.

Evolution of the Strategic Focus on Service

The focus on the patient that is provided by VMPS is further enhanced by the existence of the service pillar in the organization's strategic plan. Understanding the evolution of this work provides an important foundation for the innovation work that I will describe in the remainder of this chapter.

In the early days following the establishment of the strategic pyramid with the patient at the top, the service work was far from being able to drive innovation at the front line of care. Michael VanDerhoef, the executive sponsor of the service pillar, recalls how the Patient Relations and Service Department was initially perceived within the organization as complaint handling. "We joke that in the old days when the phone would ring and the caller ID on the manager's desk would say that it was from the Patient Relations and Service Department … they wouldn't answer."

Early VMPS workshops focused on moving the organization's thinking one small step beyond complaint handling to service recovery—dealing with complaints and issues before the patient left the facility, rather than waiting for a complaint after the fact. VanDerhoef and the team also tried to mandate certain service improvement efforts in the operating divisions, but got a cool reception from fellow executives. However, that experience created a turning point in thinking in 2009. Instead of the service team taking responsibility for service, maybe it was better to see what operational leaders were already doing (for example, hourly rounding on patients in the hospital). This redirection of effort acknowledged that executives and staff in those divisions already had responsibility and the requisite desire to provide excellent service. It focused the service team's work on enabling and sharing these good efforts to create an overall culture for service. In this way, the service team's evolving thinking paralleled that of the innovation team. The role of each is to build supportive culture and capability in operational units, rather than seeing the work mainly as that of an offline staff group executing a function.

The service team helped create an infrastructure that facilitates integration of service improvement into everyone's kaizen plans and puts the voice of the patient into VMPS workshops and Everyday Lean Idea (ELI) system efforts. Importantly, from the beginning, service leadership teams in the hospital and clinic divisions have included executive and physician leadership. Sadly, many healthcare organizations today do not have physicians actively helping to lead their service improvement efforts on a wide scale across the organization. It is difficult to impact the patients' and families' experience of care without them. Further, other staff members often look to the physicians to set the tone regarding behavioral expectations.

Administrative director Susan Haufe notes that the Patient Relations and Service Department has evolved significantly over this time period to support the strategic service work. "We now have an amazing team that serves the organization's proactive focus on the patients' and families' experience. I see the next 5 years really focused on helping the organization further integrate the patient's voice into how we do our daily work; embedding this focus on the patient in *everything* that we do." (For a tribute to Haufe's predecessor in this work, see the box "In Memory of Keely B: The Power of Patient Listening.")

The key insight here is that these efforts over time have prepared Virginia Mason to embrace customer-driven innovation, as described by von Hipple and others. In essence, the ears of the organization have been slowly retuned to hear the voices of patients and families as invitations to think differently, rather than as complaints.

**IN MEMORY OF KEELY B: THE POWER
OF PATIENT LISTENING**

Keely Brzozowicz—affectionately known simply as Keely B because no one could pronounce her surname—was a nurse by training, who became the administrative director of Patient Relations and Service. Sadly, she passed away just months before I began interviewing for the writing of this book. Michael VanDerhoef recalls her inspirational leadership. "I think we are where we are today largely because of who Keely was as a person. She helped people to see service work not as reacting to bad things, but as actually creating the good things we wanted."

Board member Lonnie Edelheit, a member of both the Innovation and Service Leadership Teams, recalls Keely's patient persistence. "I was rounding once with Keely B and we got on the elevator and immediately she's talking to a woman like she is her best friend. This woman is telling her all kinds of positive, wonderful things about the care at Virginia Mason. So we went to visit this woman's father, who was a patient. And they were both so positive. And I was just basking in it. I said to myself, 'Well, this is fun.' And then I was ready to leave, but Keely kept talking to them. And finally they brought up an issue. 'Well, there is this one problem we have had …,' they said, and that just opened up an important set of things. All of a sudden there was an issue that you can work on. And it was just so striking to me how she just knew that 90 percent of the time patients' first response is going to be nice, saying everything is fine. But she just knew that there was more there in this case, and she knew how to get it out of them. I was just in awe of how she did that. It was amazing. She was a very special lady."

The next obvious step was to acquire better methods for listening, escaping mental valleys and focusing attention.

Imported from the UK: Experience-Based Design

One of my roles as the external chair of innovation at the Virginia Mason Medical Center is to bring ideas from elsewhere. So, in reviewing the joint efforts of the innovation and service teams with Jennifer Phillips one day, my thoughts immediately went to my British friend Dr. Lynne Maher. Maher, a critical care nurse by profession, is the former director of Innovation and Design at England's National Health Service (NHS) Institute for Innovation and Improvement. One of the many things on which I have worked with her was a methodology grounded in the design science literature called *experience-based design* (EBD). She explains it this way.

The experience-based design approach is a four-stage methodology that helps staff work very closely with patients and their families to first capture, then, second, to really understand in great detail, the experience that people are having as they journey through health services. Of particular interest is understanding if there are clusters of negative or positive feelings, as indicated by their use of emotion words as they talk about certain parts of the care pathway. We call such clusters of emotional response a *touch point.* The third step is improvement, where we work with the patient and family member to co-design a new way of working that better meets their needs. The final step is measurement to verify the impact of changes.

This methodology grew out of work that Maher and her colleagues did with professional designers from other industries in efforts to reduce that frustration that research showed NHS patients were experiencing. This is yet another example of the principle that the germ of innovation in one's industry might lie in something that is quite common in another. To a designer, the ideas of co-designing with service users and focusing on improving emotional touch points in the process were second nature. To healthcare professionals, these ideas were radical and potentially innovative.

Design professionals use a three-part framework to think about the goals of design—functionality, engineering, and aesthetics. *Functionality* refers to whether a design is based on the best knowledge, science, or technology available. Evidence-based medicine has traditionally been well focused on this aspect of good design. *Engineering* refers to attributes of design that contribute to such operational variables as consistency, reliability, and efficiency. The adaptation of industrial methodologies from lean thinking, safety practice, and other fields helps us create better designs in this dimension. The element of *aesthetics* refers to the emotions elicited by the design via the look, feel, and experience it presents to the customer or service user. A designer's understanding of this term goes beyond the architectural features of a space to include the totality of the human interaction. A hospital with a beautiful lobby, but inattentive or rude staff, does not live up to what a designer means when she or he uses the phrase *aesthetics of the experience.*

Recent calls for more patient-centered care support the contention that this third element has traditionally been given less emphasis compared to the other two. Beyond simply being the right thing to do for patients, there is also a growing body of evidence showing the positive relationship between aspects of patient experience and clinical quality. Simply put, anxiety and unease impedes communications and delays healing.

The tools of experience-based design for capturing and understanding of the patient's experience in order to drive innovation—the first and second steps of the EBD approach—are relatively straightforward.

Interviews (or *focus groups* when more than one or two people are involved) are among the simplest methods for interacting with patients and family members to understand their experiences of care. "Although," Maher points out, "I tend to call it *having a deep conversation* because interviewing puts people in the mindset of research where the interviewer is mostly in control of the conversation. In EBD, we let the person tell the story." The previous box, "In Memory of Keely B: The Power of Patient Listening," was a good example of what Maher calls deep conversation.

Observation—simply sitting still and watching what is going on—is another important tool. "But we have to teach it carefully to clinicians," Maher notes. "In the way designers observe, you are literally just observing. You're not looking for a certain symptom that you can match to a diagnosis, as you are with clinical observation." Observation is also a foundational method in lean thinking. But here the focus is on the patient experience, not the process steps and other flows.

Rounding out the basic suite of tools for capturing and understanding is the *experience questionnaire.* This tool has been widely used at Virginia Mason, as we will see in examples later. It is a flow diagram depicting known touch points in the process, with a choice of emotion words listed underneath (along with a space for free-form comments). Patients and families are asked to select the emotion word that best describes their feelings as they reach each touch point along their care journey. The results can be tallied over a relatively large sample of patients and families to get an indication of where the most negative and positive feelings are being elicited in the process of care. (I will present a detailed example of this tool in Figures 8.1 and 8.2 later in this chapter.)

The third step in the EBD approach is that of real change, driven by the new focus and understanding acquired through the tools above. Lean thinking and VMPS provide concepts, tools, and structures for doing this, as we have seen in previous chapters. However, adding in the idea of co-designing services—having mixed groups of service users, service providers, and designers working side by side—brings a revolutionary drive to the evolution of patient-centeredness in healthcare. Maher and her colleagues, as well as the Cambridge, Massachusetts–based Institute for Healthcare Improvement, describe this evolution as *to … for … with.* Traditionally, healthcare service design could be characterized as doing things *to* patients. Providers wrote orders, made rules, and set schedules rather unilaterally, and patients were expected to comply. Fortunately, many healthcare organizations have now evolved to seeing themselves more as serving patients by doing things *for* them. Patients and families provide input to the redesign and improvement of services, which providers then take away for consideration when they meet among themselves in improvement teams. Co-design radically suggests a third stage of evolution where service providers redesign services along *with* patients in a true partnership.

The experience-based design approach has been used in hundreds of applications across England, Wales, Scotland, Norway, Canada, New Zealand, Australia, and Singapore. Clearly, the methodology is catching on.

EBD is linked to innovation in two ways at Virginia Mason. First, like lean thinking, importing it into healthcare from other industries, other countries, and a nontraditional literature base is an innovative act that adds to the culture. It causes staff to think "we are always open to new ways of doing things." Second, like the tools for creative idea generation, EBD methods help stimulate new ways of thinking about the details of care delivery that can then be fed into the structures of VMPS to create practical innovations. It is another wonderful combination of innovation and lean.

Experience-Based Design Meets Standard Work in a Clinic

One of the earliest examples of the use of EBD concepts was in a 2008 VMPS workshop looking at the flow of patients in primary care clinics. The workshop leader, stimulated by a presentation he had heard about EBD, told the team the story of a medical assistant he observed breaking the flow of the process to chat with a lady in a wheelchair sitting alone near the entrance. This dramatically illustrated the concept of emotional touch points and led to a rich discussion about the presence of other touch points along the value stream. These included greeting the patient in the waiting area, interaction during recording of vital signs and reviewing of health maintenance information, being left alone in the exam room, the moment the provider enters, and so on. At each touch point, the team further identified statements, questions, and behaviors that create positive experiences for patients; making them feel cared for and building rapport.

It naturally occurred to them that these empathic behaviors could be incorporated into the statements of standard work. More importantly, not doing so would constitute waste and failure to deliver value for patients. Reflecting on whether this systematic mapping and addressing of the emotions of patients in the design of a process of care was too mechanical, one team member noted that it was not any different nor more artificial than scheduling a romantic dinner, with hopefully the same positive effect. The team placed symbols of a heart and a smiley face on the standard work document in order to make the touch points and behaviors stand out amid the more technical steps of the flow.

This story also illustrates the critically important difference between a touch point and a process step; a distinction in EBD that often confuses the novice. A *touch point* is the moment in time at which something triggers an emotion in a person experiencing the process. The touch point is typically described by what is going on at that moment; for example, greeting the patient in the waiting area, the provider entering the room. It is the language and lens on what is happening *as the patient experiences and tends to remember it*. A *process step* is a name given to a collection of detailed tasks and actions that the people who designed and work within the process use to describe the major pieces of work they do in contribution to a value stream; for example, patient intake, provider visit, and so on. It is the language and lens on what is happening *as the people who work in the process think of it*. Both perspectives are valid, of course. EBD focuses our attention on the former; a perspective that is often inadvertently, but sadly, overlooked by busy healthcare professionals.

Understanding the Emotional Experience of Surgical Patients and Families

In preparation for a series of workshops to redesign flows associated with surgical procedures, Virginia Mason convened several focus groups of former surgical patients and family members to learn more about their experiences. The prompts in the focus group leaders guide shown in the box "Excerpt from Focus Group Leader's Guide: Surgical Procedures Process" give a sense of the atmosphere for dialog that can be created when using EBD methods.

While the dialogue covered thoughts that were to be expected (for example, patients love warm blankets), it also revealed some insights into which those who work in the area were typically less tuned. These more revealing insights included:

■ The common practice of escorting family members to a private room for conversations with the surgeon was often interpreted by others in the waiting area as a sign of bad news, which raises anxiety.

■ The first person that patients and families meet on arrival sets the tone for the entire experience; he or she can go a long way toward creating a sense of calm and caring, or a sense of chaos and lack of caring.

EXCERPT FROM FOCUS GROUP LEADERS GUIDE: SURGICAL PROCEDURES PROCESS

Take a moment to close your eyes and visualize your procedure experience at Virginia Mason Medical Center. Open your eyes. Think about the emotions that surface when you think about your experience.

Let's start at the beginning of your experience ... What emotions do you associate with the preprocedure experience? How do those emotions link to the experience? How could the preprocedure experience be different and/or better for you?

Imagine an ideal setting for patients and families; not just a focus on the décor. How would you describe the best experience, flow, or sequence for patients and families experiencing a procedure?

(Repeat for each major phase of the patient's journey.)

■ Patients and families become anxious when they witnessed staff chit-chat and personal conversations. They wonder if staff are more interested in their personal lives than in looking after patients.

■ Waking up to familiar staff in the recovery room is reassuring; waking up to new staff creates a sense of anxiety and disconnection.

These findings from the focus groups were fed into the subsequent weeklong improvement workshop and influenced the team's view of what was of value to patients and families as they flowed through the process, and what constituted waste.

You Can See a Lot by Looking

Unfortunately, a common problem in healthcare is that well-meaning professionals are often so busy and focused on what they are doing that they sometimes fail to notice the experiences of others around them. VMPS specialists and certified lean leaders who have been trained in experience-based design methods have learned the power of observation—simply sitting still and watching.

Communications manager, Dane Fukumoto, underscores this point in reflecting on his experience in using EBD observation methods. "It is fascinating because I learn things that I never even thought of. I observed a waiting room that I walk past several times a day and I never even noticed before how noisy and busy it was." VMPS specialist Shawna Whipple noted a similar conclusion in her observation work. "I sat in the waiting room of the emergency department and just watched. I would see patients check in and state their problems. They came to us because they thought they had an emergency, but then they had to wait in the waiting room until the nurse came to see them, which could take half an hour. What starts off as a stomach ache could be a sign of a heart attack. So it was a potentially risky situation. But we had no nurse out there to watch. So, they changed the process now where they have a nurse greet patients from the beginning and there is a nurse out there with them if they have to wait. It sounds simple, but we didn't see it before."

I Am Sure That This Is What They Will Want

Another common problem in healthcare is that sometimes well-meaning healthcare professionals who are striving to serve patients can get it completely wrong in assuming what patients want. Really listening to patients without preset assumptions, and really allowing them to co-design change, lies at the heart of experience-based design.

A Virginia Mason team looking to improve the admissions kit that patients receive containing soap, lotion, and other such basic items had three samples to try. The intent was to replace the current kit with a version that was more patient centered and could be easily used. After seeing the three samples, the team assumed patients would go for one particular bag they felt was an upgrade, looked better, and was more user friendly. Their assumption was completely busted when they took the samples out on a hospital unit, asked patients and their families to play with the bags, and then conducted interviews.

One sample kit was a large bag that could be reused as a tote bag after discharge. There were large pockets and room for other items. Some team members felt that this would be very useful. One patient put it the best, "I would rather have something I could use now in a practical way, than wait to reuse it as a tote bag for when I'm discharged." The second kit was streamlined, sleek, and opaque, similar to what one receives on a first-class plane flight. This was the kit the majority of our team selected for patients as it was the most aesthetically pleasing and seemed to be the more user friendly. However, patients had a difficult time finding items in the kit as it was difficult to manage the sleek design. The third was a simple, clear plastic kit with a handle. It was the least expensive. No one on the team wanted this kit as it was the least aesthetically pleasing and did not seem like an upgrade. However, the majority of patients interviewed chose this kit. It had a wide zipper and top so one could easily reach into it. The clear plastic made it easy to locate items, and the short handle allowed it to hang in the bathroom where patients were during their hygiene care.

While this simple story is far from the vision of patients and families co-designing entire systems of care in equal partnership with healthcare professionals, it does illustrate the potential power of this concept from experience-based design. Can American healthcare really afford to invest resources in change that doesn't meet the needs of the healthcare consumer? What better way to avoid the mistake than to truly listen and partner with patients and family to co-create what Prahlad and Ramaswamy call *experience innovation?*

The Roller Coaster of Emotion

By far, the most widely used EBD tool in Virginia Mason's early stages of adoption has been the *experience questionnaire.* As previous noted, a well-designed questionnaire can be administered to a relatively large sample of patients, yielding a metric that can be used to drive improvement—a natural link to lean methodology. An example of an experience questionnaire from a project associated with the flow of rheumatology patients in a clinic setting is shown in Figure 8.1. It illustrates the general process of constructing and using this tool.

The touch points in the value stream are listed in the first column. These were identified through interviews and observations. Patients and family members were asked to complete the questionnaire either as they go through the process

TEAM MEDICINE™	Thank you for TRANSFORMING HEALTHCARE with us. By completing this questionnaire-- YOU are helping us improve everyone's experience at Virginia Mason.							
How do you feel when you schedule your Rheumatology appointment?	Circle the BEST word that describes your feeling	frustrated	confident	okay	satisfied	insecure	afraid	happy	Comments:
How do you feel when you arrive at Virginia Mason and check in?	Circle the BEST word that describes your feeling	valued	pleased	frustrated	okay	ignored	satisfied	disrespected	Comments:
How do you feel when you are in the waiting area?	Circle the BEST word that describes your feeling	okay	ignored	disrespected	satisfied	frustrated	confident	hopeful	Comments:
How do you feel when you are being weighed?	Circle the BEST word that describes your feeling	secure	resentful	confident	guilty	pleased	okay	depressed	Comments:
How do you feel when you are reviewing your prescriptions and other issues with the Medical Assistant?	Circle the BEST word that describes your feeling	insecure	afraid	secure	frustrated	okay	safe	confident	Comments:
How do you feel during the visit with your doctor?	Circle the BEST word that describes your feeling	resentful	valued	frustrated	disrespected	okay	confident	safe	Comments:
How do you feel about the information you received about changes in your care and next steps?	Circle the BEST word that describes your feeling	frustrated	afraid	confident	insecure	okay	empowered	optimistic	Comments:
How do you feel when you call the Rheumatology Clinic in between visits?	Circle the BEST word that describes your feeling	frustrated	confident	disrespected	resentful	okay	happy	satisfied	Comments:

Figure 8.1 Experience questionnaire for a rheumatology clinic.

or immediately after completing it. They did so by circling the emotion word (in the rows) that best describes their feeling, based on their experience, at each of the various touch points. There is a space for comments, to elaborate or suggest another word that they feel fits better. The seven emotion words were selected from a standard list of positive, negative, and neutral emotions to include three positive, three negative, and one neutral emotion choice.

Consistent with the strategic plan notion that the patient is at the top, Virginia Mason defines as a *defect* any neutral or negative emotion word choices. In its usual fashion of setting stretch targets to encourage the pursuit of perfection, the goal is clearly to create only positive experiences. Tallying the number of these defects as a percentage of the total number of responses provides a score for each touch point, and an overall score for the process as a whole. When these defect scores are plotted on a graph like the one in Figure 8.2, the roller coaster of emotion that typifies so many processes in healthcare emerges.

In this case, the observation and interview methods from EBD yielded insights mainly related to facilities and staff behaviors. But inquiring deeper into the touch points also identified by these methods highlighted the fact that patients often experienced negative emotions around being weighed for their clinic visit and calling the clinic between visits. This provided an additional focal point for the clinic

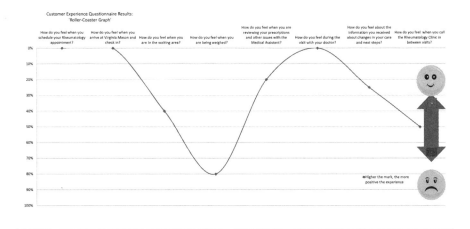

Figure 8.2 The roller coaster of emotion in the patients' experience of care.

team to improve the patients' experiences. The first issue was rather easily resolved by redesigning the weighing area to provide more privacy. The second is the subject of ongoing work around telephone access.

This simple example illustrates the power of the experience questionnaire to focus attention as a prelude to creative thinking. While initially identifying the touch points in a process requires the labor-intensive effort of observation and interviews (or focus groups), once designed, the questionnaire can be administered to dozens of patients in order to get reliable feedback from a large sample at relatively low cost. The questionnaire also easily lends itself to converting the data into a number and graphic depiction, which enables easy priority setting in the context of any of the widely used improvement or innovation approaches.

Other Virginia Mason applications of experience questionnaires have included:

- Assessing how to improve communication and reduce anxiety with critical care unit patients and family members regarding plans for transfer to another unit.
- Improving the checkout process for urology clinic patients to ensure a private, respectful process.
- Improving care coordination and outcomes for patients enrolled in the innovative Virginia Mason Intensive Primary Care (IPC) program.
- Improving way-finding and other elements of the care experience for patients and their parents in the Virginia Mason pediatric practice.

Having given some quick examples chosen to illustrate the various concepts and tools of EBD, let's now look at a more extended case study that illustrates how Virginia Mason is integrating the suite of EBD tools into the toolkit of VMPS in order to drive innovation.

The Case of the Critical Care Unit

The Critical Care Unit (CCU) at Virginia Mason Medical Center cares for some of the sickest, most clinically complex patients in the hospital. It, and the ecosystem of other units that support it, have been the focus of multiple improvement activities. The application of experience-based design methods to stimulate thinking differently about change has featured prominently in this work.

Efforts to increase throughput in the CCU without jeopardizing patient safety or clinical outcomes exposed issues concerning the following:

- Coordination of processes that delayed transfers
- Handoffs between professionals where information loss could create potential clinical risks and confusion for the patients and families
- A discouraging rate of transfers back to the CCU of patients who had only been transferred out a short time before

The emotional impact on the patients and families that arises from these issues is obvious. It was clear from the outset that EBD methods should be used alongside the traditional tools of lean thinking in order to arrive at a redesign that better accounted for the three design variables of functionality, reliability, and aesthetics.

Having conducted the observations previously described in the emergency department waiting area, Shawna Whipple also conducted some of the initial observations to inform the planning for improvement by sitting in the CCU family waiting area. "It was really noisy because of all the people and equipment traffic flowing past it. It was frustrating for people trying to make phone calls to inform loved ones, and frustrating for other people trying to have a quiet conversation. Signs were very confusing, with lots of *Do not* … rules. The furniture was very uncomfortable. There was no signal for when family members might be able to return to the bedside, so they had to keep constantly checking. It was all very unwelcoming." During a thirty-minute period, she counted 76 times that someone walked past the waiting room, and 14 times when a piece of equipment was pushed loudly past.

Whipple also recalls the sad case of an elderly gentleman who had come to see his sick wife on the Medical Telemetry unit. "He goes into the room and it is empty … and his face dropped! So he went to the nursing desk in a panic wondering what had happened. His wife had actually gone to a unit that cares for less intense patients because she was getting better. But it took a while for someone to find the nurse to explain that, and meanwhile he is panicking. No one had incorporated him into that process. So the workshop team did some really intense work on that."

It is important to note that the clinicians and managers in the care team were the same sorts of wonderful and caring professionals that one finds throughout healthcare. They were uncomfortable to learn these things about their processes of care, and even more uncomfortable to realize that *they played a role in making them that way*. They simply had not seen it so starkly before. That is often what experience-based design tools do. They bring into stark focus things that have always been there, but were never really seen by the busy caring professionals doing the work. In other words, EBD activates the attention, escape, and movement that stimulate creativity.

A series of observations and interviews with members of staff and current and former patients and family members identified five key touch points in the overall transition of patients out of the CCU onto a unit of lower intensity: getting the news of an upcoming transfer out of CCU, waiting for the transfer, communications about delays and changes of plan, transfer to the new care unit, and settling in on the new unit. Key insights gleaned from the interviews and an experience questionnaire included:

- Knowing what to expect helps patients and families feel more ready and relaxed about transfers.
- It is vital to know the reason for delays and changes of plan.
- Staff need to actively ensure that the patient does not feel alone and ignored.
- Nurses need confidence that a patient is safe to transfer.

Note that each of these insights gleaned from the EBD tools can be easily translated into a "How might we …?" or "How do others …?" statement to provoke innovative thinking. For example, How might we creatively help patients and families know what to expect? How might we more cleverly communicate reasons for delays and changes of plans? How do other industries and individuals in different settings handle similar issues?

The experience questionnaires administered prior to the workshop showed an overall defect rate across the five key touch points of 24%. That is, on average, about a quarter of the time that a patient or family member entered a touch point, they experienced a negative or neutral emotion, rather than a positive one. Considering the intensity, complexity, and riskiness of underlying illness being treated, the process of care was not appearing to be as caring as the Virginia Mason team members aspired for it to be.

These insights, with supporting details, were fed into the planning for a workshop whose goal was to "create a planned, transparent, and seamless transition for patients, families, and care teams as the patient moves from CCU to the Medical Telemetry Unit (Med Tele)." The team was determined to make the care better.

Key improvements coming out of the workshop addressed the insights and issues raised by the application of EBD methodology.

- A nurse from the receiving unit (Med Tele, in this case) now travels to CCU for a bedside handoff with the CCU nurse who has been caring for the patient. The receiving unit nurse also meets the patient and family, and can stop the line if he or she is not comfortable that both the patient and the receiving unit are ready to execute the transfer safely.

■ A goals-of-care worksheet now travels with the patient, assuring continuity and continual visibility of the plan for patients, families, and team members.

In addition to these large changes, Med Tele manager Christin Gordanier recalls many smaller, but no less important, improvements that her team made based on the study of the patient and family experience. One such insight was around the language that clinicians routinely use to describe what is happening to patients. "We say you're being *downgraded* to Med Tele, or you're going to a *lower level of care.* That is actually an improvement in their status, but it may not sound like it to them. If you were checking into a hotel and they told you had been *downgraded,* you wouldn't like it." She and her team made a simple chart to raise awareness of how the usual language might sound to a patient or family member. It suggested simple changes such as:

■ Instead of downgraded, try graduated.
■ Instead of lower level of care, try transitioning to progressive care.

Ninety days after the workshop, measurements using the same experience questionnaire showed only a 14% defect rate (cutting the original 24% almost in half); with all such defects being neutral ("OK") experiences with a touch point, and no negative experiences. While that is still not good enough, it is much better than it was. The pursuit of innovation and the perfect patient experience will continue.

Building the Infrastructure to Support Experience-Based Design

Based on these and other examples of the use of EBD methods, both the innovation and service teams became increasingly convinced of the value of their innovative British import. Beginning in 2009, the two teams worked together to create a sustainable infrastructure to support experience-based design. An initial cadre of eight individuals from the Kaizen Promotion Office (KPO), Patient Relations and Service, and Communications were trained as EBD advisors and began experimenting with the various methods, some in the efforts described above. This cadre of advisors has expanded over time and become somewhat more formalized via a training program.

Workshops were held to establish standard work around EBD tools in order to better embed them into the planning and delivery of various VMPS events. Team members also developed support materials to address frequently asked questions; for example, "What is the difference between a process step and a touch point?" In 2011, these and other items were collated into the *Virginia Mason Experience-Based Design Handbook.*

Early on in the process of awareness raising, leaders decided that EBD would not become as fully integrated into VMPS if it were seen solely as a specialty effort that only a few advisors were trained to use. This decision to mainstream the methods led to an educational series in 2011 for the more than one hundred certified lean leaders in the organization, to enable them both to do some straightforward things on their own, and also to know when to seek the help of a more extensively trained advisor.

The work has not been without some inevitable growing pains, especially around the application of the experience questionnaire. Because the questionnaire yields measurement data and enables sampling of large numbers of patients relatively quickly, lean workshop leaders naturally gravitated toward its use. The pitfall, however, is that healthcare professionals do not always know where the emotional touch points are for patients and families. Further, raising awareness of the questionnaire as a method was actually having the unintended consequence of making it seem as though talking to patients and family members face to face was not needed. A third difficulty revolved around a genuine difference of opinion about whether certain emotion words were positive or negative. For example, *surprised* can be either, depending on the circumstances.

These issues were addressed in 2011 and 2012. Leaders from the innovation and service teams worked together to create what they are calling the *EBD bundle* of methods that should be used together. The bundle comprises observations, interviews, and experience questionnaires, with focus groups added for certain efforts. It is strongly advised that they be used in the sequence listed, with interviews and focus groups being equal and circumstance dependent. In other words, teams are advised to begin with simple observation, and then progress to interviews (or focus groups) to get a richer understanding of the experience. It is only through these methods that one can reliably identify emotional touch points and thereby design an effective experience questionnaire.

The issue of the ambiguity of meaning of various emotion words was resolved via a novel research study involving over 400 patients, family members, and staff, and yielding a set of 20 positive, 1 neutral, and 14 negative words that can be categorized with high reliability. This has resulted in improved face-validity and reliability of the questionnaire as a measurement tool and refocused debate onto what actions to take to improve the experience.

Team Members Have Emotional Experiences Too!

While we have focused thus far on the experience of patients and family members, the origins of experience-based design in service delivery applications also place emphasis on the emotional experience of staff in the process. Job performance suffers if those doing the work are stressed out, or otherwise experiencing negative emotions, in connection with their work. As Susan Haufe puts it, "The perfect staff experience is what is going to allow us to consistently deliver on the perfect patient experience." The burden of work is also one of the forms of waste, *muri*, that lean thinking seeks to eliminate. Observations, interviews, focus groups, and experience questionnaires can, therefore, be just as valuable when used to understand the experiences of care team members.

Most of the projects described in this chapter also included a component aimed at staff experiences. To illustrate with one such example, consider the case of the nurses working in the Med Tele unit receiving complex, rather ill patients transferred from the CCU. Whipple recalls the situation prior to the improvement work. "Some nurses would go home in tears because it was so scary for them and so intense. They would get a patient who was really sick that they would need to spend so much time with them. But then, eventually, they had to send them back to the CCU and it really upset them. It didn't feel like anyone was fixing the problem of what they called *bounce back.*"

Med Tele manager Gordanier also recalls the subtle ways that staff expressed their emotions. "I would notice things like nurses writing things in all capitals, or double underlines, or triple exclamation points on their own data sheet. So it wasn't necessarily in the words themselves, but you could definitely read emotion into what they had written. I realized this was impacting their work and we needed to figure it out. So, we all worked together to understand what the real defect was beneath all these exclamation points and underlined words. I realize that might be a pretty loose interpretation of experience-based design. But it definitely helped our team." The interventions of bedside handoffs, where the nurse from the receiving unit could *stop the line* if she or he felt that the unit or the patient was not ready for transfer, and having a clear set of goals and plan of care travel with the patient, were based partially on these insights.

Transforming Healthcare: What Others Can Learn from Virginia Mason's Focus on Patients and Families

The Virginia Mason Medical Center experience provides strong evidence that lean thinking, innovation, and patient-centeredness work synergistically. Virginia Mason has a *management method* to support patient-centered design—the Virginia Mason Production System. It has a *strategy* that focuses on pursuing the perfect service experience. It is willing to explore outside the box of conventional healthcare thinking to seek *innovative adaptations of methods* from other professions, developed in another country, in order to sharpen its ability to hear the voice of the customer. Taken together, Virginia Mason is demonstrating that patient experience can be measured and improved upon in ways that patients and families appreciate.

CEO Dr. Gary Kaplan summed up the challenge and the opportunity that has come from the early experience with EBD methods. "Experience-based design involves being willing to come face to face with the emotions our patients are feeling, and that has the potential to be a huge breakthrough. We are good at it, but it is early still and we are not nearly as good as we *can* be. We are going to keep getting better at it."

Leaders in Other Healthcare Organizations Should ...

Be prepared to be shocked, and maybe even a bit ashamed, when they really look at their current process through a new lens that represents the patients' and families' experiences. Being initially shocked and ashamed is a feature of several of Virginia Mason's stories of innovative change. It is not something to fear. Rather, it is something to get excited about because it might very well lead to new levels of service.

- How does the culture of our leadership team and organization as a whole react to embarrassing questions, challenges to thinking, and uncomfortable insights?
- Do we tend to embrace these as invitations to innovation, or do we become defensive and dismissive?
- If we think we are ready to be innovative, then where do we plan to find the input that will generate these uncomfortable questions and insights?
- Have we ever just sat and watched some aspect of our care delivery, or just listened in a nondefensive way to patients and families tell their stories of navigating through our systems, in order to gain new insights?

Develop leaders and staff at all levels who are genuinely empathetic to the experiences of patients and families, and create ways for them to get the feedback and insights they need to stimulate new thinking. VMPS methodology requires leaders and staff to observe the work closely. With the addition of required training and use of experience-based design methods, leaders will become further steeped in a rich flow of information about what it feels like to be a patient or family member. This ultimately drives change.

- Does our organization systematically select, train, develop, and provide input to leaders in ways that cultivate empathetic leadership?
- What is the relative weight we give to content intelligence (for example, about a clinical field or finance) versus emotional intelligence in selecting leaders?

Design strategies, tactics, and methods to support the goal of achieving true patient-centeredness. Virginia Mason is continuously building these elements and underpinning them with supportive infrastructure. The organization is well placed to continue to build, succeed, and grow patient-centeredness for years to come. It is not a fleeting effort, nor one that only produces a few examples of excellence in a sea of mediocrity.

- Do we have an active strategy around service that guides decision making and provides supportive coaching and tools?
- Do we have a constancy of purpose around pursuing a perfect patient experience?
- Is *OK* good enough when it comes to the feedback that patients and families give, or do we routinely set goals for more than that?
- Do we have durable elements of infrastructure that support this pursuit?
- Are we actively looking outside healthcare to other industries and professions from whom we might learn innovative ways to create better experiences for patients, families, and staff?

Chapter 9

Looking Ahead: The Future of Innovation and Lean at the Virginia Mason Medical Center

> Lean gives us the ability to think about change … to accept change … to think outside the box … and those are the things that are going to give us the tools to be able to deal with all of the craziness that is in the world in the future. It teaches you to be able to flex with the changes that come.
>
> **—Joyce Lammert, MD**
> *Medical Director, Hospital, Virginia Mason Medical Center*

While success is already evident, the journey of lean and innovation has only just begun at Virginia Mason Medical Center. It turns out that while this is a journey with a clear destination, it may well be a journey without an end.

Virginia Mason neurosurgeon Dr. Farrokh Farrokhi returned enlightened to this fact from his Japanese study tour. "The Toyota people, who have been at this for forty or fifty years, say they've still got work to do. It is not as deeply ingrained in their culture as they would like for it to be. It is one of those never-ending journeys. So, we have an urgency to get this done, but we also need to recognize that this is infinite. That actually brought me a lot of peace because I now realize that, paradoxically, what you need is *patient urgency*."

The clear destination is perfection. The journey is about the ongoing pursuit of the perfect patient experience; the highest levels of quality, service, and people development; and the attainment of a culture that totally supports innovation and learning—all elements of the Virginia Mason strategic plan pyramid. Like Toyota, and its Japanese and American industrial followers, Virginia Mason is experiencing the journey in the same way as the turtle in the diagram in Figure 3.2. It is a journey that consists of both slowly climbing the hill of incremental improvement (kaizen), and occasionally rocketing to a higher level via innovation.

The journey is also about making continual questioning and tradition-busting the norm. As Virginia Mason Institute executive director Diane Miller put it in reply to my request that she define the term *learning organization,* the proper attitude for the journey is, "We are not perfect, we are always asking." The previous chapters have cited dozens of examples of what can happen when the tools of lean and innovation are integrated into a culture that supports such an attitude (see the box "Virginia Mason's Most Innovative Ideas Yet").

Any consideration of what the future holds for Virginia Mason's journey must be framed in this understanding of where the organization has come from in its thinking. In this final chapter, we will see that the basic answer to the "What's next?" question at Virginia Mason is to *stay the course, but be open to opportunities.* It is a modern version of what W. Edwards Deming taught the Japanese in the 1950s when he stated his first principle as *establish constancy of purpose.*

VIRGINIA MASON'S MOST INNOVATIVE IDEAS YET

I posed the following question to leaders I interviewed: "What do you think are the most innovative things that Virginia Mason has done thus far?" The six most frequent responses were:

- adaptation and implementation of lean thinking into the Virginia Mason Production System
- flow stations and flow managers in clinics (Chapter 3)
- the Spine Clinic and other clinical value streams developed in partnership with employers (Chapter 2)
- geographic nursing cells for staff–patient assignment and work design in the hospital (Chapter 3)
- adaptation and application of experience-based design methodologies from the UK (Chapter 8)
- space design in hospital and clinics, for example, Jones Pavilion clinical areas and the Kirkland clinic with no waiting areas (Chapters 3 and 8)

plus dozens more honorable mentions.

A Strategic Plan That Stands the Test of Time

The Virginia Mason strategic plan pyramid has remained largely untouched since its conception in 2002, a fact that CEO Dr. Gary Kaplan and other leaders are pleased to point out. The fundamental focus remains putting the patient first and striving for operational excellence, as indicated by harmonious flow and the elimination of waste. No one is suggesting that any change is needed. As past board chair Carolyn Corvi put it, "the first thing we should *not* do is deviate too much. I think that we have established a really strong foundation."

A level down, strategic plans for quality, service, people, and innovation are updated regularly, and organizational goals are revisited annually. "The role for leaders," says Chief Operating Officer Sarah Patterson, "is setting a direction and saying what are our priorities. If we are going to innovate, where are the areas and what are the big dots we are trying to move?" At this level, leaders have many visionary ideas (see the box "Potential Targets for Future Innovation at Virginia Mason").

It is fair to say that Virginia Mason's list of potential innovation targets is not unique. I have heard similar items from leaders in other healthcare organizations. What might be unique, however, is what is *not* there. Note that leaders at Virginia Mason do not see their future intimately bound up in trying to make the right mergers and acquisitions, as is the case for many other healthcare organizations. Virginia Mason leaders see the pathway to growth and economic sustainability as built on the twin concepts of attracting patients based on a stellar reputation for quality and service, and creating added capacity within current resources through the relentless removal of waste. Lean and innovation are the tools for maintaining that pathway.

The integration of lean and innovation methods also enables a two-pronged strategy for finding the ideas that can take a healthcare organization into a brighter future. Clinic Medical Director Dr. Donna Smith notes, "VMPS [Virginia Mason Production System] enables us to look out in the environment and see what others are doing, and then quickly adapt and imitate the best ideas … and [with directed creativity tools] I think we can also make a real contribution to pushing the envelope in healthcare ourselves."

The innovation pillar strategic plan underpins all of this as Virginia Mason continues its journey into the future. The current evolutionary threads of increasing clarity about innovation, creating capability, and directing focus to high-impact issues remain valid. The board- and executive-level Innovation Leadership Team continues to set challenging stretch targets in these areas. In addition to work already underway, two areas for future development noted by executive sponsor for innovation, Lynne Chafetz, are better infrastructure for "listening to the voice of the future," and more systematic stage-gate business processes to manage breakthrough innovation, both of which we will return to at the end of this chapter.

POTENTIAL TARGETS FOR FUTURE INNOVATION AT VIRGINIA MASON

I posed the following question to leaders I interviewed: "Where do you think the innovation effort at Virginia Mason should be focused over the next three to five years?" The most frequent responses fell in three categories:

Patient Experience of Care

- Making things as easy as possible for patients
- Bringing care to the patient via the Internet, mobile, and sensor technology (rather than relying on them visiting us)
- Bringing care out into the community, and into homes, schools, and the workplace
- Truly listening to the voice of the patient and having the courage to change in response
- Understanding what motivates behavior change in patients
- End-of-life care
- Optimizing care transitions; for example, from clinic to hospital, hospital to home, or hospital to skilled nursing facility
- Eradicating hospital-induced delirium

New Business Relationships

- Working directly with employers on new models of care

Internal Processes

- Accelerating the execution and spread of change
- Creating breakthrough innovation through a systematic approach
- Creating the culture that supports learning and innovation
- Creating seamless value stream flows from home, to clinic, to hospital, to home
- Better connectivity and information mining from currently disparate IT systems

The list of potential innovation targets in the box suggests both an outward-facing and an inward-facing set of strategic opportunities for capitalizing on the foundation of innovation and lean. We will look first at what the future might hold with regard to the inward-facing opportunities for innovation.

Further Embedding Innovation Methods in VMPS

Previous chapters have provided many examples of how the concepts and tools from the creativity and innovation literature are being integrated into VMPS workshops and daily work. That integration will continue as more leaders are trained and more staff experience the use of these tools. Further, the literature on tools for stimulating creativity is large and there are many other methods that will be adapted over time. Online and tablet-based apps offer the promise of a *creativity facilitator-in-a-box* that could be used to further stimulate thinking at a moment's notice.

While lean and innovation methods are becoming well integrated into VMPS workshops, which are often spawned by organizational goal setting, Kaizen Promotion Office (KPO) administrative director Linda Hebish cites the need to better integrate these methods into the up-front development of the goals themselves. "There is an optimistic hope that if the leaders advocating these goals are trained well enough, they will think to pull these tools into their goal-setting work, but we don't really know how well that is happening now."

Perhaps an even bigger challenge for Virginia Mason as it moves forward lies in better harvesting the ideas that it already generates. The Center for Innovation has launched a study to trace flows and leaks in Virginia Mason's idea pipeline. This study supports one of the goals in the strategic innovation plan and follows directly from the innovation literature concept of the idea funnel. It aims to learn how the circumstances of generating, packaging, socializing, and sponsoring ideas impacts the chances of an innovative idea at least undergoing a fair test. Findings will further enhance Virginia Mason's ability to capitalize on the creativity of its nearly 5,000 team members, and countless patients and family members.

A final challenge for the future in this domain is to build further on the Everyday Lean Idea (ELI) system and the Idea Supermarket. Virginia Mason is nowhere near the Toyota benchmark of 100,000 tested ideas per year. Not all work groups actively participate in these systems, but it is hard to know exactly what that means. Anecdotally, leaders know that there is much more improvement in daily work going on than what is documented in the Idea Supermarket. Further, the organization realizes that patients and family members represent a vast, untapped reservoir of creative ideas that could potentially transform the care experience. Work to build further the communication, education, and information technology infrastructures to advance this work is already underway.

Creating More Capability through Culture Development, Education, and Infrastructure

Virginia Mason leaders acknowledge that more work also needs to be done in enhancing the organization's capability to be innovative. As Dr. Farrokhi observed at Toyota in Japan, an organization can never rest in its efforts to enhance its culture. New leaders and staff are constantly entering the mix and new challenges and stresses constantly test resolve. However, few healthcare organizations have Virginia Mason's board-level indicator of culture that supports innovation, underpinned by more detailed workgroup-level measurement, feedback, and improvement aids.

Further, few healthcare organizations have a CEO like Dr. Kaplan with such a firm, ongoing commitment. "I want to see us moving the big dot metrics on building the culture for innovation, because if you do that you create a flywheel effect that accelerates progress. It is going to make us stronger, and better able to create robust and actionable ideas from our people. I think the marketplace is crying out for disruptive innovations that will create better, faster, more afford-able services."

The education curriculum for leaders is also being constantly refreshed and enhanced while executives are communicating their expectation that all leaders complete the curriculum at a faster pace than sometimes occurs today. More front-line staff are registering for the Promoting Innovation course, and that is likely to pay off in more innovative ideas in the future.

Although the topic of centralized resources for innovation comes up from time to time in the Innovation Leadership Team and other forums, Virginia Mason leaders remain firmly committed to keeping the infrastructure small. Miller sums up the theory underlying the strategy best in saying, "This is similar to our deci-sion to not become overly reliant on KPO for knowing our improvement method. It is only when our leaders truly understand VMPS and therefore also innovation that we will change our culture. That will not happen if we are reliant on a group of experts." As I have pointed out, this direction runs counter to the emerging trend in other healthcare organizations to form centralized, well-staffed innova-tion centers, and it remains to be seen which approach creates the most transfor-mational benefit.

One area of infrastructure that might be expanded in the future is that sup-porting the moonshine and clinical informatics work described in chapter seven. In companies like Boeing, where a large percentage of employees are engineers or crafts persons, mocking up new devices and production tools as part of daily work is a reasonable expectation. Similarly, information technology moonshine occurs naturally in a company like Google or Apple, where both the necessary equipment and skills are a natural part of the environment. Such is not the case in a healthcare organization, and the best way to fill that gap will be an active topic of discussion at Virginia Mason in the coming years.

Enhancing the Implementation of Experience-Based Design Methodology

Having imported experience-based design (EBD) from the United Kingdom, Virginia Mason leaders have become convinced of its value and want to do even more. Three strands of effort are planned going forward to further explore the power of these methods.

The first involves embedding EBD into the work on strategic and operational goals. Starting in 2013, each organizational goal has an assigned EBD advisor team. The expectation for the accountable leaders is to actively apply the EBD tools bundle to allow the *voice of the customer* to inform all the improvement work associated with that goal. The high profile and sense of urgency surrounding these goals will heighten awareness and accelerate learning about experience-based design.

A second strand involves fully embedding EBD concepts and methods into all VMPS training and certification processes. Just as leaders in Virginia Mason are expected to demonstrate lean, innovation, and continuous improvement skills, they will now also be expected to demonstrate skills in understanding and improving the emotional experiences of patients, family, and staff. This will take the work beyond the occasional seminars for certified lean leaders that were previously the vehicle for this education.

The third strand is perhaps the most bold—more full-scale, active involvement of patients and family members in improvement and innovation work. VMPS workshops have always had a provision for involving a patient or family member, when it was deemed appropriate, but the full concept of co-design in EBD provokes a challenge. It involves deliberately empowering multiple patients and family members to be equal partners in decision making and detailed design, training them to be assertive, and engaging them in large numbers so that they feel even more empowered. "It gives people the shivers," says executive sponsor for service Michael VanDerhoef. However, if the innovation literature is any guide, yielding power and fully engaging patients and family members in the executive decision making and management of design and improvement will undoubtedly lead to innovative change that those within healthcare cannot possibly imagine. As we discussed in Chapter 8, it opens the way for what Eric von Hipple called the *democratization of innovation*, and is an example of C. K. Prahalad and Venkatram Ramaswarny's *co-creation of value*. Getting to full co-design may still lie further out in Virginia Mason's future, but the organization is committed to taking initial steps that seem to head in that direction.

Looking Outward to Innovate

Capitalizing on these inward-facing, capability- and culture-building efforts, Virginia Mason leaders will also continue to look outside their walls to bring ideas in to create transformational experiences for patients and families. Several leaders that I interviewed noted the ongoing value that the organization derives from the several senseis that it has engaged to advise periodically on the lean and innovation journey.

Leaders also noted that several of the Virginia Mason innovations that I have described throughout this book have come from insights gained from looking open-mindedly outside the organization's walls. VMPS itself came from outside. The original concepts behind Virginia Mason's intensive primary care (IPC) model came from interactions with Boeing and work originally done at the California Health Foundation. The drive-through influenza vaccine process was an adaptation from the fast food industry and the Patient Safety Alert™ system came from observation in a Japanese factory. These and other successes have made it more natural for the organization to search outward in the future, rather than hiding behind the old saw, *we're healthcare, we're different,* that I sometimes encounter at other organizations.

Creating Breakthrough Innovation to Transform the Healthcare Marketplace

The direction for the future that has the potential to create the most impact is the strategic innovation plan goal to differentiate Virginia Mason as a breakthrough innovator. The organization has put in place the infrastructure to support this goal. Capitalizing on that capacity will be a key challenge in the coming years as it pursues its mission to transform healthcare.

The longest standing piece of infrastructure is the Center for Healthcare Solutions at Virginia Mason. The Center's work alongside employers in creating an innovative clinical value stream for low back pain was presented in Chapter 2, and its ongoing efforts with employers and their health plans in innovative *marketplace collaboratives* was described in Chapter 7. The Center has worked with employers and health plans to create innovative value streams for migraine headaches, breast concerns, depression, and several other conditions. Each has resulted in faster access to care, faster return to work, lower costs, reductions in wasteful care, and high levels of satisfaction.

Virginia Mason is now sharing its work and actively participating in new efforts nationally through its participation with sixteen other leading healthcare organizations in the National High Value Healthcare Collaborative. This collaborative includes organizations such as the Mayo Clinic, Intermountain Healthcare, Dartmouth-Hitchcock, and Denver Health. The suite of innovative, but evidence-based, value streams that Virginia Mason and its new partners will create over the next several years may well become the new standards for care in a transformed healthcare system.

A second piece of infrastructure to support breakthrough innovation in the future is the recently introduced process of targeting a few specific organizational goals for breakthrough thinking. As described in Chapter 2, current targets for breakthrough include rethinking care transitions and making hospital-induced delirium a thing of the past. This work will employ the definition of breakthrough innovation described in Chapter 2 and the stage-gate model depicted in Figure 7.1. Virginia Mason leaders will identify new target areas periodically as part of the organization's annual goal-setting process.

The Innovations Grants process is the third piece of infrastructure that has recently been put in place to support breakthrough innovation. Plans for future rounds of grants will be made based on learning from the initial round. The key point is that this process makes it possible for *anyone* at Virginia Mason to contribute the proverbial *next big idea* with the potential to transform healthcare.

A fourth piece of infrastructure that has the potential to support breakthroughs in thinking about healthcare delivery is Virginia Mason's web portal. Leaders admit that the organization was late to the game in this arena, but they have rapidly caught up in terms of enrollment, thanks in large part to the discipline of lean. "We have done a fantastic job of promoting the portal as well as integrating it into staff workflows, which is something that our vendor told us has not always been done at other medical centers," explains director of E-Health, Isaac Phillips. "We have created standard work that makes any staff member who touches a patient capable of enrolling that patient in MyVirginiaMason. In a few short months, we had the second-highest enrollment rates in the country, according to our vendor. They tell us we are rapidly gaining traction at a rate not seen with any other clients."

While the phase one portal design offers only basic features, such as online appointment request, viewing nonsensitive lab results, secure messaging with providers and medication refills/renewals, the vision for this new element of infrastructure at Virginia Mason goes well beyond that. "Our longer-term vision for the portal," explains Chief Financial and Information Officer Sue Anderson, "is for it to be a way to engage more fully with patients on *their* terms, and at times and places that suit *their* needs." It is a vision consistent with Prahlad and Ramaswamy's experience innovation, as well as Virginia Mason's embrace of experience-based design and its commitment to put the patient at the top of the strategic pyramid.

Isaac Phillips adds further, "And the vision isn't limited to a patient portal, but really looks out for several key audiences: consumers in general, our patients, consumers who might become our patients, our staff, and referring clinicians. The long-term vision is to provide an interface for each of these audiences that integrates all the information that needs to be shared across those audiences."

Consistent with Virginia Mason's philosophy that line leaders should drive infrastructure elements, not the other way around, the web portal vision is being crafted in enthusiastic partnership with executive and clinical leaders. Clinic Medical Director Dr. Donna Smith says of the potential for the web portal, "I think the areas that are most crying for innovation are really partnering with patients in a meaningful way and really understanding what is health *for them*. But it is not just co-designing your clinic visit as it exists now to make it nicer for you. It is asking the questions, 'What do you need in your life and where does that show up for you?'" Vice President for Clinic Operations Shelly Fagerlund points out, "If you think about the patient's current contact points with us, the healthy patient may not contact us at all, and the chronically ill patient we may see for only fifteen to twenty minutes every six months. So what kind of impact are we having in terms of their whole health? We are probably only a very tiny fragment of the information and advice they are getting about their health. We have a huge opportunity to become much more connected in building relationships for better health."

The discussion of the web portal, and the ongoing application of experience-based design principles, is leading Virginia Mason into what Prahalad and Ramaswarny called the third "competitive space for innovation"—*experience space*. In the current two spaces, products and services, organizations seek to differentiate themselves on quality and cost from others with similar offerings. The goal in experience space to is create and integrate flexible networks of products, services, and information flows that allow the user to co-create unique experiences that meet his or her needs in the moment.

While other healthcare organizations have similar visionaries, Virginia Mason may have a combination of capabilities that could result in more than what is possible in other organizations. It has both the discipline of lean, and the creative thinking tools that build potentially transformational ideas into everyday workflows and standard work. This will likely enable Virginia Mason to test, implement, spread, and sustain transformational change at a pace not possible in other organizations. Add in the sensitivity to the patient, family, and staff experience that comes from the application of experience-based design methods, along with the informatics team's abilities to rapidly prototype, and Virginia Mason has a potentially powerful engine for transformation. Only time will tell how well that engine performs.

Hearing the Voice of the Future while Avoiding the Siren Call of Technology Alone

Practitioners of improvement science speak of the importance of listening to the *voice of the customer* and the *voice of the process*. Innovators add a third voice— the *voice of the future*. Companies that look ahead and spot trends in technology, lifestyles, demographics, politics, finance, the environment, education, building sciences, and so on, have the opportunity to get a head start on innovations that serve tomorrow's needs. They also are better able to avoid making decisions today that leave them with unproductive assets in the future. As noted in Chapter 2, the voice of the future concept is incorporated into the environmental scanning process that feeds annual planning at Virginia Mason.

However, just as it is Virginia Mason's view that operations should drive any future infrastructure development, leaders also believe that operations and the patient experience should drive technology choices, not the other way around. Like most other medical centers, Virginia Mason invests in the latest IT, diagnostic, and treatment technology. The organization is keenly interested in breakthrough developments such as those that might occur at Boston's Center for the Integration of Medicine and Innovative Technology (CIMIT) and also actively supports the search for medical breakthroughs at its own Benaroya Research Institute at Virginia Mason. However, the sad fact is that healthcare often takes twenty-first century technology and embeds it in service delivery processes that have not changed much since the 1970s.

Virginia Mason leaders see the relationship of futuristic technologies and care delivery differently. CEO Kaplan puts it this way: "I believe that we will continue to innovate through new approaches to surgical intervention and new medical approaches. But I don't believe that that, *alone,* will be the silver bullet. Especially given what we have seen historically with many of these innovations. In too many cases, technology has *driven up* cost significantly." Virginia Mason's philosophy is to integrate technology acquisition with evidence-based, lean and innovative care delivery system redesign. The former might initially inspire thinking about the latter, but in the end, the latter needs to drive the change.

Once again, this is thinking that Virginia Mason Medical Center leaders learned from Toyota and their Japanese lean *senseis* who say, "Relying on outside [technology] providers to do the *thinking* and *doing* for us, is *not* a course we should follow. Having others design their processes is a mistake that many companies make as they attempt to become world-class competitors. *You cannot successfully buy your way towards 'world-class' by purchasing the latest technology.*" (Italic emphasis preserved from original).

Spreading the Word to Transform Healthcare

The 2013–2017 strategic innovation plan added a new goal to "share our knowledge to transform healthcare." Virginia Mason is serious about this aspect of its mission, and that passion is communicated throughout the organization. When I innocently asked primary care director of strategic initiatives, Carolyn Cone, to tell me what she did as I began my interview with her, she replied, "When people ask me, 'What do you do?' I say, 'I am on teams at Virginia Mason who are being strategic about how we are going to stay viable in healthcare reform, and in fact, how we are going to *lead* and transform healthcare reform.' I am very, very pleased to be working in that kind of area."

To support the innovation plan goal to get the word out, Virginia Mason has established the Center for Health Services Research with the charter to transform healthcare by sharing the results of our quality, safety, and other improvements in the academic literature. This is in addition to the many presentations given by Virginia Mason team members at professional conferences and the several major television and print-media reports on the organization's work. The new Center, under the leadership of its director Dr. C. Craig Blackmore, hopes to publish several papers a year for the foreseeable future.

The main outreach effort to the healthcare industry comes from the Virginia Mason Institute (VMI), whose mission revolves around providing education and training to others who wish to adapt the Virginia Mason Production System to their organizations. In 2012, VMI hosted visitors from forty-eight states and sixteen countries. On average fifty visitors a week come to learn about Virginia Mason's approach to transforming care.

VMI's outreach efforts have an interesting internal side effect of spurring on the sustainable implementation of lean and innovation at Virginia Mason. VMI executive director Diane Miller points out, "If we are speaking to groups about what we are doing here, we better be *doing* it. And we better be inventing the *next thing* because people are now expecting us to help guide their way about how to transform healthcare."

Moon Shots for Management

In 2008, management guru Gary Hamel assembled a group of scholars and business leaders to "lay out a roadmap for reinventing management." Just as President Kennedy's 1963 proclamation that the United States would put a man on the moon and return him safely by the end of that decade created a vision that catalyzed technological innovations, this group was charged with identifying the elements of a vision that might amount to a "management moon shot."

In order to successfully address the limitations of modern management philosophy, the assembled experts agreed that leaders needed to:

- "First, admit that they had reached the limits of Management 1.0 …
- Second, cultivate, rather than repress, their dissatisfaction with the status quo; creating a little righteous indignation … and
- Finally, have the courage to aim high …"

The group went on in its *Harvard Business Review* report to challenge leaders to, among other things, "reconstruct management's philosophical foundations … redefine the work of leadership … dramatically reduce the pull of the past … and further unleash human imagination."

Virginia Mason Medical Center has clearly launched its management moon shot. Having established the foundations of lean thinking, linked it to the passionate pursuit of the perfect patient experience, and overcome the myth that lean and innovation cannot coexist, the organization sees its continuing journey as one of:

- Strengthening the foundations of quality, service, people development, and a culture of innovation and learning.
- Continually scouting for new ideas that can be adapted through application of the discipline of the Virginia Mason Production System.
- Stimulating and supporting homegrown breakthrough innovation.
- Sharing the learning and spreading the word.

The need for transformation in healthcare is clearly being felt across American healthcare. While the journey is likely to never really end, Virginia Mason has come a long way. Fellow travelers are welcomed.

Source Notes

Initial drafts of the manuscript were reviewed by a Virginia Mason committee comprising Lynne Chafetz, Linda Hebish, Gary Kaplan, Diane Miller, Sarah Patterson, and Jennifer Phillips. Most of the material for the book comes from a series of seventy-two interviews I conducted in the period October 2012 through March 2013. The list of those interviewed includes: Barry Aaronson, Jeff Anderson, Sue Anderson, Julia Arp, Chris Backous, Andy Baylor, Robbi Bishop, Karen Blankenship, Alvin Calderon, Lynne Chafetz, Katerie Chapman, Joan Ching, Jordan Chun, Carolyn Cone, Carolyn Corvi, Jim Cote, Theresa Craw, Debbie Cutchin, Bill DePaso, Celeste Derheimer, Keith Dipboye, Pete Doyle, Denise Dubuque, Lonnie Edelheit, Shelly Fagerlund, Farrokh Farrokhi, Val Ferris, Becky Foley, Dane Fukumoto, Rich Furlong, Cathie Furman, Karen Gifford, Mike Glenn, Christin Gordanier, Susan Haufe, Linda Hebish, Mark Hutcheson, Andrew Jacobs, Gary Kaplan, Mark Lacrampe, Joyce Lammert, Bob Lemon, Amy London, Debra Madsen, Sharon Mann, Lynne Maher, Robert Mecklenburg, Diane Miller, Laurel Morrison, Dana Nelson-Peterson, Henry Otero, Sarah Patterson, Jennifer Phillips, Issac Phillips, Jennifer Phillips, Kim Pittenger, Catherine Potts, Eli Quisenberry, Jennifer Richards, Dennis Rochier, Sundance Rogers, Francis Salinas, Donna Smith, Michael Spohnholtz, Chris Stewart, Charleen Tachibana, Deborah Tombs, Amy Tufano, Michael VanDerhoef, Mike Westley, Shawna Whipple, and Roger Woolf. Many of these individuals reviewed drafts of selected sections of the manuscript and offered additional comments. I also reviewed internal documents supplied to me, mainly by Jennifer Phillips.

The concepts of lean thinking described through this book are explained in more depth in Ohno (1988), Womack et al. (1991), Black (1998), and Womack and Jones (1996). A search on an Internet bookselling website will reveal many more.

The methods and tools for directed creativity described throughout this book are explained in more depth in Plsek (1994, 1997, 1998, 1999) and Maher, Plsek, and Garrett (2008). There are numerous general books on creative thinking techniques, for example de Bono (1992) and Michalko (2011). A search on an Internet bookselling website will reveal many more. All such tools are embodiments of the three mental actions of attention, escape, and movement, as described in Plsek (1997). The term DirectedCreativity™ is a trademark of Paul E. Plsek & Associates, Inc.

Chapter 1

Sources of results cited include key executives, internal improvement project reports, and Virginia Mason's blog at http://virginiamasonblog.org/. The other hospital to earn the Leapfrog Group's distinction as a Top Hospital of the Decade is the University of Maryland Medical Center. The history of the development of the Toyota Production System can be found in Ohno (1988) and Womack et al. (1991). The history of the involvement of American quality improvement experts with the Japanese following World War II can be found in Juran (1995). For a general overview of the science and methods associated with creative thinking, see Plsek (1997) and Sternberg (1999). The models and definitions in the section "Creativity and Innovation Basics" are more fully developed and described in Plsek (1997). Research establishing the nonlinearity of innovation processes is presented in Van de Ven et al. (1999)

Chapter 2

The review of health policy documents from several countries was reported in Bate et al. (2004). The promise of healthcare reform is taken from a March 17, 2010 publication of the United States Senate entitled "The Patient Protection and Affordable Care Act: Detailed Summary" and posted at http://www.dpc.senate. gov/healthreformbill.healthbill52.pdf. The health and healthcare statistics quoted are taken from a summary by PBS and posted initially on October, 22, 2012 at http://www.pbs.org/newshour/rundown/2012/10/health-costs-how-the-us-compares-with-other-countries.html. Deming's fourteen principles are explained in Deming (1986). With regard to the point about the ill-fate of banks who continued to invest capital in traditional buildings at the advent of the ATM era, a similar point can be made about the video rental and recorded music industries.

Chapter 3

In Figure 3.2, Imai's contribution was the main concept of the innovation and kaizen stair step. The Japan Human Relations Association simply added the turtle when they adapted it for their book *Kaizen Teian 1*. While the subsection-leading statements in the section "Integrating Lean and Innovation: Natural Overlaps in Tools and Methods" present a contrast for explanatory purposes, it is not the intent to create a stark dichotomy. For example, in the first subsection ("Lean continuous improvement tools raise awareness of and challenge specific mental valleys with respect to flow and waste, creativity tools extend this challenge to all types of mental valleys.") it should be noted that other mental valleys beyond flow and waste are challenged in lean thinking Production Preparation Process (3P) workshops. Shigeo Shingo's methodology for thinking about rapid changeover in manufacturing operations is described in Shingo (1985).

Chapter 4

For a deeper look at many of the concepts outlined in the early sections of this chapter, see Argyris (1993). Herbert Simon first described the biological and evolutionary basis behind the concept of satisficing in Simon (1947). He coined the term in Simon (1956). For a review of this work, see Brown (2004).

Chapter 5

For a more complete explanation of the research described in the section "Dimensions of Culture that Support Innovation," see Maher et al. (2010b). The systematic review mentioned in the Information dimension is Smith et al. (2008), while the Harvard Business School forum is described in Amabile and Khaire (2008). The quote in the Targets dimension is from Amabile (1998). For more intrinsic motivation and understanding of what makes people do what they do, see Amabile (1998), Kohn (1990), and Hornsby et al. (2002). The study of aerospace firms mentioned in the Relationships dimension is in Clegg et al. (2002). At the time of this writing (June 2013), Virginia Mason was considering changes in its staff satisfaction survey vendor that may necessitate modifying the survey it uses to measure culture for innovation. The full set of items originally used in the United Kingdom version of the survey is available from the author. The phrase *culture kaizen* is the author's terminology, not Virginia Mason's.

Chapter 6

The information presented in the section "Examples of Innovation Infrastructures in Leading Healthcare Institutions" is based on descriptions of the three healthcare innovation centers as provided on the Internet (accessed by the author April 19, 2013). See http://xnet.kp.org/innovationcenter/index.html (Kaiser Permanente), http://www.mayo.edu/center-for-innovation/ (Mayo Clinic), and http://www.cimit.org/ (CIMIT). The author assumes full responsibility for any inaccuracies in the information in these brief summaries. For more about how simple rules guide the evolution of complex systems, see Plsek and Greenhalgh (2001). For a summary of the work of the Center for Health Care Solutions at Virginia Mason, see Blackmore et al. (2011).

Chapter 7

For more about the pioneering work of Virginia Mason anesthesiologist Dr. Daniel Moore, see Mulroy (2011). For more about stage-gate models and the research supporting them, see Cooper (2011). Teresa Amabile's research on meaning in work is summarized in Amabile and Kramer (2011).

Chapter 8

Bate and Robert (2007) provide the academic background and research underpinning experience-based design, while the NHS Institute for Innovation and Improvement (2009) provides practice guidance and tools. The concept of touch points in service process was first articulated in Carlzon (1987), where he called them *moments of truth*. For a systematic review of evidence on the links between patient experience and clinical safety and effectiveness, see Doyle et al. (2013).

Chapter 9

For more about the National High Value Healthcare Collaborative, see http://www.highvaluehealthcare.org. The quote from Japanese senseis about the fallacy of relying on technology from outside vendors is taken from a Production Preparation Process (3P) training manual available from consultants Shingijutsu Corporation. They point to Womack et al. (1991) for what they call "a great example of the truth of this statement."

Bibliography

Amabile, T. M. (1998). How to kill creativity. *Harvard Business Review* 76(5):77–87.

Amabile, T. M., and Khaire, M. (2008). Creativity and the role of the leader. *Harvard Business Review* 86(10):100–109.

Amabile, T., and Kramer, S. (2011). The power of small wins. *Harvard Business Review* 89(5):70–80.

Argyris, C. (1990). *Overcoming Organizational Defenses.* Allyn & Bacon.

Argyris, C. (1991). Teaching smart people how to learn. *Harvard Business Review* 69(3):99–109.

Argyris, C. (1993). *Knowledge in Action: A Guide to Overcoming Barriers to Organizational Change.* Jossey-Bass.

Bate, P., Robert, G., and Bevan, H. (2004). The next phase of healthcare improvement: What can we learn from social movements? *Quality and Safety in Health Care* 13(1):62–66.

Bate, P., and Robert, G. (2007). *Bringing User Experience to Health Care Improvement: The Concepts, Methods and Practices of Experience-Based Design.* Radcliffe Publishing.

Bessant, J. (2003). Challenges in innovation management. In Shavinina L., ed. *The International Handbook on Innovation.* Paragon.

Black, J. (1998). *A World Class Production System.* Crisp Publications.

Blackmore, C. C., Mecklenburg, R. S., and Kaplan, G. S. (2011). At Virginia Mason, collaboration among providers, employers, and health plans to transform care, cut costs and improved quality. *Health Affairs* 30(9).

Brown, R. (2004). Consideration of the origin of Herbert Simon's theory of "satisficing" (1933–1947). *Management Decision* 42(10):1240–1256.

Carlzon, J. (1987). *Moments of Truth.* Ballinger.

Christensen, C. M. (2000). *The Innovator's Delimma.* HarperBusiness.

Christensen, C. M., and Anthony, S. D. (2004). Cheaper, faster, easier: Disruptive innovation in the service sector. *Strategy & Innovation.* January–February. (Harvard Business School reprint number S0401A)

Christensen, C. M., Bohmer, R., and Kenagy, J. (2002). Will disruptive innovations cure health care? *Harvard Business Review* 78(5):102–112.

Clegg, C., Unsworth, K., Epitropaki, O., and Parker, G. (2002). Implicating trust in the innovation process. *Journal of Occupational and Organizational Psychology* 75(4):409–422.

Collins, J. C., and Porras, J. I. (1994). *Built to Last: Successful Habits of Visionary Companies.* Harper Business.

Cooper, R. G. (2011). *Winning at New Products: Proven Roadmap for Success, 4th Edition.* Basic Books.

Damanpour, F. (1991). Organizational innovations: A meta-analysis of effects of determinants and moderators. *Academy of Management Journal* 34:355–390.

Deal, T. E., and Kennedy, A. A. (1982). *Corporate Cultures: The Rites and Rituals of Corporate Life.* Basic Books.

de Bono, E. (1969). *Mechanism of Mind.* Penguin Books.

de Bono, E. (1992). *Serious Creativity.* Harper-Collins.

Deming, W. E. (1986). *Out of the Crisis.* Center for Advanced Engineering Study.

Doyle, C., Lennox, L., and Bell, D. (2013). A systematic review of evidence on the links between patient experience and clinical safety and effectiveness. *BMJ Open* 2013;3:e001570. doi:10.1136/bmjopen-2012-001570.

Gawande, A. (2012). Big med: Restaurant chains have managed to combine quality control, cost control and innovation, can health care? *The New Yorker.* August 13.

Hamel, G. (2009). Moon shots for management. *Harvard Business Review* 87(2):91–98. (HBR reprint number R0902H.)

Hornsby, J., Kuratko, D., and Zahra, S. (2002). Middle managers' perception of the internal environment for corporate entrepreneurship: Assessing a measurement scale. *Journal of Business Venturing* 17:253–273.

Imai, M. (1986). *Kaizen: The Key to Japan's Competitive Success.* McGraw-Hill.

Institute of Medicine. (1999). *To Err Is Human: Building a Safer Health System.* National Academy Press.

Institute of Medicine. (2001). *Crossing the Quality Chasm: A New Health Care System for the 21st Century.* National Academy Press.

Japan Human Relations Association. (1997). *Kaizen Teian 1: Developing Systems for Continuous Improvement through Employee Suggestions.* Productivity Press.

Juran, J. M. (1964). *Managerial Breakthrough.* McGraw-Hill.

Juran, J. M. (1995). *A History of Managing for Quality.* Irwin Professional Publishing.

Kenney, C. (2011). *Transforming Health Care: Virginia Mason Medical Center's Pursuit of the Perfect Patient Experience.* Taylor & Francis.

Knowles, M. (1990). *The Adult Learner: A Neglected Species, Fourth Edition.* Gulf Publishing.

Kohn, A. (1990). *The Brighter Side of Human Nature: Altruism and Empathy in Everyday Life.* Basic Books.

Kotter, J. P. (1995). Leading change: Why transformation efforts fail. *Harvard Business Review.* March–April:59–67.

Krafcik, J. F. (1988). Triumph of the lean production system. *Sloan Management Review* 30(1):41–52.

Kuhn, T. S. (1962). *The Structure of Scientific Revolution.* University of Chicago Press.

Maher, L. M., Plsek, P. E., and Garrett, S. (2008). *Thinking Differently.* NHS Institute for Innovation and Improvement.

Maher, L. M., Plsek, P. E., and Bevan, H. (2010a). *Creating the Culture for Innovation: A Guide for Executives.* NHS Institute for Innovation and Improvement.

Maher, L. M., Plsek, P. E., Price, J., and Mugglestone, M (2010b). *Creating the Culture for Innovation: A Practical Guide for Leaders.* NHS Institute for Innovation and Improvement.

Michalko, M. (2011). *Creative Thinkering: Putting Your Imagination to Work.* New World Library.

Mulroy, M. F. (2011). Daniel C. Moore, MD, and the renaissance of regional anesthesia in North America. *Reg Anesth Pain Med.* 36(6):625–629.

NHS Institute for Innovation and Improvement. (2009). *The EBD Approach: Using Patient and Staff Experience to Design Better Healthcare Services.* NHS Institute for Innovation and Improvement.

Ohno, T. (1988). *Toyota Production System: Beyond Large-Scale Production.* Productivity Press.

Pedler, M., Burgoyne, J., and Boydell, T. (1991). *The Learning Company: A Strategy for Sustainable Development.* McGraw-Hill.

Plsek, P. E. (1994). Directed creativity. *Quality Management in Health Care* 2(3):62–76.

Plsek, P. E. (1997). *Creativity, Innovation, and Quality.* ASQ Quality Press.

Plsek, P. E. (1998). Incorporating the tools of creativity into quality management. *Quality Progress* 31(3):21–28.

Plsek, P. E. (1999). Innovative thinking for the improvement of medical systems. *Annals of Internal Medicine* 131(6):438–444.

Plsek, P. E., and Greenhalgh, T. (2001). The challenge of complexity in health care. *British Medical Journal* 323:625–628.

Prahlad, C. K., and Ramaswamy, V. (2003). The new frontier of experience innovation. *MIT Sloan Management Review* 44(4):12–18.

Rogers, E. M. (1962). *Diffusion of Innovations.* Free Press. (A fourth edition, updated in 1995, is also available.)

Schon, D. A. (1983). *The Reflective Practitioner.* Basic Books.

Schon, D. A. (1987). *Educating the Reflective Practitioner.* Jossey-Bass.

Schrage, M. (2000). *Serious Play: How the World's Best Companies Stimulate Innovation.* Harvard Business School Press.

Senge, P. M. (1990). *The Fifth Discipline: The Art and Practice of the Learning Organization.* Doubleday.

Shewhart, W. A. (1931). *Economic Control of Quality of Manufactured Product.* Van Nostrand.

Shingo, S. (1985). *A Revolution in Manufacturing: The SMED System.* Productivity Press.

Shingo, S. (2007). *Kaizen and the Art of Creative Thinking: The Scientific Thinking Mechanism.* PCS Inc. (English language translation of original published in Japanese in 1959.)

Simon, H. A. (1947) *Administrative Behavior: A Study of Decision-Making Processes in Administrative Organizations.* Macmillan.

Simon, H. A. (1956). Rational choice and the structure of the environment. *Psychological Review* 63(2):129–138.

Smith, M., Busi, M., Ball, P., and Van Der Meer, R. (2008). Factors influencing an organisation's ability to manage innovation: A structured literature review and conceptual model. *International Journal of Innovation Management* 12(4):655–676.

Smith, R. (2007). *The Seven Levels of Change: Different Thinking for Different Results, 3rd Edition.* Tapestry Press.

Sternberg, R. J., ed. (1999). *Handbook of Creativity.* Cambridge University Press.

Tushman, M. (1977). Special boundary roles in the innovation process. *Administrative Sciences Quarterly* 22(4):587–605.

Van de Ven, A. H., Polley, D. E., Garud, R., and Venkataraman, S. (1999). *The Innovation Journey.* Oxford University Press.

von Hipple, E. (1988). *The Sources of Innovation.* Oxford University Press.

von Hipple, E. (2005). *Democratizing Innovation.* MIT Press.

Womack, J. P., and Jones, D. T. (1996). *Lean Thinking: Banish Waste and Create Wealth in Your Corporation.* Simon & Schuster.

Womack, J. P., Jones, D. T., and Roos, D. (1991). *The Machine that Changed the World: The Story of Lean Production.* HarperCollins.

Yasuda, Y. (1990). *40 Years, 20 Million Ideas: The Toyota Suggestion System.* Productivity Press.

Glossary

3P: *Production Preparation Process,* a five-day event in which a team focuses on building a production system for a new facility, process, or service.

5S: A strategy that helps to keep the workplace safe and organized. It is a foundational element of the Virginia Mason Production System (VMPS). Includes sort, simplify, sweep, standardize, and self-discipline.

A3 tool: A method associated with *hoshin kanri,* an approach to planning widely used in companies using lean manufacturing methods. It provides a succinct and clear answer, on one A3-sized piece of paper, to the following questions: What is the problem? Why does it require organizational resources? What are the metrics that you can use to measure success?

assumption busting: A tool of directed creativity in which assumptions, mental models, mental valleys, traditions, and so on are surfaced so that alternatives can be examined.

be someone else: A tool of directed creativity that invites individuals to approach a problem from the perspective of someone with different background or training.

creativity: The connecting and rearranging of knowledge—in the minds of individuals who allow themselves to think flexibly—to generate new, often surprising ideas that others judge to be useful.

defect: A mistake that is passed along to the next step in the process or to the customer.

Everyday Lean Idea (ELI) system: A formal method to capture staff ideas about removing waste in their work unit and develop them with their manager.

experience-based design (EBD): A collection of concepts and methods for identifying and understanding the emotional experiences of patients, families, and staff. It includes the concept of co-designing improvements and innovations with patients, families, and staff.

experience questionnaire: A tool from EBD for surveying patients, families, and staff regarding their experiences at various touch points in a process.

EBD bundle: The four key tools from experience-based design (EBD) for identifying and understanding the experiences of patients, families, and staff—interviews, focus groups, observation, and experience questionnaire.

Final Report Out: A report given to the organization that includes a formal method for presentation that is intended to inform people of the work and inspire future improvements.

gemba: Where the work actually happens.

harvesting: The process of selecting ideas for further consideration from among the many ideas expressed in a brainstorming session. Typically, this is done on the basis of preagreed criteria, using a group consensus process.

home team: The workers that are not part of the improvement team, but whose work is affected by the changes. They are encouraged to participate by providing real-time ideas and honest feedback during planning, the event, and implementation.

hoshin kanri: Methods for policy and goal planning and deployment, popular among organizations adopting lean thinking methods.

idea notebook: A format used in directed creativity for documenting the best ideas from a brainstorming session.

innovation: Directed creativity implemented.

innovation funnel: A concept from the innovation literature that suggests that the ratio of brainstormed ideas to innovation is about 100: 1. Brainstormed ideas must be harvested, further developed, tested, and evaluated in ever-decreasing numbers over time because of resource constraints, thus creating a funnel effect to go from the 100 brainstormed ideas down to the one successfully implemented innovation.

kaizen: Continuous incremental improvement.

kaizen activity: Events intended to meet one or more improvement targets in a value stream.

kaizen event: A one- or two-day event focused on a particular process in which people who do the work are empowered to eliminate waste and reduce the burden of work.

KPO: Kaizen Promotion Office, the department responsible for the deployment and application of the Virginia Mason Production System tools, methods, and concepts.

lean: A general term describing methods similar to the Toyota Production System.

leaping: A tool from directed creativity in which participants are asked to generate ideas based on an extreme scenario using the principle that necessity is often the mother of invention.

mental benchmarking: A tool from directed creativity in which participants seek to adapt concept and practices common in other organizations or industries to their situation.

mental valleys: The collection of concepts, assumptions, and images that are conjured up when a word is heard. The cognitive process of creating mental valleys is central to language processing, but it can lead to repeated thoughts when new, creative thoughts are desired.

mistake: An inadvertent error.

mistake-proofing: A method that aims to prevent defects.

Rapid Process Improvement Workshop (RPIW): A five-day workshop focused on a particular process in which people who do the work are empowered to eliminate waste and reduce the burden of work.

sensei: A term used to show respect to someone who has achieved a certain level of mastery in a skill. At Virginia Mason, it specifically refers to the consultants (not necessarily Japanese) who are regarded as masters of all or part of the elements of the Virginia Mason Production System.

seven levels of change: A framework, developed by author Rolf Smith, for thinking about change on a range from the logical and linear to the creative and lateral.

seven ways: A tool from the Toyota Production System that asks participants to come up with at least seven ideas in response to a provocation. It facilitates mental movement, a necessary element for creativity.

standard operations: A specific method of observation and analysis to determine and document the most efficient way to complete the work.

standard work: An agreed upon, repeatable sequence of work assigned to a single operator at a pace that meets customer demand.

touch point: A moment in time at which something triggers an emotion in a person experiencing the process. It is a central focus in experience-based design.

Toyota Production System (TPS): Toyota's specific application of kaizen.

trystorming: To produce prototypes rapidly for the purpose of testing, learning, and further development.

value stream improvements: Actions that focus on increasing value from the perspective of the customer by decreasing waste.

value stream: The entire set of activities that encompass the transformation of a patient or product from beginning to end.

value stream map: A visual tool to help see and understand the flow of process, information, and material.

value stream mapping: A process of understanding and depicting the transformation of a patient or product, then identifying and implementing improvements necessary to add value.

Virginia Mason Production System (VMPS): Virginia Mason's management method, based on the principles and practices of the Toyota Production System and lean.

VMPS flows of medicine: The fundamental components of any process that flow together to create the patient's experience—patients, providers, family and relationships, medications, supplies, equipment, information, and process engineering.

waste: Any task or item that does not add value from the perspective of the customer. Taiichi Ohno identified seven types, including time, processing, defects, inventory, motion, overproduction, and transportation.

wordplay: A method from directed creativity that invites participants to explore a topic using words that they do not normally associate with the topic. The purpose is to active different mental valleys in thinking.

Index